Muus vs. Mu...

Muus vs. Muus

THE SCANDAL THAT SHOOK
NORWEGIAN AMERICA

Bodil Stenseth

EDITED BY
Kari Lie Dorer

TRANSLATED BY
Kari Lie Dorer & Torild Homstad

MINNESOTA HISTORICAL SOCIETY PRESS

NORWEGIAN-AMERICAN HISTORICAL ASSOCIATION

The publication of this book is supported by an anonymous endowment for Norwegian American History in Minnesota.

Author Bodil Stenseth has received financial support from the Norwegian Non-Fiction Writers and Translators Association and the Fritt Ord Foundation (Stiftelsen Fritt Ord).

mnhspress.org

The Minnesota Historical Society Press is a member of the Association of University Presses.

Published in cooperation with the Norwegian-American Historical Association, naha.stolaf.edu.

Manufactured in the United States of America

10 9 8 7 6 5 4 3 2 1

♾ The paper used in this publication meets the minimum requirements of the American National Standard for Information Sciences—Permanence for Printed Library Materials, ANSI Z39.48-1984.

International Standard Book Number
ISBN: 978-1-68134-298-6 (paper)
ISBN: 978-1-68134-299-3 (e-book)

Library of Congress Control Number: 2024938109

MUUS VS. MUUS

Part II: Family Trials

Part III: Disgrace

"her complaint is at present a pycological [*sic*] enigma
which may or may not be solved at some future time."
Pioneer Press, January 26, 1880

PROLOGUE

February 18, 1880

BEGINNING IN THE EARLY MORNING, spectators had streamed in through Holden Church's front door to secure seats. Long before the meeting actually began, the great church on the prairie was packed full. It didn't seem to matter to the spectators that they had woken up to falling snow and difficult driving conditions, or that it was a weekday. No one wanted to miss this meeting. Nearly a thousand people arrived, many of them curious outsiders, newspaper reporters, and others who otherwise never attended the church.

Newspapers had already written about the case for a long time—both in America and in Norway. On this day, three Norwegian Lutheran Church congregations in Goodhue County, Minnesota, were to meet in an open congregational meeting to discuss the marriage between their pastor Bernt Julius Muus and Oline Muus. One of the most prominent leaders of the Norwegian American community in Minnesota and founder of St. Olaf College, Pastor Muus spoke with authority. He had been active in religious debates for two decades. The pastor's wife, Oline Muus, was among the leading women of the rural community, a role model for the entire congregation. Now embarrassing and personal details from the couple's life together were to be discussed thoroughly, in front of everyone. What had really happened between the spouses? Could Pastor Muus continue as Holden's pastor even after charges were brought against him? And would Mrs. Muus be put under church discipline as a result of her unruly behavior? The day's events would be more entertaining than going to the theater.

Holden Church had been financed by the congregation and built by a construction company from Red Wing. The building had a high ceiling, so it couldn't have been very warm in the church that January day, despite the crowd, which was a sea of men. In all the rows of pews, even on what was usually the women's side, there were men as far as the eye could see. At the front, under the altar and pulpit, sat even more men: pastors and the church council burdened with the seriousness of the moment. Only three women were present: Oline Muus herself, and two companions she had been allowed to bring with her. In the minutes before the meeting began, there was both great excitement and uncertainty, as no one really knew what to expect. The only certain thing was that only the men would speak during the meeting; they would debate, discuss, and scrutinize the matter publicly. Of the nearly one thousand people in the room, the main character would not be allowed to speak. Oline Muus, on whom the day's discussions would center, who had put everything in motion by submitting a written complaint against her husband to the civil court without bringing it to the congregation first—she would be silenced.

PREFACE

THERE IS A SCENE ENGRAVED on my mind from Emanuele Crialese's film *Nuovomondo* (2006), which tells the story of a poor family
of farmers who emigrated from Sicily to America in 1913. At the harbor
of Ellis Island in New York, where the large wave of immigrants arrived
and were kept in temporary custody, the Sicilians witnessed a group of
Orthodox Jews sitting together, deep in prayer. This sight of religious
devotion moved the Sicilians to prayer, and together they recited both
the Ave Maria and Pater Noster, the most beloved prayers brought
from their homeland.

This scene, with the immigrants at the threshold of the new world,
hanging on to their religion from the country they left, searching to
find safety and strength, was the seed that sprouted this book project.
What was it really like to build a new life in an unfamiliar world? What
does religion mean for individuals who have emigrated and established
themselves in a foreign place? What is the relationship between the
immigrants' own community and the larger society that takes them
in? What does it actually mean to become assimilated—and how long
does the process take? This book centers on all these questions.

Muus vs. Muus takes place during the largest mass emigration in Norwegian history. In the period from 1830 to 1920, as many as 800,000 people emigrated from Norway, most of them traveling to North America.
The Norwegian emigrants left a land that did not have full religious freedom, a place with extremely tight connections between church and state
at all levels of society, a country that through many hundreds of years

was characterized by a strong—if not totalitarian—religious Lutheran culture. In the United States, one was seemingly entirely free to develop one's own religious identity, to create new religious communities. How did these Norwegian immigrants make use of this opportunity?[1]

From the history of migration, we know that two main tendencies manifest in these situations. Religion—with its articles of faith, rituals, and rules—can actually become more important for the immigrants than it was in their home country. Migrants and their religious communities can go through what researchers call a puritanization process. In a new and ambiguous situation, with vague borders defining both the majority culture and other immigrant groups, the religious community's set of rules can be an important support for creating safety, sustaining vulnerable traditions, and strengthening the community internally. In such situations religious practices quickly become stricter and more conservative in the immigrant community than they were back in the homeland. But among the newly arrived immigrants the opposite tendency can also be seen. In a foreign country, they can reject the religion they grew up with and venture out on the religious market to find belonging in another religious community or in various forms of secular identity. Both of these processes can be observed in this story of Bernt and Oline Muus and the community to which they belonged.[2]

The work on this book began in 2011. The original plan was to gather nine short biographies of Norwegian immigrants to America from 1850 to 1914, individuals who illustrated the religious, historical, and sociological themes I sought to research. But soon it was clear that one of the biographies stood out, and in a way that could encapsulate all the others. It was the story of Oline Muus (1838–1922).

First and foremost, Oline Muus's rebellion against her husband, Bernt Julius Muus, created a sensation in the Norwegian American community and ignited intense debate both in Norway and in America. Oline Muus's story directly or indirectly impacted several individuals I had planned to include in my portrait: they read about and became engaged in the conflict between the couple, and they participated in the debate around the scandal. A few of them also met Oline Muus personally and established their own relationship with her.

The conflict between the married couple—and the debate it generated—also directly affected the religious and social questions I hoped to research. Was it Norwegian or American law that should be applied in the inheritance settlement at the center of the complaint? What should weigh most heavily: the Norwegian Lutheran immigrant church's religious traditions, or the majority culture's civic standards and ideals? How did Oline Muus, her husband, and the Norwegian American community around them handle these differences?

Oline Muus's rebellion against her husband also provided access to unique primary sources, as the church and civic proceedings are extremely well documented. This religious process, in which many members of the congregation actively participated at the same level as the Norwegian Synod's pastors, gives a valuable entry into studying the role religion played in a settlement of Norwegian American immigrants, both for individuals and for how they organized as a community.

The tensions found in the local church proceedings and the extensive public debate makes Oline Muus's story especially well suited to illustrate the breadth of and the contention within the Norwegian American milieu during the last half of the 1800s. The conflicts between Oline and Bernt Muus played out in a Norwegian culture that the majority of us today know very little about. It is a culture that we, somewhere along the line, have forgotten: an early immigrant culture where Norwegian language, beliefs, and traditions wrestled with new landscapes, new traditions and belief systems, and a new society. At the same time, this Norwegian culture was also a common transatlantic culture, wherein both people and ideas traveled back and forth between the old Norway and the new Norway abroad for several decades. Today these connections are long lost or exist only as a distant memory. But, for Oline and Bernt Muus, these connections were an important basis for their existence.

Last but not least, the story of Oline Muus gives access to a distinct human fate—and to a peculiar and puzzling love story. This book is constructed as a wide-reaching account of social history, but it is organized around this love story. The book is divided into three parts. Part I: "Hand in Hand" centers on the period between 1838 and 1879, in which Oline Muus's life in Norway and the first twenty years of her life in America is woven together with the history of the Norwegian settlement of Holden and the Holden congregation in Goodhue County in Minnesota. Who was Oline Muus—and who was Bernt Muus? Why did they end up together? Why did they emigrate? What were their lives like as pastor and pastor's wife in Norwegian America? The source materials about Oline Pind (her name prior to marriage) are scant, but many rich letters that shed light on Oline and Bernt Muus's life prior to their big crisis in 1879 were preserved.

By contrast, for Part II "Family Trials," there is an enormous amount of source material about Oline Muus. This section centers on a two-year period; however, these years are extremely dramatic and eventful. They involve the American legal proceedings between the couple, the long series of congregational meetings in Holden in the first part of 1880, and the extensive debate about the conflict in both Norway and America. Why did Oline Muus file a lawsuit? What consequences did it have for her as a pastor's wife, a wife, and a mother? In this section members of the congregation assert themselves in the story—along with a good many others in the Norwegian American community, in the larger American society, and in Norway. What reactions did the case create in the outside world, and what were Norwegian American community members' opinions about the issues it raised?

Section III "Disgrace" focuses on the four decades after Oline Muus left Holden in the fall of 1881. What became of her in her new life? What became of her husband, the Holden parish, and the religious community? As in the first section, the sources from Oline Muus's last forty years are meager, but what is available gives a fascinating glimpse into both her and her husband's fate. The name "Oline Muus" wasn't engraved on her tombstone in the fall of 1922; strangely, it was something quite different.

I owe my interest and research on this subject to Kathryn Ericson's fascinating article "Triple Jeopardy: The 1879 *Muus v. Muus* Case in Three Forums" (1987) in *Minnesota History*, which initially led me to dig further. Additionally, I am indebted to Joseph M. Shaw's expansive

biography *Bernt Julius Muus: Founder of St. Olaf College* (1999), which
contains multiple chapters on the couple and the Muus family. These
two texts are the foundational accounts I have relied on. For the remaining sources, please refer to the book's bibliography.[3]

The many individuals who traveled to America from around the
world in the 1800s had a variety of different motives to emigrate. The
majority traveled due to lack of opportunities in their homeland. A few
fled religious and political oppression. Others left because of a spirit
of adventure. For the Sicilian family in Crialese's film, the dream of a
better life leads them to the nuovomondo [the new world]. Because
the film ends on Ellis Island, we don't find out how things went for the
Sicilians and whether they held on to their Catholic faith. In contrast,
we do know quite a bit about the Norwegian immigrants who ended
up in the Holden settlement in Minnesota. Parts of their stories are
now gathered in this book.

Muus vs. Muus: The Scandal that Shook Norwegian America is essentially a story of how immigrants came together to form their own community: an Evangelical Lutheran congregation where their Norwegian
language as well as Norwegian traditions and values were replanted in
American soil. But the story also contains interesting contradictions.
After an extraordinary amount of research, writing, and editing, I
hope this book can provide some answers to the questions about the
Muuses, about the Norwegian immigrant community in Holden and
Minnesota, and more generally about what religion means during a
time of immigration. The answers point in all different directions: what
I initially believed to be straightforward and obvious turned out to be
puzzling, complicated, and full of contradictions.

Many individuals have assisted in this project. A special thanks from
the author of the original Norwegian version goes to Knut Kjeldstadli,
who has been an academic support from the start; Øyvind Tveitereid
Gulliksen, who read and commented on the manuscript several times;
and law consultant Ola Mestad. Thanks to those who have provided
counsel and assistance: Arne Bugge Amundsen, Ingeborg Kongslien,
Alexis Logsdon, Sverre Mørkhagen, Marta Norheim, Jeff M. Sauve,

Taru Spiegel, and Dina H. Tolfsby. Thanks, also, to the Norwegian Non-Fiction Writers and Translators Association and the Fritt Ord Foundation, which have given financial support to this project. And last, but not least, a big thanks to my editor, Trygve Riiser Gundersen, for inspirational teamwork.

....

Shortly after my book was published in Oslo in August 2019, Kari Lie Dorer contacted me, eager to translate the book. And the rest is history. Tusen takk, Kari.

Bodil Stenseth
Oslo, Norway

PART I

Hand in Hand

Oline Pind, 1857.
From Alfred Muus and Bernt J. Muus,
Niels Muus's Æt: Muus-slegten i Snaasa, 1642–1942, 72.

To America

IN THE SPRING OF 1857, Oline Pind, the nineteen-year-old daughter of a district official in Fet, was photographed for posterity. She conducted herself properly, sitting in front of the camera as if she had done it many times before. Not quite facing forward, she looks at the photographer as she rests her head lightly against her right hand.

Her hand is slim, pale, and unblemished. Her eyes are large and captivating, while her round face seems small. Dark, shapely brows accentuate the beauty and depth of her eyes. Her high cheekbones give her a Mediterranean look. Her gaze makes a lasting impression—that and her thick, black hair. Her mouth is short, her lips narrow, and her nose both too long and too large. Her hair, her pride, is attractively styled for the occasion. With a precise part down the middle, it falls beautifully over her temples and ears and is gathered in a loose and full bun at the base of her neck.

Her dress, black and decorous, reflects her sophistication. It is lavish, embellished with a wide white lace collar and a small brooch. From her elbows to her wrists, her sleeves are fitted with white silk flower ruffles that undoubtedly took a considerable amount of material to make. It must have cost a small fortune. Only an experienced seamstress could have conjured such a work of art with a needle and thread.

Originally baptized as Kathrine Christiane in 1838, as a small child she began to call herself Oline—the name of a sister who only lived to be four. Her parents could have, as was the custom, formally named her after their daughter who had died. But Kathrine Christiane, who was their last in the brood of four children, made her own choice to be called Oline.[1]

On Tien Farm in the wooded farmland of Fet, Norway, twenty miles east of Christiania (present-day Oslo), Oline grew up in grand circumstances. Her father, Johan Christian Pind, was the local district official and, together with the pastor and the bailiff, constituted the village's authority. He belonged to the first generation of civil servants after 1814, when Norway adopted Europe's most democratic constitution and then was forced into union with Sweden. Pind was a wealthy landowner. In addition to Tien, he owned several other farms, which were run by managers and a large workforce of farmhands. Pind also owned a mill and was involved in real estate. His administrative duties were conducted from Tien Farm, where there was both a courtroom and a jail. There, Oline gained an early glimpse into the folly and the evil of the world. From the cook and the servants in the kitchen, she may have heard about everything from ghosts and thieves to ax murderers and poisoners. And, at the dinner table, she must have heard her father's commentary on everything from local business to fraud, inheritance disputes to politics.

In 1849, when Oline was eleven years old, "Thraneria," as authorities called it, raged. Marcus Thrane, the son of a merchant who had been imprisoned for embezzlement, was regarded by those like Pind as a political agitator, a dangerous revolutionary. In the following years in Fet, as in other areas in eastern Norway, craftsmen and cotters joined Thrane's workers' associations in large numbers, demanding the right to own land and the right to vote. There were cotters who refused to do their obligatory duties on the owner's land, and in some places, they chopped down trees in the owner's forest. In 1851, the authorities crushed the rebellion. Later, many of Thrane's supporters, with their entire families, emigrated to start a new life on the other side of the Atlantic.

Oline's parents would do anything for her. When Oline's siblings one by one grew up and moved away, she became in practical terms an only child. If she wanted to go to the capital, she did so with her mother, Hanna Louise (née Poulsen), as a travel companion. Oline cherished her visits to Christiania, where the shops were filled with everything she could want and where there was a thriving social life not found in Fet. During one of these visits to the city, at the age of eighteen, she met the love of her life, Bernt Julius Muus. He was a theology student and six years older than her. They became engaged in the spring of 1857.

A photo from the 1850s gives an impression of Bernt as a stern man. In front of the photographer's camera, he sits like a statue, serious and reserved. He seems a little hesitant, with one eye wide open and the other half closed. Undoubtedly, he is uncomfortable with the situation. Being photographed was demanding. The actual picture taking required several minutes, and Bernt had to concentrate and not even blink. He absolutely could not smile, for it was important to show his true self.

Bernt was a joyful and witty man, though he hides it well as he sits with his hands in his lap. His hair is cut short at the neckline and along his ears. His dark, full head of hair is elaborately combed to the side with water or oil over his broad, high forehead. His cheeks are narrow and smooth, his chin round and forthright, and his mustache powerful and bristly. Bernt Muus was a man of strong convictions, someone who easily fell out with others. His black suit jacket is obviously tailored, and the white shirtfront is immaculate. The giant black silk bow tie knotted artfully under his shirt collar testifies that he was also vain. In his left hand he holds a dark tube with a white end piece—probably his meerschaum pipe. If there was one thing the theology student couldn't live without, it was tobacco.[2]

Most men in the Muus family were tall and large-boned, like Bernt's father, Ingebrigt Muus. Bernt, however, was well proportioned and slender. He was good-looking; a friend described him as a handsome man, physically strong. In his youth, he was often in the mountains and in the woods, and in the winter, he would go skiing. He came from an old and influential family in Snåsa, located in the northern region of Trøndelag. His ancestor Niels Muus (1642–1737), who was of Danish origin but born in Hedmark, held the position of pastor of Snåsa parish for sixty-five years and was buried at the church in Snåsa, in the Muus family chapel. A man born into the Muus family had a lot to live up to.

Bernt Julius Muus, 1850s.
From Alfred Muus and Bernt J. Muus,
Niels Muus's Æt: Muus-slegten i Snaasa, 1642–1942, 71.

Bernt's father, Ingebrigt, was a prominent leader in Snåsa, and the family's Krogsgården was the parish's most splendid farm. There, Ingebrigt had built a huge farmhouse and buildings for all of his businesses, including an inn and a general store, thanks to the royal privileges he received. There were rumors about Muus's business dealings; among other things, he once managed to sell a large batch of chamber pots as porridge tureens. Ingebrigt also asserted himself in politics. He was a longtime member of the municipal executive council and deputy mayor. With the Alderman Act of 1837, Norway had gained local autonomy. This law likely helped to consolidate class differences, as only men who were property owners and civil servants could be elected to government office and to the Parliament.

But Bernt, the firstborn son of Ingebrigt Muus, had not grown up on the Krogsgården farm. When his mother died after giving birth to his sister Birgitte, the two children were sent to live with their grandparents at Snåsa parsonage. Their father, who lived for a few years as a widower, remarried in 1840, and the eldest son in his new family, Martinius, would eventually inherit Krogsgården farm. Bernt, on the other hand, was to be university educated; his father gladly paid for him to follow in his grandfather's footsteps. Perhaps the idea was that Bernt in time would become the pastor at Snåsa.

His maternal grandfather, Jens Rynning, Snåsa's pastor at the time, was concerned with more earthly things: road construction, the education system, and responsible agriculture. From the pulpit he raged at people who immigrated to America: Norwegians must live where they were born; their Christian duty was to work for the progress and prosperity of the fatherland. After his own son, Ole, left Snåsa, Jens thundered with anger even more often. In 1837, Ole Rynning, Bernt's uncle, led a group of immigrants who established a colony in Illinois. But the land they bought was marshy, and most of the immigrants died of malaria. Ole Rynning, however, survived and wrote a book before he died in 1839. The book, *Sandfærdig Beretning om Amerika til Oplysning og Nytte for Bonde og Menigmand [True Account of America for the Information and Help of Peasant and Commoner]*, did not calm his father, Jens Rynning. Jens had only one good thing to say about America:

wheat bread. In America people could eat wheat bread, while in Norway they had only flatbread. Other than that, America, with its snakes and unhealthy air, was the worst place on earth; in many states, the law even allowed slavery.

In 1849, when Bernt Muus began his studies at Royal Frederik's University in Christiania at the age of seventeen, his uncle's book had been printed in ever-new editions and the first great wave of emigration from Norway had just begun. A decade later, in 1859, it had by no means subsided. In April of that year, Bernt wrote a letter to Laur. Larsen, who had become a pastor for a congregation in Wisconsin, and would soon serve as the founding president of Luther College. Bernt wrote about his intention to accept a call from the Holden congregation in Goodhue County, Minnesota. Was it easy to find servants there? How was the climate? How would they secure a place to live? His letter contained many questions, questions his prospective in-laws had asked and that he himself could not answer. Still, he believed he'd arrive in America as a married man.[3]

2

A Call from God

....

OLINE PIND AND BERNT MUUS first met at a revival meeting in the capital. There, as in Kristiansand, Stavanger, and Tromsø, hearts were on fire. Across the entire country from east to west, from north to south, the revival movement of the 1850s gained ground. Only in a few towns and rural hamlets, including Bernt Muus's home hamlet of Snåsa, did cooler heads prevail. Even old-fashioned rationalists and ardent skeptics had to examine themselves and ask if they were only "nominal Christians," as the revivalists claimed.

The revivalists considered themselves enlightened as true Christians. They were "brothers" and "sisters" and constituted a community of friends. They read the Bible themselves, interpreted the Bible themselves, were accountable to no one but God, and lived in accordance with the gospel. The friends would meet regularly in private homes or public meeting rooms. People who attended such meetings could share their experience of deep joy and peace, the glory and grace of God. Through belief in the Savior, they were forgiven of their sins, and the darkness departed from the light. The saved became, as they said, "blessed in the faith." Being converted was akin to being born again. After a long struggle with oneself, both crises and nervous breakdowns could occur before the great thing—the celestial awareness of God's presence—happened. A new reckoning began, and the redeemed stuck close to their friends. From then on, there were two groups of people: the believers and the nonbelievers.[1]

"My dear, precious Oline! Doubt not, my dear," began Bernt Muus's letter on October 23, 1857. The couple, who six months previously had promised to be faithful to each other until death, lived in different parts of the country: she in Fet, and he in Christiania. In his letter, Bernt worried that Oline didn't understand that he was writing to her in sincerity, that she believed he didn't love his own soul nor hers. He explains that because she was given unto him, therefore, wouldn't he hurt himself by not being candid with her? He asserts that, because he is human, he might be mistaken, even unconsciously, but hopefully that wouldn't be true too often. He assured her that he rejoiced in having found a soul who was steadfast in "the Law," one who wouldn't let herself be carried by the wind, one who wouldn't blow away from others or him.[2]

The two were clearly in love; their moods could suddenly shift from happiness to sorrow, from hope to despondency. "I think you like me a little, because you call me by so many dear names, and that is something you like to hear from the one you love," wrote Bernt. It was as if he couldn't quite believe she would be his forever. He comforted himself with their common faith: "Christ is our Savior and our Teacher, both yours and mine. And see how good it will be to follow him, hand in hand, if we even once could see his face." When they followed Jesus's example, the love between them would grow even stronger. Hand in hand, the two would travel to America.

Oline Pind was nineteen when she made the biggest decision of her life. The plan was that the two of them, he as pastor and she as pastor's wife, would follow their call and go to America. But the plan wasn't well received by her parents in Fet. "You have already begun to endure unpleasantness for my sake," Bernt admitted on October 23, 1857.[3]

America—that was the problem. Her mother and father believed Oline was in support of the plan, though they accepted their daughter's chosen one. Her mother especially seems to have grown fond of Bernt; in letters, she refers to him as "my son." Bernt, who came from a long line of pastors and was to become a pastor himself, was not a bad match. The two elder Pind daughters had both safely settled in marriages: one with a justice of the peace in Grimstad, the other with a doctor in Kongsberg. Now Oline desired to become a pastor's wife, and if it wasn't for the plan to go across the Atlantic, to America, everything would have been well received. In his letter, Bernt was upset that Oline's parents blamed the emigration plans on her, for he had, long before their engagement, told the Pinds of his intention to take a call in America. But Bernt wasn't surprised that Oline's parents wanted to keep her at home in Norway. "It must be very hard for them," he wrote, "and we couldn't help but see them doing what they can to move us to reconsider our decision." The plan also wasn't easy for Bernt. For Oline, who had hardly gone beyond her family's farm, the journey to the foreign, faraway country would be difficult. Perhaps the best thing would have been for her to follow her father's wishes. Bernt, in his letter, comforted himself that she, like him, would consider it an honor to serve the Savior, wherever he might call them. Besides, Bernt continued, life's happiness does not always depend on what is familiar. Oline had, after all, confirmed that she would join him. When he heard "the cry from the American churches" as a call from God, it was also her calling.[4]

The pietistic revival, with its worship of Jesus as the Savior and emphasis on a deeply personal relationship with God, was a modern project. The revivalist movement of the 1850s, unlike that of Hans Nielsen Hauge in the 1790s, also gained momentum among the upper classes, especially among the young. Even one of Bernt Muus's theology professors, Gisle Johnson, became a revivalist. He had the students read Søren Kierkegaard, whose writings criticized the ritualism of the state church and spoke out for its abolition. And Professor Johnson himself caused a scandal when, during a meeting of the Students' Society, he thanked God that he had never become a pastor because the state church made the duty of the church and the individual—to fulfill the evangelical ideal—difficult.[5]

The revival movement, which centered on the individual and the role of the individual within the family and society, was also a manifestation of another modern phenomenon: the so-called spirit of association. This pervasive process brings people together in societies and clubs, associations and organizations, and also drives the development of newspapers and magazines. America led the way. By 1830, the United States had the most newspapers and organizations of all the countries in the world. Bernt was himself an active participant in this process. In 1857, with fellow student T. H. Bernhoft, he had started the journal *Norsk Kirketidende*, to which Professor Johnson contributed. The first serious theological journal in Norway, it was also an opposition periodical. According to the two editors, theologians in office were too minorly engaged in the great questions of the day, namely, "the ecclesiastical movement," and the journal was intended to address this deficiency.[6]

In the fall of 1857, Bernt Muus had not yet graduated from his practicum, a prerequisite for being ordained a pastor and to answer a call. But did he want to become a pastor? In Christiania, he made a living as a teacher while also having other irons in the fire. Nevertheless, in his letter to Oline on October 23, 1857, he asked her to adjust as best she could to the plan to journey to America. "And good night, my love!" he wrote after long, heartfelt confessions. "Yours to the grave, Bernt Muus."[7]

3

Land Rush and Pioneer Life

....

SOON AFTER SETTLERS HAD colonized lands in the "West," they began to establish congregations, even before the territories had acquired statehood. So began the story of the Norwegian settlement of Holden in Goodhue County, Minnesota. In 1854, the first groups of young men, with or without a wife and children, arrived in covered wagons drawn by oxen. Two years later, on September 23, 1856, eighty-seven Norwegian men and one woman met to found Holden church. Two more years later, in 1858, Minnesota would become the thirty-second state admitted into the Union. Like most new settlements, the congregation lacked its own pastor. Bernt Muus knew the situation, though he was not yet ready to respond to the invitation.[1]

Drawn on the map as a triangle, Goodhue County is named after Minnesota's first newspaper editor, James Madison Goodhue. Red Wing, the administrative center of the county, located on the banks of the Mississippi and named after the legendary Dakota leader, was where groups of white settler-colonists flocked to purchase land. The land rush had begun. The Homestead Act of 1862 granted 160 acres (sixty-five hectares) of surveyed government land for $1.25 per acre. With a purchase contract in hand, settler-colonists knew it was essential to arrive as quickly as possible, preferably before other immigrants. Rumors spread about how rich and fertile the soil in Goodhue County was. In all of Minnesota, which is comparable in size to Trøndelag, Norwegian immigrants hoped to end up in Goodhue County.[2]

Besides lakes, rivers, and waterfalls, the area offered prairies with their vast grasslands stretching farther than the eye could see and forests rich in timber, birds, and game. All this splendor, it was said, was beyond the edge of civilization. The Indigenous peoples, the Mdewakanton Dakota, were driven westward by government treaties and the influx of settler-colonists. The Dakota were given inferior land or received promises of compensation that were never honored. The price of Euro-American advancement, relentlessly demanded by the United States, was high. The confinement of America's Indigenous peoples to reservations had just begun in 1857. Yet they weren't completely gone: they hunted and gathered on their old homelands as they had for centuries, while white immigrants put down roots in farming colonies.[3]

One of the Norwegian settlements in Goodhue County was named Holden because the majority of immigrants there came from Holden in Telemark. This was the pattern. People from the same place in Norway sought out each other and together created a new community in their adopted, foreign country. Among the many tens of thousands of emigrants between the years 1840 and 1850, a striking number came from mountainous communities in eastern Norway or from the hamlets on the inner fjords in western Norway. The men from these places, farmers who had often also worked as carpenters and craftspeople, were well equipped for the settler-colonist life. The ability to take on multiple types of work came in handy for them and for their wives. The woman of the farm was a housewife, a milkmaid, and a farmhand; often, she walked from chore to chore with her knitting, which she could hang from a hook on her belt. She had her own handicraft business, carding, spinning, weaving, and sewing. Whatever her extended family needed—from undergarments to outer layers of clothing—she would knit and sew herself. These early immigrants who did well in America were hailed by the generations that followed as "pioneers."[4]

One of the immigrants who helped found the Holden church was Knut K. Finseth, who also became the pastor's faithful supporter. As a result, Knut's life story ended up in print, in an obituary written by his friend Pastor Bernt Muus. In 1849, twenty-four-year-old Knut had traveled from destitute conditions in Hemsedal to America; the eldest son, he was to investigate opportunities and report back. He first arrived in Rock Prairie, Wisconsin, where he found work with an American farmer. Knut, quick to learn, soaked up all the new things he saw and heard. Often a Baptist pastor came to the farm, and Knut, having been raised in a God-fearing home, was moved when he heard the minister preach. He learned that baptismal water must be used in abundance for it to have spiritual worth, and that man can only be baptized in adulthood and then reborn a Christian. Knut worked for another American farmer, and then another. Everything was so different from his home in Hemsedal. Here there was carpet on the floors and a thresher on the farm; even a farmer himself could vote for the president. And Knut could be a Christian in a different way, which appealed to him deeply.[5]

After two or three years in Rock Prairie, the day came when Knut's relatives arrived from Hemsedal, as planned. But his family firmly believed in what they had learned about God at home in Norway and couldn't bear to listen to his interpretations of water and spirit, faith and baptism. That a man can vote for whom he wants as president was all very well and good, but that one can decide for oneself how to gain eternal salvation—on that they could not agree. In the end, after reuniting with his relatives and beginning their new life together, Knut acknowledged that he had gone astray. Religious training during childhood was the greatest blessing the Evangelical Lutheran Church brought to the Norwegian people in America. Bernt Muus wrote in 1870 that Knut came to his senses, compelled by the obedience of his faith. When Knut and his relatives had put down enough money to purchase land in 1855, they left Rock Prairie and traveled west, to the new settlement of Holden.

For people from poor rugged mountains and fjords, Goodhue County was like a paradise. Peder Langemo, a member of one of the first small groups to arrive in the summer of 1854, and who managed to build a log house by winter, compared Holden to "the land of Canaan." "Apparently these pioneers did not find the houses full of everything good, as the children of Israel found it, when they took the land of Canaan," he recalled at the age of seventy-three when giving a talk on the fiftieth anniversary of the Holden congregation. Peder had been a member of the congregation from its founding in 1856, and in Holden, he cleared land and built up one of the largest farms.[6]

The founding of settlements also created conflicts. Some newcomers circumvented the law by setting boundary stakes claiming land they neither were entitled to nor had paid for. They also swindled more land than the legal 160 acres. The land rush certainly didn't bring out the best in people, and in some places the "law of the land," the self-justice of the settler-colonists, prevailed. In Holden in 1855, the law was tested in a veritable brawl that became known as the "battle of the clubs." It all began with the Talla brothers, Henrik and Tøge, who put boundary markers outside their legally purchased land. When newcomers arrived to claim their own parcels, they were told that the Talla brothers' law prevailed and anyone who tried to claim the land the Talla brothers had taken possession of had to fight for their right to it. The Tallas drew up their own law, known as "club law," to control who would start new lives in the settlement.[7]

Then a man by the name of Store Sven (Big Sven, or Sven Nordgaarden) set his claim in the area the Talla brothers had marked out but didn't have the legal right to, which led to the infamous brawl. In *Drømmen om Amerika [The Dream of America]*, Sverre Mørkhagen gives an account of the defeat of the brothers, a shortened version of which follows: Sven knew when he saw the crowd coming that they did not come to welcome him so he told his hired man to take the gun and hide among the trees and to fire it into the air on a given signal. Tøge Talla was the spokesman for the crowd. He stepped in front with a club on his shoulder and told Sven in not very complimentary language that he could not remain there but had to move on. Sven, who always had a good supply of words not fit to repeat, made liberal use of them and as the discussion was growing hot and blows were momentarily expected to fall, all of a sudden a shot sounded behind them and all turned around to see what it meant. Sven watched his chance and gave Tøge a rap over the neck with a stout stick and laid him out. The rest of them took to their heels.

The old timers who took an active part in this scrap never cared to talk much about it. The hickory clubs are said to be preserved in the courthouse in Red Wing. The battle of the clubs of 1855, which had a legal consequence, ended with the Talla brothers losing. They each, however, retained their own farm and their own 160 acres.[8]

Despite the land rush, the "Norwegians," whether they came from Hemsedal or Sogn, kept apart from "the others": Yankees and German and Swedish immigrants who had also acquired land in the same settlement. But when the Norwegians eventually became the settlement's most numerous group, they made life so miserable for the others that they gave up and moved on. "Damn Norwegians," the Yankees said.[9]

An immigrant without nearby relatives was ill equipped to cope with the struggle for existence. He had to continue working as long as it was light, and when family joined him, his wife and children would labor as well. While the sons followed their fathers to work in the fields, the daughters helped their mothers at home. In a family's first farmhouse, a primitive log house with ten- to twelve-foot-tall walls, there was always room for relatives and others who arrived later. In these log houses, two or three families could often live together for long periods of time. The extended family constituted a work collective, in which everyone contributed to the group's success and prosperity. The immigrants were proud of progress and betterment, and they competed against each other. The land of Canaan that Peder Langemo spoke of also provided a breeding ground for envy and hostility, bickering and strife.[10]

Moreover, this new life brought trials of all kinds: sickness, untimely death, homesickness, and drunkenness. Old drinking habits followed the Norwegian immigrants to America. They would take a dram at work, one on the road, and another when guests arrived. As soon as administrative towns were founded where immigrants settled, whiskey merchants established general stores or saloons. And as soon as the government financed road construction so the settler-colonists could continue farther west, still other whiskey merchants turned up. "Give me whatever you have, give me a brandy," offers a widely used pocket phrasebook, *The Little American: Den lille Amerikaner*. A newcomer who demanded brandy at the country store probably soon learned that in America one drinks whiskey. Maybe he also learned the polite phrases "please" and "thank you very much."[11]

4

Oline's Disfavor

....

WHEN LOUISE PIND WROTE from the farm to her prospective son-in-law, Bernt Muus, in Christiania on February 28, 1858, she had maternal concerns. The scarf she had knitted for him might not be to his liking. She had a lot to say about the scarf, but she was mostly worried about Oline, who was visiting the capital and had stayed there longer than planned. Oline's parents certainly understood why she stayed in Christiania, where life was more exciting. Her mother didn't begrudge her some fun. It was good for Oline, as the monotonous and quiet life on Tien Farm became dull for someone her age. And, Louise Pind noted, "the time will soon come for Oline, as for all of us, when she will have to do without the amusement and entertainment that she can now enjoy." Hopefully, Oline didn't stand in the way of Bernt's work. One day they would be able to repay the hospitality Oline experienced with her friends in the city. Was Oline reasonably careful about her health? Was the medicine the doctor had prescribed her left unused? Louise wrote that when Oline came home, they would be able to catch up. "God grant," she continued, referring to the medicine, "that it might accomplish its purpose for Oline to be really well."[1]

The message was that her daughter had to come home, and soon. The mother added, tellingly, that Oline wouldn't lack company—the parliamentary representatives were to meet at Tien, and the meeting would take place already on Tuesday. Louise asserted that Bernt must notify Oline about the gathering, as Louise didn't want to risk being in "Oline's disfavor." The youngest daughter was obviously the kind of person with whom it was best to remain in good standing. It almost looked as if her mother, and her father too, were so afraid of making Oline unhappy that they would let her do whatever she wanted. But they still opposed her determination to emigrate. In the letter, Louise Pind didn't write a word about America.

In closing, Louise wrote that Tien was as it had always been, and thank goodness the family was healthy. She and her husband talked daily about the young couple in the capital, about how well they had it there. "God bless you and our beloved Oline," she wished, with many warm greetings from "Your Devoted Mother L. Pind."

Was the America plan shelved? Probably the departure was postponed, and there were several reasons for that. The letter indicates that Oline was not entirely healthy. It may also be that Oline, who in the winter of 1858 was still only nineteen years old, lacked the necessary skills for a pastor's wife, the most honorable position a woman could occupy. Within Oline Pind's social sphere were young women who absolutely aspired to become a pastor's wife; the duties imposed upon a pastor's wife were more extensive and significantly more important than those of an ordinary wife. Parsonages around the countryside were like cultural centers. Even if the clergy were not always adored, they enjoyed respect in their position as public officials.[2]

While the prospective pastor was preparing for his position studying at the university, the soon-to-be pastor's wife also had to make sure she learned everything required of her. She had to be familiar with the scriptures and the creeds, and she had to be among the confirmands who passed the pastor's catechization in front of the congregation with flying colors. When her husband was away, the pastor's wife had to lead the confirmation instruction and help out in the congregation. The pastor's wife had to be able to manage a large household from beginning to end and be experienced in all kinds of work that it required. Often a pastor's wife acquired experience by living and working in a parsonage. The youngest daughter from Tien could undoubtedly learn how to run a large farm from lending her mother a hand. However, it's unclear whether Oline actually trained in this way. On her journey to America, she brought an older, experienced servant girl, who resided with the Muuses for several years.[3]

Oline was hardly among the young women who dreamed of becoming a pastor's wife, or who realized this dream by hunting down an eligible pastor. When she became engaged to Bernt Muus, it was because they were in love and shared a common faith. He made sure he was prepared in the English language, the common language of trade at the time. In 1857, he translated *Parables from Nature*, which became *Fabler fra Naturen*, by Margaret Gatty, the famous Victorian children's book author who was also a self-educated biologist. One of the fables is about a dying butterfly mother worrying about her little ones, the eggs she's laid on a cabbage leaf. Before she dies and flies up to heaven, she spots a little caterpillar, whom she asks to care for the little ones by giving them morning dew and honey. How to meet this request the larva doesn't understand, until a lark comes to its aid. The caterpillar must give the little ones the same thing to eat as what they lie on: namely, cabbage leaves. Even though the caterpillar has a hard time believing what the lark says, it follows through. And out of the eggs on the cabbage leaf creep the larvae, who eventually become butterflies.

Bernt likely drew from these types of parables about God's wonderful creations to teach his youngest students the fundamentals of Christianity. At the same time as they learned about Almighty God, about how wisely He had designed all things, about faith, hope, and charity, they also learned about nature itself. Bernt was, at that time, an educational innovator. Yet he held fast to the religious training of his youth, the Articles of Faith, and all the other things in Luther's *Small Catechism* that children had to practice and memorize. Religious training in childhood was and remained essential, something that couldn't be forgotten. For Bernt, modernity and tradition were integrated in their own unique manner, which often led to difficulties in his ministry.

The fact that he actually translated a book by a female author might have been notable at the time. Norway in the 1850s was a society of men; it was men who spoke and wrote, and it was men who fought with or against each other in public. But, in this decade, a handful of women began to make their presence felt. In 1852, Aasta Hansteen, the daughter of a professor, established herself as a portrait painter in Christiania. She was the country's first woman to receive training and become a professional artist. In 1855, astonishingly, she was chosen to represent Norway at an international art exhibition in Paris. Norway's first novel was also written by a woman. *Amtmandens døtre [The District Governor's Daughters]*, with its biting criticism of arranged marriages, became a scandalous success. The novel was published in 1854–55 under a pseudonym, but everyone knew who the author was: Camilla Collett, sister of Henrik Wergeland, a prolific writer who is considered one of the greatest Norwegian poets and a symbol of revolutionary ideology.[4]

Whether Oline got hold of Camilla Collett's book is unknown. But the possibility isn't especially likely. Bernt's letters to her only occasionally mention a poem or a novel, or even a song or music book—so in her early years she may not have been very well read or cultured. But we know that she became quite accomplished later in life. According to Andreas Ueland, a close acquaintance later in 1879, Oline was richly endowed, a skilled pianist, and very knowledgeable in Norwegian literature. Although Oline and Bernt belonged to the circle of revivalists, they didn't reject worldly pleasures.[5]

In the Lutheran tradition, entertaining literature and song, such as theater, dance, and card games, were commonly considered adiaphora—worldly pleasures that are neither sinful nor virtuous in their own right. The religious distinction was made between those communities in which adiaphora was permitted and those who believed such pursuits drew time and attention away from the much more important life of faith, which, in the worst case, could quickly lead to sin. Those who lived strictly according to the law and the gospel took pride in their life of piety and renounced such things. When they met for scripture readings and hymn singing, prayer and spiritual conversations, they sought to support one another against such temptations. "There is no peace for the wicked, says my God," the revivalist's godfather, Professor Gisle Johnson, often reminded his followers. He said this in a quiet and feeble voice, proclaiming the grace in Christ that was available to those who indeed experienced the faith and surrendered themselves to it. Professor Johnson, Bernt's teacher and mentor, demanded the complete dedication of all who followed Christ.[6]

In Christiania, there was a story about one of the upper-class wives who was known as a skilled pianist, but after she was awakened she put "her tempter," the piano, away in the attic. She would never again play the piano. But Bernt's betrothed became a pastor's wife who played the piano and who later even became a piano teacher.[7]

5

The Lay People's Church

....

IN THE FALL OF 1858, the Holden congregation was still without a pastor. Two years had passed since the church council sent a letter to the theology faculty at Royal Frederik's University in Norway calling for a pastor. But no one besides the theology candidate Bernt Muus allowed themselves to be persuaded, and the Holden congregation received only this one response. The Norwegian clergy were minimally infected with America fever: their calling must remain in the fatherland; anything else was unpatriotic.

The Norwegian Church—the state church—was clear on one point: it would not send missionaries to America nor set up mission stations there. When certain pastors, proper pastors who had been ordained in Norway, went to minister to Norwegian congregations in America, it wasn't with the state church's blessing. One of the first to leave was twenty-six-year-old Herman Amberg Preus. In 1851, he along with his wife, Linka (née Keyser) Preus, became a pastor and pastor's wife for a congregation of Norwegian immigrants in Spring Prairie, Wisconsin. One of the pastors who followed was twenty-seven-year-old Ulrik Vilhelm Koren. His mission was farther west, in Washington Prairie, outside of Decorah, Iowa. At Christmas in 1853, when Koren and his wife, Elisabeth, arrived in Washington Prairie, he observed that there were "no shepherds and hundreds of wolves."[1]

Preus and Koren, young enthusiasts and shrewd strategists, quickly became powerful figures among the Norwegians in the new country.

In 1853, Preus, along with four other clergymen, established the Norwegian Evangelical Lutheran Church in America, also known as the Norwegian Synod or the Synod. Preus later became the Synod president, and Koren eventually became secretary. The two also became inseparable friends. The church in Holden belonged to the Synod from the time when a visiting pastor, Pastor Hans Andreas (H. A.) Stub, had assisted the congregation to formally organize on September 12, 1856. Although the new church was Norwegian, with a Norwegian pastor, it was separate from the state, since in America there was no state church. As a result, the Norwegian immigrants gained two unfamiliar new democratic institutions: congregational meetings and church councils. The state church in Norway, which from the days of the Reformation had been an authoritarian church, was for the first time allowed to hold a congregational meeting in 1873. And not until five decades later, in 1920, did Norwegian law allow for church councils. The Norwegian American churches were themselves examples of the new and modern trend in the growth of organizations. The Norwegian immigrants also participated in their congregations in a democratic experiment.[2]

The founding of a congregation was a very important event, signifying community organization, representative government, and democracy in the new Norwegian American community. Laypeople united to found a church; laymen assembled in congregational meetings; and laymen, through their elected church council, governed and made decisions. On September 12, 1856, Knut K. Finseth and Peder Langemo were signatories of the Holden Church bylaws, which gave the laymen democratic rights both in the congregation and in the church as a whole. The congregation hired the pastor and, if he did not meet expectations, fired him. Bernt Muus was to learn from the very outset that his clerical authority was not a given at Holden Church.

But even though laymen enjoyed both democracy and autonomy within the congregation, they didn't have unlimited power. At this historic meeting of the Holden congregation, a member cried, "I traveled to America to get rid of the pastor, and now the same pastor has come after me." Pastor Stub, the representative sent on behalf of the Synod, felt sorry for the man. In Holden's congregation, as in the other churches belonging to the Norwegian Synod, the laypeople, according to their bylaws, governed democratically. At the same time, according to the church bylaws, the pastor hired by the congregation was still the highest authority, and he exercised his power on several levels.[3]

For example, a man who applied to join the church first had to be approved in a congregational meeting. He had to present "a pastoral reference." Those who didn't have one were rejected at once. The reference, a letter of good conduct issued by the pastor at home in Norway who confirmed the individual, stated how well that person had fared on their confirmation examination, whether they were a diligent church-goer, and so forth. But a good reference from the pastor was not enough. Upon admission to the congregation, under oath, one had to answer yes to several questions, such as, "Will you submit to the order of the church, as determined by the church ritual of our fatherland, Norway?" It was essential to cite the Norwegian church rituals. On American soil, Holden Church, through its membership in the Synod, would also have to adhere to the practices of the Norwegian State Church, and thus also the ecclesiastical rules of the pastor as undisputed authority. Another question required the applicant to promise not to have any other ordained pastor and to show obedience to the pastor of the congregation, the clerical authority.[4]

Was a Norwegian church ritual and the ecclesiastical order imposed on laymen against their will? Even if some opposed the pastor's author-ity, it seems the laymen simply wanted to hold tightly to the ceremonies of the state church and also to their childhood religious training. Doing so would allow the immigrants to continue practicing the religious cus-toms with which they had grown up, creating security by holding close that which was near and dear to them, and thus creating a Norway in the foreign land. But if the church was a safe space, it was also occasion-ally a battleground, where words were weapons of contention among laymen and between laymen and clergy. For the laypeople, the congre-gation, even with its ecclesiastical rules, also functioned as a school in democracy. The men who would participate in the infamous Holden Church meetings in 1880 were experienced in the democratic organi-zational culture.

The Norwegian Synod was not alone in preserving the home country's pietist church practices. The ordained theologians from Norway had to fight for souls in the new settlements. In Goodhue County, lay preachers who called themselves pastors and who originated in the Haugean churches had arrived first. These self-taught pastors who preached in the spirit of Hans Nielsen Hauge were quite enterprising and founded many churches. Both in Red Wing and in Holden were congregations that belonged to the Haugean Synod or, as it was called in 1846, the Evangelical Lutheran Church in North America. The Haugean Synod didn't have the word "Norwegian" in its name, but rather focused on the swift integration of Norwegian immigrants into their new country. In the Holden settlement, two churches would be constructed a few years later: the Haugean Church in Aspelund and Holden Church belonging to the Norwegian Synod. The churches were only a stone's throw apart.

In America, the revivalist movement and the state church followers developed, respectively, into an American low church Haugean institution and a Norwegian high church institution, which were constantly in bitter conflict with each other. Both churches were Evangelical Lutheran, maintained their childhood religious training, confessed to the same scriptures, and sang the same hymns. But among the greatest areas of contention were the definition of a pastor and what a true life of piety was. In Norway at the time of Hans Nielsen Hauge, in the revivalist movement there had been a social uprising against the clergy and public authorities. A generation later in America, the Haugean Synod continued that social uprising in the fight against the high church Synod, headed by Pastors Preus and Koren.

The Haugeans earned the nickname "crows": "We call them crows. A crow is entirely black and screams horribly!" Preus declared in 1871. Lay preachers most likely dressed in black, though they wore neither clerical vestments nor a ruff (the clerical collar typical of the time). Like card games, alcohol, and music and dance, pastoral garb was considered a sin. But the Norwegian Synod also got an insulting nickname from the Haugean church: the Norwegian State Church Party.[5]

The childhood religious training that the emigrants had impressed upon them in their homeland and that had saved Holden Church's Knut K. Finseth from his Baptist delusions was very old. Ever since the Reformation, Luther's *Small Catechism*, in continuously updated Danish translations, had been a textbook and ABCs for generations of schoolchildren. This training continued in the Norwegian settlements in America. The *Small Catechism*, with its general examination questions for the teaching of children, including a simple confession according to Luther's true meaning, as well as *Sentences of God's Word for the Reinforcement of the Faith for the Innocent*, as the elaborate title read, was the first Norwegian—or rather, Danish—book printed on American soil. Its content was the children's curriculum. At the age of fifteen or sixteen, boys and girls were to be examined by the pastor, to be catechized, as it was called. Individuals who could answer by heart the questions posed to them secured a good reference from the pastor.

One of the questions: how many parts are there in the catechism and childhood religious teaching? The answer: five—the Ten Commandments, the Articles of Faith, the Lord's Prayer, the sacrament of baptism, and the Lord's Supper. Of the commandments that were the core of the childhood teaching, the eighth in particular, thou shalt not lie (or thou shalt not bear false witness against thy neighbor), would be of great relevance during the Holden congregation proceedings in the winter of 1880. So would the fourth and seventh commandments: thou shalt honor thy mother and thy father, and thou shalt not steal.

In Holden, before the immigrants founded the church, they provided board and lodging to an itinerant schoolteacher, Ole Solberg, who was tasked with teaching these lessons to the children. When the men of the Holden congregation constructed a schoolhouse, a log building with room for seventy students, religious education took a more organized form. And when Minnesota became a state in 1858, the American public school could also utilize Holden's schoolhouse. With statehood, Minnesota's many counties and towns had to be formed as administrative units with government officials. Men, and only men, had the right to vote, and from their midst elected a bailiff and other officials. Through this process, the immigrants became involved in a larger society beyond the settlement. In Holden, Ole Solberg, the religious schoolteacher, was elected as town treasurer. "However, it is not as a government official, we remember, esteem, and honor Ole Solberg," Peder Langemo would later say in his address at the congregation's anniversary celebration in 1906, "but for the skill, fidelity, and patience he demonstrated as a religious teacher for our children."[6]

Even though Holden had a public school and an American school-teacher, the church continued to run its parochial school. Christianity was not a part of the public school curriculum. There, the children of Norwegian immigrants learned English language and grammar, American history and social studies, mathematics and science—everything other than religion.

6

"My Lost Arlien"

....

FOR WEEKS ON END, Bernt Muus spent his days in Christiania preparing for his exams. After living with a family for a couple of years, he now lived by himself—and he was burdened with loneliness. He worried about Oline, who was not well, and even when he thought about how they would enjoy all their days together, not every thought was uplifting. He wrote to Oline in a letter dated November 16, 1858, that he was anxious about beginning his life in the clergy; he felt unsuitable. He never went to bed with a clear conscience. He always felt that he could have done things better, that he could have behaved more wisely. He brooded over his own sinfulness, and it made him uneasy. Nevertheless, he was afraid of losing this uneasiness; if he did, indifference would prevail. He knew his thoughts would frighten Oline, he wrote, but she should bear with him, for she was interested in everything that concerned him.[1]

Their relationship, he continued, had certainly brought her many disappointments. She hadn't found him communicative enough. She had lived in the hope that he would change, become more candid. In religious and other respects, she hadn't received much benefit either. He admits that he is, by nature, cold. He was sorry that she hadn't found embers of greater affection from him. It pained him to give her catechesis in life's disappointments, yet he still believed she loved him. He was ashamed to even write the words, for he was aware of how few reasons she had to love him.

Bernt soon enclosed a copy of "My Lost Arlien," a short serial article that had left an impression on him, in a letter to Oline. In it, a man has married a young girl whom he loves. Arlien is cheerful and innocent; as Bernt wrote in his note, she is childlike. Her demeanor makes the husband happy; he loves his wife's good spirit. But one day it dawns on him that his wife is too childlike, and that her personality is incompatible with their "joint personality." What did Bernt mean by the phrase "joint personality"? Did he think a wife must deny her own will, her own desires, and everything that was hers and live through her husband? When a woman promises at her wedding to be submissive to her husband, must she give up her personality and individuality? Bernt Muus may have thought that in marriage a wife must submit completely to her husband. In his ministry, he would assert a marriage doctrine in which the wife's submissiveness must be undisputed.

In this fictitious marriage, the husband begins to act coldly toward his wife, and several times he offends her affectionate heart by treating her unkindly. The more the husband saw that his wife felt hurt and offended, the more his pride resisted confessing his faults and changing. The story stops there, as the rest of the letter is not preserved. "My Lost Arlien" hardly had a happy ending; as the title suggests, the husband lost his wife, whatever that implied. Does Arlien leave her husband and home? Does she become fatally ill, or does she kill herself?

"My Lost Arlien" was a strange story for Bernt to send to his beloved. Why had he included this piece with his letter to her? And did Oline fear that her marriage would be like the one in the story? We don't know how Bernt intended the account to be read, nor how Oline interpreted it. But the partially destroyed letter sheds some light on the young couple's relationship.

"I long to be clear with your parents," Bernt wrote a month later, on November 18. Had the Pinds suddenly persuaded Oline to change her mind? If so, she was not alone in her doubts regarding the call to go to America. In a letter three months earlier, Bernt had indicated that he didn't know if he would seriously follow through with his plan. He had heard a great deal about the conditions in America from a pastor who served there and who was now visiting Christiania. What he had learned was downright discouraging. If the descriptions were reliable, he could no longer be so sure about his decision.[2]

In the fall of 1858, Bernt successfully passed his university examinations. He received high marks with laud as his final grade. Now there remained only one exam before Bernt could be ordained and prepare for his departure to America. But would Oline go with him? As Christmas approached, he was finally sure of his decision, though it seems something about their relationship was unclear. He kept waiting for her letters. More than a week at a time could pass without him hearing from her. He hoped that "their affairs" could be handled satisfactorily so they could celebrate a pleasant Christmas. It might be their last in old Norway.[3]

Christmas at Tien was not without uncomfortable moments, as Bernt admitted in a letter just after the new year, on January 13, 1859. Still he thought the holiday had been peaceful in several respects. His soul was more calm when he was with Oline, he wrote. If he had gradually missed something, it was proper employment, for when he didn't have work, he was haunted by an unpleasant feeling of living like a good-for-nothing. He thanked Oline, "you my flower," for all her kindness and love. Maybe she would get him to loosen up a bit if they had the chance to spend a little more time together.[4]

Six months later, on July 12, 1859, their wedding was held at Tien. On that stormy day, it was barely possible for the bride and groom, family, and guests to cross the Glomma River by boat to get to Fet Church. When the pastor asked the bride if she would obey her husband in all things, through good days and bad, and be faithful to him until death parted them, she answered yes.

7

Before Darkness Came

THAT SAME YEAR, 1859, after several weeks at sea, the newlyweds and their traveling companion, a hired girl by the name of Karen Christophersen, were finally able to set foot on dry land again. Their port of arrival was likely Quebec, and after the three had collected themselves, they boarded another steamship. This one set course southward—across the Great Lakes, through canals, and on to the great Mississippi. In La Crosse, a settlement in the westernmost tip of Wisconsin, the group rested for a time from their travels. At a Norwegian Synod assembly, Bernt Muus met several of the pastors who were to become his colleagues in America, some of whom he certainly knew from Christiania. The Muus couple's arrival with their own hired girl was undoubtedly noticed by the ministerial meeting participants. It wasn't common that a young couple could afford to hire a servant, especially one who traveled with them from Norway.

In all likelihood, Oline's parents had paid for Karen's services, feeling reassured that their daughter would be accompanied by an experienced servant. In this foreign place, their daughter would have a mother figure. The two had become acquainted in Christiania; they were sisters in spirit. It didn't matter that one was a servant and the other a pastor's wife; they were on a first-name basis with each other.

Perhaps Oline hadn't yet had time to acquire all the skills expected of a housewife on a large farm. If so, Karen, who stayed with Oline for four years, had plenty of time to teach her the skills she needed—everything from slaughtering and baking to candle making and preserving food. Karen could probably also give the young pastor's wife advice on how to manage the parsonage's tenants, servants, and farmhands. And the pastor's wife must be prepared for her first baby to arrive within a year of the wedding. An enormous job awaited the twenty-one-year-old Oline, who would be housewife and administrator, wife and mother, and also her husband's assistant in the church.[1]

From La Crosse, the small group continued on into Minnesota. In Rochester, near the Zumbro River, a large tributary that flows into the Mississippi River, they were met by a man from the Holden congregation, the sexton, Saave Knudson Groven Aaker, who had emigrated from Brunkeberg in Telemark. They embarked on the last leg of the journey, their crates and trunks hoisted up on yet another method of transport, this time a wagon pulled by two yoked oxen, which would carry Pastor Muus and his party all the way to Holden. It took a long time, as oxen don't have nearly the same stamina as horses. The entourage stopped frequently along the way so the oxen could graze.

The roads were long and straight, stretching far into the horizon. Road and bridge construction were governmental priorities, making the wilderness more accessible to the flow of newcomers in search of their own land. In 1850, the white population of Minnesota consisted of 6,077 individuals; ten years later, it was twenty-eight times larger. Among the 172,023 people recorded in the 1860 census, a significant portion were of Norwegian descent. The immigrants from Norway were largely rural people, and they remained rural dwellers in the new country. Goodhue County and the surrounding area contained a sizable Norwegian core.[2]

The prairie landscape in Minnesota through which the Muuses traveled resembled Oline's home area of Fet in many ways. But while the plains, forests, and hills of her native district always had an ending point, it didn't seem like that here. Here, the sky was so much higher, the light so much brighter, and the distances so great, so vast. In October, the sun hangs low and colors the landscape with deep shadows. The plains glow a golden brown, and the deciduous trees burst like fire in red, yellow, and orange. It's as if nature is giving thanks before the long, cold Minnesota winter covers everything in snow.

Soon, the travelers noticed no more than two or three houses on either side of the road, except for the town of Wanamingo, which lay midway between Rochester and today's Twin Cities, St. Paul and Minneapolis. In Wanamingo Township, where the new farms were spread over a vast area, the Muuses were to find their home. Before nightfall, the oxcart stopped at a farmyard, but it was not the Holden parsonage. In fact, the congregation had neither the time nor the money to build a parsonage. For the time being, Pastor Muus and his wife were to live on the farm of Knut Pedersen Haugen, the church treasurer.

The first arduous immigrant period was behind the Haugen family. The farmland was cultivated with fields and pastures. The farmyard had been built in a traditional Norwegian style, with a barn, stable, pigsty, and storehouse. The first primitive log house had been expanded with several additional rooms. Pastor Muus and his wife received their own room, where the two could be completely alone. They were given food and lodging and resided there as guests. On All Saints' Day, a few days following their arrival, Pastor Muus delivered his inaugural sermon to the congregation at Holden. The ceremony took place at the home of Ole Olsen Huset, one of the settlement's prominent farmers.

The new life Bernt and Oline Muus had talked and written about for as long as they had known each other had finally begun. Although Bernt was, according to the standards of his time, a well-traveled man, he had never journeyed as far away as America. When he was on his way home in the fall of 1857, after a nearly two-month study trip to Germany, he was homesick. "I have also experienced, as have so many travelers before me, that nothing is as beautiful as our native land. But you don't really know what you have, until you compare it to what is foreign," he had written in a letter to Oline. He longed for home and didn't think he would have peace before he set foot on Norwegian soil: namely, on the Norwegian steamship in Kiel. Oline, on the other hand, had hardly been farther from home than the Norwegian capital. The luggage they brought with them contained only the most essential things: clothing and books, a medicine chest, and small personal items.[3]

What did Oline think when they were welcomed at the Haugen residence? The living room she entered had a dirt floor, and the walls were dark with soot and dirt. Here the housewife cooked dinner, here everyone in the large household sat on benches around the long table at mealtimes, and here several of them slept. The stench of hardworking bodies that had not been near soapy water for far too long, fried pork that was the daily staple in America, and everyday uncleanliness must have struck her. Had it not been for the size of the house, which had several rooms, it could have been mistaken for one of the poorest farmers' cottages in Fet. Though accustomed to only the best, Oline was to live here, and when she and her husband acquired their own home, it would be much like this one. She may have come to grips with the simple conditions with courage and good humor. Or was she someone who experienced the transition from the pleasurable life of luxury to the spartan immigrant life as harrowing and unbearable?

There are no preserved letters from Oline from the time immediately following their arrival, so we don't know what she thought or felt. Until the parsonage was built, she had to spend her days as best she could with Karen. Her husband, on the other hand, had his hands full. He was constantly on the road. In the winter when the driving conditions became impossible, he could still get where he needed to be on skis; the skiing abilities he developed in Snåsa came in handy. Within a few years Pastor Muus would serve as many as twenty-eight congregations, the majority of which he had helped found. They were scattered throughout the lower half of Minnesota and eastern Wisconsin, over an area comparable to the size of Denmark.[4]

Hellfire and Damnation Sermons

"EVERYTHING WAS ENJOYABLE and we had a lot of fun," Ole Huset recounted in his letter on January 16, 1860, to friends from home in St. Paul. Gunder Næset had married, and it was an incredibly large wedding. And yes, the pastor and his wife were there, too. Ole himself participated in the celebration until Tuesday, but some partied on until Thursday night. Among the guests were Hans and Christen Westermoe, Gunder Huset, Halvor Huset, Gunder Hestemyr, and many others. Twelve of the guests stayed overnight.[1]

The immigrants in Holden were faithful to their traditions. As in the old country, a farmer's wedding lasted at least three days. This custom wasn't the only one they carried over with them to their new country. Like the community they came from, Holden was a patriarchal society. In Huset's rattling off of wedding guests, only men were mentioned by name. He didn't mention who the bride was because his friend in St. Paul already knew about her. Nor was the pastor mentioned by name, but the letter's recipient undoubtedly knew it was Pastor Muus. Whether the new pastor was liked or not by the congregation, the letter writer doesn't say. The most important thing was that the congregation had gotten its own pastor and that he should match what people were accustomed to from home. Was Bernt Muus such a pastor? From day one at Holden, difficulties began to pile up for him.

Back in Christiania, Bernt had thought that in America he would be like a father, and his wife like a mother, for their parishioners. But that relationship did not develop. At church, Bernt was given the title of "Pastor." He was addressed as Pastor Muus and Bernt Muus, his wife as Fru [Mrs.] Muus and eventually Mrs. Muus. "I sat yesterday and enjoyed thinking about how you would fill the motherly role, when you join me in America as my wife," he had written to Oline before their departure in the winter of 1859. "For a pastor's wife," he explained in his letter, "is the mother of the congregation, as the pastor must be its father, especially to those who are poor, sick, or suffering in some other way." The most beautiful aspect of the ministry, in which both the pastor and his wife take part, is to help those in need.[2]

But the old social order in Norway would not apply in America, where laypeople were neither the pastor's flock nor his subjects. According to the church's charter of September 12, 1856, the pastor was dependent on the congregation; he had to have the majority on his side. At the same time, according to the same charter, each and every member of the church had to obey the pastor. Who was more powerful? It's hard to say.[3]

In 1870, when Bernt had been a pastor at Holden for ten years, he spoke his mind. Surprisingly enough, in Knut K. Finseth's obituary, printed in the Synod's publication Kirkelig Maanedstidende [Church Monthly Times], Bernt strongly criticized the Holden congregation. Conditions there had been not at all good for such an inexperienced pastor. The most hardened indifference to all true Christianity dominated the congregation. People were controlled by "the abundance of drink, tumult, and carousing." There were devout Christians in the congregation of course, but in the pastor's eyes, they were mostly hidden. Preaching the word of the Lord was the surest way to silence everyone. With few exceptions, it was as if people didn't care much about whether their pastor lived or starved to death. Within the congregation there was no willingness to work for the church or for the school.[4]

During services Pastor Muus preached in a way that he hoped would cause the congregation to feel shame and repent, or become so angry they would chase him away. But nothing happened. He came to understand that people were accustomed to hearing what they called hellfire and damnation sermons. In the old country, churchgoers heard nothing but harsh words from their pastor; a sermon had to be unsettling to the congregation. A pastor wasn't a proper pastor unless he unnerved the congregation. In doing so, he proved he was worthy of his salary and gifts. But, Bernt reminisced, even before the closing prayer was offered, people had already shaken off all his hard words. Out in the churchyard, people talked about the weather, horses, and business, and before they had traveled half a mile, they had a clear conscience again.[5]

He quickly realized he had exaggerated notions of the Holden congregation. Bernt, who had long since taken a stand against the Norwegian State Church, believed members of a free church would be the opposite of nominal Christians. Most members of the Holden congregation felt it was enough to attend church services, and when they needed a pastor to perform a baptism or confirmation, a wedding or funeral, they paid him generously.[6]

In 1857, when Bernt became cofounder and coeditor of the Norwegian paper *Norsk Kirketidende [Norwegian Church Times]*, he had become the spokesman for the free church, for the living congregation, and for church discipline. In particular, he was preoccupied with the confession associated with church discipline. Back in Norway, "traditional church discipline" was no longer widely practiced. This antiquated custom consisted of a public confession before each individual came forward to receive communion. Bernt wanted to revive this dormant practice, though in a slightly milder form. At least twice a year he wanted each member of the congregation to confess to the pastor—that is, to him alone. The purpose of the confession was to help those who were indifferent become true Christians. By making confession mandatory for all members of the congregation, he was also able to strengthen church discipline. It's natural to interpret Pastor Muus's campaign as the result of a puritanization process, but he could also have been influenced by pietism despite his affiliation with the Synod. It was his way to encourage people who lived unchristian lives to become good Christians, while at the same time strengthening and consolidating unity within the congregation.

But many in the congregation were unwilling to confess, even when coerced. As Bernt put it, confession was uncomfortable because many respectable men and women had to admit to the pastor that they didn't know the way to salvation. Besides, they didn't trust the pastor to observe confidentiality; they were afraid others would find out about their transgressions. At the same time, some circulated lies about the matters Pastor Muus had discussed with them in the confessional. From the very outset, this ritual caused a stir. Nonetheless, the congregation had to put up with practicing confession the way Pastor Muus wished.[7]

However, in Norwegian America, laypeople knew how to demonstrate their power, and the pastor had to understand that it was different here than in Norway. From the church council's call letter, it was evident the pastor would receive a fixed salary, in addition to a parsonage with one hundred acres of arable land. He was also supposed to get a travel allowance, and steamship tickets across the Atlantic were expensive. But, as months passed, Bernt received neither a fixed salary nor the funds to travel, and there was no sign of a parsonage. By winter 1860, he had nevertheless become "a well-off man," and he owned a good horse and a cow. The reason he had a livable income was partly because of all the baptisms he had performed in his congregation. As in the old country, it was customary for a child's parents to compensate the pastor with cash. The larger the gift, the more the child's future and the parents' standing in the congregation were secured.[8]

Not until the spring of 1860, after more than six months living with the Haugen family, when the pastor's wife was expecting a baby, did the congregation begin to make headway on construction of the parsonage. Building the farmhouse was a community project; each man in the congregation brought with him a certain number of logs and planks. The work of building the walls, raising the roof, and laying the floor went quickly once it was started. During the summer, the parsonage's farmhouse, a log house measuring eighteen by twenty-six feet, was partially ready for occupancy. The parsonage at Holden, only the second Lutheran parsonage to be constructed in Minnesota, was valued at $6,000. The year before a parsonage was constructed in Spring Grove, Minnesota's first Norwegian settlement, valued at $5,000.[9]

In late November, Oline Muus gave birth to a daughter, named Birgitte after her paternal grandmother. Bernt Muus, who had become motherless when he was only a year and a half, now had a little Birgitte. Bit by bit the household belongings beyond the most necessary were accumulated, and family life in the parsonage could begin.

At War with the Dakota

THE EARLY SETTLER-COLONISTS in Goodhue County never felt entirely safe. Neither did the Dakota, the Indigenous people of the prairie. Each lived in constant fear of the other. The Dakota were starving. American authorities hadn't kept their word; the Dakota didn't receive anywhere near the financial settlement they had been promised. The compensation for the vast lands they were forced to relinquish was pitiful; on their new lands, there was neither game nor crops sufficient for them to survive.[1]

One of the stories that circulated from the settlement's founding era was about Margrit Finseth Bakke, the first white woman in Holden, who went to the well one day to fetch water. She was home alone with her newborn son; he was asleep when she left the house. But when she returned, her son was missing. Terrified, she ran outside, fearing the worst: that the child had been stolen. Suddenly, she heard a child's cry from a thicket a short distance away. When she reached the spot, there was her son in the lap of a Dakota woman. Without hesitation Mrs. Bakke bent down and grabbed her son. She squeezed him close while she ran home as fast as her legs could carry them. As she slammed shut the door, she thanked God that she didn't see any trace of the Dakota woman. That story ended well, but in the years that caravans of white settler-colonists forged their way west, tales were constantly told of children and women being abducted by the Dakota and other nearby Indigenous groups.[2]

Franklyn Curtiss-Wedge notes in *The History of Goodhue County* that any account of relations between the Indigenous peoples and immigrants in Goodhue County would be incomplete without mention of the Spirit Lake massacre, which took place across the border in Iowa. Following a harsh winter, in March 1857, the Dakota leader Inkpaduta and a group of fourteen men attacked settlements in the northwestern territory of Iowa near the Minnesota border. They sought revenge for the murder of Inkpaduta's brother, Sidominadotah, and his family. These men were not under the authority of the tribal leader, but rather a small group driven away from their own people but still living in the region.[3]

The attack resulted in the death of thirty-two white men, women, and children and the abduction of four women, of whom two were killed, one released voluntarily, and one ransomed. And, although the events took place more than a hundred miles away, a group of white men from Red Wing went to bury the remains of the murdered immigrants. They certainly brought back gruesome tales of the aftermath they encountered, resulting in a real fear of Indigenous people among the early settler-colonists. Though the immigrants of Goodhue County were not immediately impacted in the attack of 1857, it created a tremendous scare. They would constantly ask neighbors for news and would believe almost any rumor they heard.[4]

The Spirit Lake massacre occurred just two years prior to Pastor Muus's arrival in Holden. Three years after that, in 1862, events unfolded that added to the growing unrest. On a farm near Litchfield, some forty miles west of Minneapolis, members of an immigrant community were killed by a small group of young Dakota men. The story, as told in a rural chronicle long afterward, was as follows: Four men from the Dakota tribe had come to a settler-colonist family farm. They were hungry and stopped at the fence of the chicken coop, where they spotted a nest full of eggs. One of the men suggested that they steal the eggs, but he was contradicted: it was wrong to steal. The men began to argue about who was afraid of the white men. One of them took the rifle from his shoulder and began shooting the people on the farm to prove he wasn't a coward; one by one, three men, a woman, and a teenaged girl were killed.[5]

When the young men returned to their camp, the older men found out what they had done. One elder, Tayoyateduta (which translates to His Scarlet Nation, though he was better known as Little Crow), admonished them, and a dispute arose as to whether it was right to take the lives of others or whether they themselves should starve to death. Tayoyateduta warned that the American army would bring its wrath down on all of them regardless. There was only one thing they could do: go to war against the white man, drive the white man out of Minnesota, before the army could arrive. The Dakota would die anyway, and it was better to die in battle than to die of hunger.[6]

Groups of Dakota men set out to kill Euro-Americans in their settlements around Minnesota. The conflict, later referred to as the US–Dakota War, had begun. Men, women, and children were murdered and their farms set on fire. Nearly five hundred people were killed, and hundreds escaped to settlements outside the war zone.

The Aaker Saga: A Family History recounts the impact of the Dakota War on Holden: "In 1862 rumors that Indians on the warpath were on the way thoroughly alarmed the community. Most of the settlers threw a few necessary belongings into their wagons and started for Red Wing." The Muus family was among those who received news of the unrest and fled their home to seek refuge. A local by the name of Cleng J. Dale gave this account:

> One evening about 7 o'clock there came a warning that the Indians were coming and that they were murdering our next neighbor and his family. It was difficult to say what to do.
>
> The thought of saving anything of our possessions we immediately gave up. We thought it wisest to flee just as we were. With our one-year-old daughter, my wife and I went eastward to Osmund Wing, who was busy getting his family into a wagon. We decided to go in an easterly direction to Torger Rygh, a devout old countryman, where people frequently held meetings.
>
> Here we soon gathered a whole company. The women and children occupied the second story, while the men remained below and armed themselves as well as we could with axes, pitchforks; firearms we did not have. Those of the men who were the most Viking-like took their places as sentries about the house during the night. However, the

Indians did not come. In the morning we sent out two spies to examine how matters stood in our homes. They returned with the report that as far as they could see and hear, everything was quiet and our homes were in the same order in which we had left them. Then we returned. At this time B. J. Muus was pastor of the Holden congregation. He removed his family to Red Wing. Mr. Muus, however, returned, and continued his labors.[7]

War had broken out in Minnesota, even as in the South the Civil War entered its second year. Holden was far from the battlefields, but like other Norwegian settlements in Goodhue County, it was heavily involved in the Civil War. Goodhue recruited the most soldiers for the "Blue Jackets," President Abraham Lincoln's unionists, out of all Minnesota counties. In 1862, one of Bernt Muus's Synod colleagues, Ludvig Marinius Biørn, became the chaplain for the Norwegian Regiment, the Wisconsin Fifteenth Regiment, with Colonel Hans Christian Heg in command. Pastor Biørn, then a newcomer to America who served two congregations in Wisconsin, would eventually become a close friend of the Muuses. The companies in the Fifteenth Regiment called themselves "St. Olaf's Rifles," "Wergeland Guards," and "Odin's Rifles." The soldiers from Holden and the other Norwegian settlements fought for the Union in America, their new homeland. Norwegian America was one of the great bastions of the Republicans and, above all, President Lincoln was the settler-colonists' hero. The Homestead Act of 1862 opened up a new land rush—and this time homesteading didn't cost a cent.[8]

Abraham "Abe" Lincoln, the son of settler-colonists from Illinois, was a giant of a politician, standing at an impressive six feet and four inches. Born in 1806, he had sparse schooling in his youth, later studied law, and eventually became a lawyer. As a statesman and public speaker, Lincoln was second to none; his November 1863 address at Gettysburg became legendary. His hope, he proclaimed, was that a government "of the people, by the people, and for the people" must endure. The speech was reproduced in *Emigranten [The Emigrant]*, the most widely read newspaper in Norwegian America. Each week *Emigranten* brought news and eyewitness accounts from the battlefields of the South. The

Civil War was the first war followed by journalists and press photographers, and those at home could also monitor the war closely through letters from sons and relatives who participated in the fighting.

Military units that were being formed to fight in the South were redirected to western Minnesota. They met with fierce fighting in the territory that had been captured, but after two months many Dakota warriors and their families fled to Dakota Territory. Dakota people who had, for the most part, not engaged in battles were forced to surrender. The men were taken to Mankato. The army marched almost 1,700 Dakota elders, women, and children to Minnesota's capital of St. Paul, and detained them in a prison camp at Fort Snelling. Not only the warriors but the entire Dakota tribe would be punished.

Shortly after the fighting stopped, Ole Berg recounted his experience as a soldier. One evening toward dusk his company was making camp, and while watching for the enemy, they discovered a moving object way out on the horizon. As the object came nearer, they saw that it was a man on horseback, and when the stranger finally rode up to camp, Mr. Berg recognized the stranger as Pastor Muus. He was out looking for the poor scattered residents who were left behind or who had returned to their destroyed homes, seeking to give them what help and solace he could.[9]

After cursory trials, a total of 303 out of 393 of the Dakota men were sentenced to death by hanging. President Lincoln, in Washington, DC, was shocked by the number of death sentences. Nevertheless, he was persuaded to agree to thirty-nine of the executions because the governor of Minnesota insisted that the sentences be carried out or a mob would take action and the state would erupt in violence. On December 26, 1862, thirty-eight Dakota men accused of being perpetrators were executed en masse. Only one individual had been exonerated. The mass execution took place in Mankato, just sixty miles west of Holden.[10]

The reckoning with the Dakota was far from over. In April 1863, Congress decided to set an example. Its members voted to revoke the annual compensation for land ceded by the Indigenous peoples, and the Dakota were forced into new internment camps called reservations.

As white settlers steadily moved west to establish new colonies, new reservations were established farther and farther west.

In 1863 Christmas peace finally descended upon Minnesota's many settlements. The war in the north had come to an end, though in the South the Civil War raged on. *The Emigrant* continuously printed lists of fallen Norwegian soldiers in the Fifteenth Regiment. At the bloody Battle of Chickamauga on September 19, 1863, Colonel Heg was seriously wounded; he died the following day. Half of Heg's original forces, officers and soldiers, were either dead, wounded, or missing. In April 1865, the same month the Confederacy surrendered, Pastor Muus eulogized one of the soldiers from Holden, Andreas Aaker. The son of church Cantor Saave Aaker had only lived to be seventeen.[11]

Historian Bruce White has warned that the accuracy of accounts of white and Indigenous interaction during the settlement era is difficult to gauge, noting that many stories passed from one person to another through the filter of the white perspective. These accounts do not depict the experiences of the Indigenous peoples of the area, but they do illuminate the attitudes of the Norwegian immigrants at the time.[12]

Due to the high proportion of Norwegian Americans settling in rural areas, scholar Betty Bergland points out, we can't fully understand Norwegian migration without further engaging in the history of the structures that enabled immigrants "to claim land and pass it on to subsequent generations." And "because of these same policies, indigenous peoples faced dispossession and displacement: lost land, removals, expulsions, starvations, and generations of historical trauma. These intersecting histories deserve more attention."[13]

10

The Churching of Women

FIVE YEARS AFTER THE FOUNDING of the Holden congregation in 1861, the church council, with Pastor Bernt Muus urging them on, had collected sufficient funds to begin building the church. The congregation had long since set aside a plot for the church and cemetery; it was close to the parsonage, just down the road. The lumber company Hill & Simmons in Red Wing was commissioned for the job; with that, the church was said to have become an American Norwegian construction—because Hill was an American and Simmons a Norwegian immigrant. Construction went smoothly at first. The entire large building with walls, ceilings, and steeple was erected, and the floor was laid, but then everything came to a halt. The church funds were depleted.

Although stories had quickly begun to circulate about how astute Pastor Muus was in getting the men of the congregation to give far greater sums than they had intended, Holden Church remained unfinished for several years. The church stood there like a large empty shell, without an altar, pulpit, or organ. Pastor Muus had to use a table as an altar and pulpit. When the sexton was the cantor during the church service, in the absence of an organ, he struck the note on a psalmodicon, an old-fashioned one-stringed instrument. The church also lacked pews. The congregation had to make do with long benches, both on the men's side and on the women's side. Seating indicated one's status and strictly reflected who was who. Not all were equal when they sat in church. Those relegated to the back benches were not the congregation's

Holden Church, 1891.
Ole G. Felland collection, courtesy St. Olaf College

faithful churchgoers nor the respected individuals in the settlement. The foremost benches were reserved for the members of the church council and the most successful farmers, those who bestowed the largest offerings during the collection and the largest gifts for religious ceremonies and holidays.

Travelers could use Holden Church as a landmark from far away, and as they got closer the church was so impressive that even the most well-to-do farmers' houses seemed small. The church was colossal, with a seating capacity of about five hundred. It was known far and wide as stor kjerke [the large church]. Building the church had been a lengthy project that was lavish in every way. In the free church in America, unlike in the Norwegian State Church, the church building was utilized for more than worship; it was also a meetinghouse for the congregation. Holden Church must be grand and stately, with a church steeple and bell that could be heard from a great distance. Muus is noted to have "caused the erection of a church of such magnitude and usefulness" that it served as a sanctuary for the Holden congregation for forty-nine years.[1]

In the nave's north section, on the women's side, the farmers' wives and daughters sat in the same status order as their husbands or fathers. In the foremost row sat the pastor's wife. Like the others, she was dressed in black and reserved. But, as the daughter of a wealthy landowner in Fet, she likely stood out both by finer attire and her manners. And how she could sing! When Oline sang her voice lifted up the entire chorus of voices on the women's side. Later in life one of the women of the congregation shared her fond memories of Mrs. Muus, who founded and directed the Kolibrien sangkor [the hummingbird chorus], named after the tiny bird that was so abundant in America. The world's smallest bird has to fly constantly because it can't walk. But it can fly backward and sideways and swiftly dive deeply down to flowers to suck their nectar. The hummingbird needs nectar to survive, and when a male wants to attract a mate, he sings alluring melodies. In the church, the woman said, Mrs. Muus's choir resonated like an organ.[2]

A pastor's wife had higher status than the other wives, yet Oline Muus and the other women in the congregation found themselves in

similar circumstances. They didn't benefit from the church's democracy because they were required to remain silent as the scriptures
ordered. The right to vote on or be elected to the church council was
reserved for the congregation's men. The patriarchal order was self-
evident and undisputed, in the church as well as in the community.
But a man without a wife was a man without a future, and his wife
was his future if she bore him heirs. Her world was the farm and the
community, where she could continue to speak her native language,
a rural Norwegian dialect. It is telling that the cows on Norwegian
American farms had names like those at home in the old country—
Fagros, Dagros, and Litago. The men, on the other hand, had to learn
the language of the new land. If they couldn't read and write it, they at
least needed to speak and be understood. Fairly good skills in American English were necessary when the men went to town with their
grain and conducted other business there. In Norwegian American
settlements, men's expensive driving horses had aristocratic names
such as King, Queen, and Duke.[3]

It isn't known whether it was customary for the women of the settlement to have their own driving horse. In any case, Mrs. Muus did not.
If she needed to go to the general store or into town, she asked her husband for permission to use his driving horse. Travel outside the home
was limited. The immigrant wives lay frequently in childbirth. Year
after year they brought children into the world. And in the Holden congregation Pastor Muus welcomed the child into the Christian community through the sacrament of baptism. Children were a gift from God,
and a married couple who had many children was blessed. Whether
a woman was a farmer's wife or a pastor's wife, the obligations of the
marriage bed must be fulfilled.

Marriage and family were institutions laden with values through
religious ceremonies and emphasized the woman's subordination to
her husband. The marriage ceremony in the church, where she said
her wedding vows with the congregation as a witness, was the first and
most important ritual. Then, when she had given birth and completed
her required confinement, she had to go before the pastor for what was
called inngangskone, or the churching of women. This very old custom

was widespread in many faiths; in Norway, it had been practiced since Catholic times. Its roots were in the Old Testament, where it states that a woman who gave birth is considered unclean. She must therefore undergo a cleansing to be washed clean of her sin, the original sin of which Eve in the Garden of Eden was guilty. For forty days following childbirth, a woman is excluded from the church. After forty days, the same number that Jesus fasted in the wilderness, she can be readmitted to the congregation.

Since the Holden congregation was large, the rule about restoring a woman's purity after forty days could hardly be strictly observed. But the ceremony always took place before the church service began. The women had to use the side door in the sacristy, and there the pastor blessed them and cleansed them of all sin. Only then could the women enter the church; hence the Norwegian word for this rite: *inngang* meaning entrance and *kone* meaning wife. They were greeted by the pastor and the congregation, they participated in the church service, and when the final hymn was sung, they exited out the front door like the rest of the congregation.

Before the Lord all women were equal, and all men were equal, while the Lord's servant, Pastor Muus, was the head of the entire congregation and its minister. Thus, for Oline Muus, at church Pastor Muus, her husband, was also her head and pastor. When she was churched, Pastor Muus cleansed her of sin and welcomed her back into the congregation. When she received Holy Communion, Pastor Muus offered her the sacrament. Her husband held a special authority over her.

"I realized immediately who this must be, and quite rightly, there stood Mrs. Hjort with her baby and Mrs. Muus with her two-year-old girl," Elisabeth Koren, Pastor Koren's wife, wrote in a letter on December 2, 1862, to her stepmother in the old country after a visit. This was the first time Mrs. Koren and Mrs. Muus met. Christiane (Janna) Otteson Hjort was an old acquaintance, a lively addition wherever she went. Mrs. Koren immediately felt at home and was very sociable. That Mrs. Koren enjoyed her visit was clearly thanks to Mrs. Hjort. But Mrs. Muus made little effort. Mrs. Koren didn't mention Oline Muus's condition; in November 1862, she was seven months pregnant, and it wasn't polite to write about such things. Mrs. Koren did note that there was something so dreary and sad about Mrs. Muus, and that she was very quiet the entire time. She also mentioned Bernt Muus; he is, she wrote, a very capable man. Early in January 1863, Oline gave birth to a son who was named Nils after his paternal ancestor.[4]

11

A Norwegian Rabble-Rouser

....

"WARNING TO ALL CHRISTIANS against Marcus Thrane's Norwegian American," the headlines proclaimed in bold type. The front page of *Kirkelig Maanedstidende* in September 1866 resembled a broadside. Seventeen full pages were devoted to *Marcus Thrane's Norske Amerikaner [Marcus Thrane's Norwegian American]*, a paper that was simply "satanic." It ridiculed Christianity and the true God, it slandered pastors and teachers, it incited rebellion against authority, it offended morals, and it spoke with profound contempt of Norway and Norwegians. The matter was so serious that the two editors of *Kirkelig Maanedstidende* had to break with their principle of not engaging in politics; they had to call out and testify to the poison the satanic newspaper spread.[1]

Marcus Thrane was a known quantity. In Norway, the clergy, led by the bishop of Christiania, had tried in vain to have Thrane convicted under the blasphemy section of the constitution. In *Arbeider-Foreningernes Blad [The Workers' Associations Newspaper]*, founded by Thrane in 1849, he called Jesus a true socialist and urged tenant farmers, servants, and craftsmen to speak out against the clergy, government officials, and the bourgeoisie. The working class, as Thrane called all common people, should acquire their own land and become a power in society with the right to vote and other democratic rights. In 1850, Thrane had persuaded thirty thousand working men to join the workers' associations.

However, the long arm of the law apprehended Thrane and other leaders of the workers' associations, and the *Workers' Associations Newspaper* was shut down. In July 1851, Thrane, along with several others, was arrested and put in custody. The authorities feared that he and the leaders were planning a revolution, but the rumors were untrue. He was eventually sentenced to hard labor and was released in 1858 after being imprisoned for seven years.

Thrane left Norway in December 1863. He was a forty-six-year-old widower and the family breadwinner. When he and his four daughters, Markitta (twenty-one years old), Camilla (seventeen), Vasilia (twelve), and Helene Sophie (nine), landed in New York, they were destitute. Thrane, who had learned the art of photography, worked for lousy wages in a factory that mass-produced portrait photographs. Markitta became a domestic servant for strangers, and the younger daughters tried to earn money with their needlework. When the family's son, Arthur, eventually arrived in New York, he found his lonely father down and out in a rented tenement in the city's immigrant slums.

Thrane was rescued from his desperate economic circumstances in New York by a group of Norwegian businessmen who hired him to start a new newspaper in America. In Chicago, which soon would transform into a city of millions because of immigrants streaming in from all over Europe, Thrane came back into his element and was reunited with his family. They were able to start a new, American life together.

On May 25, 1866, he greeted his fellow countrymen, those who had been nourished by the republican spirit and lived under the sun of American freedom, with his new paper *Marcus Thrane's Norske Amerikaner.* In the first issue, the editor appealed to his former followers. As in the old days, Thrane hoped they could once again work together for a great and noble cause: namely, religious freedom. Many of his followers had acquired much of what they had fought for in Norway—their own land, voting rights, and so on—but one thing they hadn't obtained was religious freedom. Thrane had already become a freethinker in Norway, but without proclaiming it to the whole world. Certainly in the Norwegian American settlements were other freethinkers, although they were tight-lipped about it. People were religious, whether they were immigrants or Americans, and they stuck to the church.[2]

However, Thrane's newspaper didn't appeal in vain to those he called his countrymen. The newspaper likely quickly reached two thousand subscribers. *Kirkelig Maanedstidende* had every reason to come out with its sharp warning to all Christians. Imagine: Thrane wrote that the Norwegian Lutherans in America were so simpleminded, the stupidest of stupid, that they allowed themselves to be bullied by their pastors. Norwegian Americans were controlled by their clergy. In response, the paper reproduced word for word what Thrane wrote in his newspaper and countered his claims. Thrane also claimed that the clergy was "old school"; that they distorted and misused Christianity to keep people in ignorance. Thrane called the Norwegian Synod's doctrine of hell nothing more than a lie. The Norwegian Synod's clergy had made an enemy, one who gave both the Haugean lay evangelists and so-called pastors a run for their money.[3]

Nor did the two editors of *Kirkelig Maanedstidende* spare any insults when they refuted Thrane's description of the state of the Norwegian Lutheran church in America. His paper was the work of the devil; it was filled with lies upon lies in black and white. That the Lutheran Church was as authoritarian as the Catholic Church was an outrageous allegation. In the Catholic Church, the editors declared, not a grain of liberalism is to be found. It was certainly not true that the Synod's pastors promote sectarianism that destroys people's reason. On the other hand, it was true that Thrane was the leader of a sect. He was familiar with "the new school" and the "notorious theologian" Henry Ward Beecher.

Beecher, a Congregational pastor, was popular among the progressive Yankees on the East Coast. In a portrait from his glory days in the years after the Civil War, he looks more like a man about town or an entertainer. As a preacher, he established a new standard for delivering a sermon. He used everyday language that everyone could understand, had a distinct sense of humor, and commented on everything from current news to sensational inventions. But first and foremost, Beecher gained his reputation because of his three central political agendas: social reform, women's rights, and the abolition of slavery. And he was the brother of a world-famous writer. Harriet Beecher Stowe's novel *Uncle Tom's Cabin*, published in 1852 and constantly reprinted, brought even Queen Victoria to tears. The edition marketed by a Norwegian publisher in America, under the title *Onkel Toms hytte*, won many readers, including within the Norwegian Synod.[4]

From the pulpit, Henry Ward Beecher praised God's boundless love and rejected the doctrine of hell. He didn't believe that God had created the world in six days either. Supported by Charles Darwin's theory of evolution, Beecher maintained that the world was infinitely older than the six thousand years on which biblical theologians insisted. With the 1859 book *On the Origin of Species* Charles Darwin had ignited a fierce debate in Christian circles. Beecher was not among the clergy who raged against Darwin, and long before the theory of evolution became popular belief, he utilized it in his sermons. Beecher was a theologian of the new school, with all that implied for biblical criticism, and was zealous for reform in all areas of society. However, he was not completely in line with the American women's movement, which had been organized at a landmark meeting in Seneca Falls, New York, in 1848. The women's movement was far too radical for Reverend Beecher.[5]

"Declaration of Sentiments," written by Elizabeth Cady Stanton, was based on what could be called biblical feminism. It states that all men and women are created equal by God and with certain inalienable rights. The champions of women's rights knew their Bible. They read the scriptures in a new way and argued against the church's marriage doctrine, that the wife should be submissive to her husband and he should be her master, just as the enslaver is the enslaved's master. The American movement for the emancipation of women sprang out of the movement to abolish slavery.[6]

Beginning in the 1830s, Stanton and Lucretia Mott, along with many other women, worked diligently to abolish slavery. The two met in London at the World Anti-Slavery Convention, Mott as a delegate and Stanton accompanying her husband; because they were women, they had been banished from the meeting room. Thus, they experienced what they defined as the complete subjugation of half of the human race under the other. Eight years later, in 1848, biblical feminism resulted in the Seneca Falls declaration. There, Stanton and Mott listed how men and patriarchal society throughout history have tyrannized and oppressed women. Women are without a voice and have no right to participate in elections, neither in politics nor in church. For a woman marriage is civil death; her husband becomes her master and can rule as Jehovah himself. A woman is barred from higher education and offices, and she is relegated to a life of sacrifice, submission, and dependency. Instead, they demanded that in both society and family women must have equal rights with (white) men, which presupposed a fundamental change in how women as well as men were viewed. Among the many legislative reforms contained in the declaration were women's voting rights, the married woman's right to own property, and the extension of her right to dissolve her marriage.[7]

In the American women's rights movement, biblical criticism and biblical feminism went hand in hand. The approach was radically new; it implied a breaking of ties with the old school of theologians, and it gave some substance to the new school of thought that Beecher represented and that Thrane believed in. But in September 1866, when Kirkelig Maanedstidende printed the warning against Marcus Thrane's Norske Amerikaner, it was Thrane who was scrutinized. The editors wrote satirically that if one is a fool of the old school, then one flees freedom, as children flee from their father who disciplines them. The wife flees from her husband; she flees from the chains of marriage and the burden of housework and parenting.

Thrane's approach from beginning to end, according to Kirkelig Maanedstidende, was untruths and slander. As if the Norwegians in America had thrown away their freedom and allowed themselves to be dominated by the clergy! As if the hand that had held them down in the country where they were born had followed them to their new home! As if the Synod's pastors were hiding behind a sanctimonious mask in order to deceive people! Kirkelig Maanedstidende asserted that the clergy who had come from Norway to America had forsaken many worldly goods and shared the burdens of immigrant life. The pastors had worked to the detriment of their health to spread the saving gospel among flocks of immigrants, who were like lambs without a shepherd. It wasn't true, as Thrane claimed, that the pastors in America were missionaries sent from the Norwegian government. The pastors had traveled over with funds donated by private individuals.[8]

Nor is it true, continued the newspaper, that Norwegian clergy nourished a strong dislike for America's religious freedom and school system. Though the Synod couldn't honestly consider the American public schools to be good, as religion was not a part of the curriculum, it was a vile insinuation to claim that the pastors were opposed to children learning English. According to Thrane, one of the Synod's pastors had publicly stated that God doesn't hear prayers in the English language. In that case, declared *Kirkelig Maanedstidende*, the pastor was alone in his opinion.[9]

12

In Sickness and in Health

IN THE YEARS AFTER Karen Christophersen, the Muus's hired servant, said goodbye to her "beloved Olline" [*sic*], the two had kept their intimate friendship alive through letter writing. When Oline Muus's father died late in the fall of 1863 and her mother in the new year of 1864, Karen had recently returned home to Christiania, and she was quick to write letters of condolence. She was homesick for all of them, especially the two little ones, Birgitte and Nils, whom she had known since their births. She tried to comfort her friend and she reminisced about their times together in Holden, the individuals she had since met, and her new life back in Norway.

In her letters, Karen prayed that the Lord would restore health to everyone in the family, and she was happy to hear that Pastor Muus could be at home more often. Oline had even sent a photograph of her husband; Karen wrote that it was wonderful to see him again. When Oline also sent a portrait of Birgitte, Karen began to cry: she somehow had gotten the impression that Birgitte had died. Karen felt old herself, and there were many around her who had passed away. She thanked God that she was healthy and was well-off here in this earthly world. Her "dear Olline" had to promise to greet all of Karen's friends, whom she listed by name. And Karen asked Oline to please excuse that the letter was poorly written, but she was tired and clumsy. "God bless you and yours. Live well in the Lord, greet the pastor and all the children, and don't forget me, Karen." This letter was probably the last Oline received from her.[1]

Meanwhile, the news in Holden was that the Muus family would soon get a larger house. The parsonage had improved enough that Oline wanted some of the nice things she had left behind in Norway, like her silverware and other items she hadn't thought she would need in the foreign land. In the fall of 1864, she asked her sister Pauline, in Kongsberg, to send the silver with an acquaintance traveling to America. They needed it, because Birgitte and Nils would soon welcome a baby brother to the family. In January 1866, Oline had another baby, who was baptized Jens. At last, the men in the congregation took the time to continue construction of the parsonage, bringing enough logs to build an office for Pastor Muus, a meeting room for confirmation instruction, and several additional rooms. Similar to an immigrant's farmhouse, the pastor's residence would have been divided into two floors; it's possible that construction of the rooms on the second floor began in the summer of 1867. In any case, the Muus home became quite spacious over time, with as many as seventeen usable rooms.[2]

By 1867, life at the parsonage was bustling. Birgitte was now seven, Nils was five, and Jens was a year and a half. There could be several reasons why there were four and a half years between child two and child three. Pastor Muus had a hectic travel schedule and was away from home for extended periods of time.

When the pastor was traveling, Oline had more to do in the congregation. She also had to manage the parsonage, the farm, and the household and be responsible for the care and upbringing of three small children. In the summer of 1867, she turned twenty-nine; even though she was still young, the work and responsibility were exhausting. Moreover, the family was constantly haunted by illness. In Holden, as everywhere else, sickness didn't discriminate between poor and rich. Babies and small children were taken too soon; children and adults died from tuberculosis or typhus; women died in childbirth. For a woman, childbirth and the time immediately afterward was the most dangerous of her life. Maybe that's why women's letters and memoirs rarely mention anything about childbirth. During pregnancy some women lived in constant fear of the impending birth; more than a few had mothers who were lost in childbirth. But Oline must have been robust. Her mother had also given birth to four children and lived to an old age. Oline herself was to have six children: in 1872 Paul came into the world, in 1874 Petter, and in 1878 Harald.

Oline was seldom anywhere other than at home; there, she kept up with her husband's work in their own congregation and probably in his many other congregations as well. It's likely that in order to stay informed she read the Synod's paper, to which her husband subscribed, and presumably was well informed about women's emancipation, the theological conflicts, and other great controversies of the day.

13

The Mustard Seed of St. Olaf

IN 1869, HOLDEN ACADEMY, a Norwegian-language religious school, began at the parsonage with the intention of providing a more complete education than either the congregation's religious instruction or the public American school offered. With money from his own pocket, Pastor Bernt Muus paid a teacher's salary and an expansion of the parsonage to accommodate a schoolroom. Tuition was set at ten dollars for a three-month term. Torsten Jesme, a graduate from Luther College, the Synod's school in Decorah, Iowa, was its sole instructor. The first term drew just three students.[1]

In December of the same year, Pastor Muus announced in *Kirkelig Maanedstidende* that Holden Academy would continue for a second term in January 1870. According to the announcement, knowledge of the scriptures and doctrine, church history, and singing lessons were high priorities. The ambitious curriculum also included secular subjects such as history and arithmetic, geography and physics, Norwegian and English. Since students were to have equal instruction in both English and Norwegian, the academy in Holden must be said to have been founded as a bilingual high school. But, according to Muus, Norwegian had to take precedence, because it was the native language of the immigrants. The religious teachings immigrants received as children in Norway must be passed on to their descendants in America, and these could only be understood in their mother tongue.[2]

Holden's second term did not fare better than the first. So few students enrolled that drastic cuts in teaching had to be made in order to focus on writing and arithmetic. Pastor Muus suffered a substantial personal financial loss when the academy failed. He admitted this in a longer article in *Kirkelig Maanedstidende* later that same year.[3]

It has long been speculated that location of the academy was a factor in its closure. In *High on Manitou*, William C. Benson points out that "Holden was at that time located twenty to thirty miles from any water or railroad transportation system, students from outlying areas could not be expected. Muus seems to have concluded that the location of the school at some point with railroad connections would be one of the prerequisites to the success of any future attempt to establish an academy." But in addition to its location, a heated debate regarding public schools sparked attention, with Pastor Muus as the firebrand.[4]

Throughout the 1830s and '40s most Norwegian American immigrant children attended public schools. In 1838, a short time after Norwegians began immigrating to the United States, Ole Rynning noted that he anticipated a quick transition to English, as the Norwegian language seemed destined to die with the parents. However, in the late 1840s, "Norwegian-American critics seized upon palpable defects in the common school as targets for their criticisms and they took cognizance of these defects." During the 1850s, despite the Synod's skepticism, most Norwegian immigrants continued to send their children to public schools.[5]

The Norwegian Synod discussed and adopted a school policy during the 1850s. This guidance, influenced by the conservative Missouri Synod, which in 1853 had helped their Norwegian colleagues with developing their organization, doctrine, and theological education, would preserve their native language for generations to come. One fact was indisputable: through religious education the pure Lutheran doctrine and the parents' native language was impressed upon the children. The Missouri Synod was exemplary, with many congregations that operated their own parochial school, but in many German American communities parochial schooling had actually become the children's only school option. This Synod policy was in contrast to the

Haugean church, which maintained it was important that Norwegian immigrant children learn English, so they could be quickly integrated into their new country. Elling Eielsen, a leader in the Haugean movement, had consequently provided an English translation of Luther's *Small Catechism*.[6]

The expansion of parochial schools spread slowly among the Norwegian Synod's congregations. Like many Norwegian American communities, the compactness of Norwegian settlement in Goodhue County did not induce the immigrants to learn the language of their new country. Very few of the original immigrants spoke any English. The parochial school wouldn't become a serious competitor to the public school for several reasons. One was that, despite the pastor's admonitions, the laity often didn't support the parochial school's ideology. Another reason was probably financial. When people had to pay taxes to operate the public school, it was unnecessarily expensive to simultaneously finance an alternative school.[7]

In 1858, at a Norwegian conference on parochial schools at Coon Prairie, Wisconsin, attended by parochial teachers and Synod preachers, the problem of religious education was discussed in detail. Adolph Carl Preus, the resident pastor of Coon Prairie and the first Synod president from 1853 to 1862, was the spokesman for the conference. He rejected the idea of rapid Americanization and maintained that religion should be taught in Norwegian. At a second conference later that year his views were unanimously endorsed.[8]

The editors of *Kirkelig Maanedstidende* followed up with a report stating that Norwegian parochial schools had far too little support. Since the immigrants wanted their children to learn English, they were enrolled in the public school. In addition, many parents believed that religious schooling with Norwegian as the language of instruction would hamper their children's progress as well as their "Americanization," or integration into American society. When members of the congregation sent their children to the public school instead of parochial school, it was also a quiet protest against the clergy and the Church.[9]

Synod leaders recognized that it is useful for Norwegian immigrant children to learn English. Still, to believe that the public school provides sufficient knowledge for children was wrong because none other than one's mother tongue can be the language of religion. Or, as the editors of *Kirkelig Maanedstidende* put it, referring to the Synod meeting on the school question, "the mother tongue is the language of the heart." The idea was that children would only understand the Lutheran doctrine if they were taught in their parents' native language. The subtext was that the American school, which doesn't have religion in its curriculum, would teach students to become ungodly. As stated in *Kirkelig Maanedstidende*, children taught religion in a foreign language often forget what they learn. If the congregation's parochial school also had secular coursework in its curriculum, the children wouldn't have a need for public school.[10]

Kendric Babcock notes that early American immigrants were believed to fall into three categories: "those who powerfully re-enforce the strength and virtue of the nation, those who supplement its defects with desirable elements, and those who lower its standards and retard its advancement." Norwegians, unlike their Scandinavian counter-parts, were considered by many to fall in the third category, slowing the advancement of civilization. Education—more specifically, educa-tion in English—was generally considered the cornerstone of Amer-ican democracy; public schools had "long been recognized as one of the central institutions that sustain a democratic society. Long before there were public schools, in the early days of the Republic, the Found-ing Fathers agreed that a democratic society requires an educated citizenry."[11]

From the larger American society's point of view, conditions among the Norwegian Americans were alarming. In 1869, the school superin-tendent in Minnesota's local administration, H. B. Wilson, came out with a report that harshly criticized the Norwegian pastors. The report, which was reprinted in several Norwegian-language newspapers, alleged that Norwegian American pastors were extreme opponents of the public school. There was very low student attendance in school districts with large populations of Norwegian immigrants. According to Wilson, the reason was that the Norwegian immigrants followed their pastors through thick and thin. The pastors alleged that the public school was a heathen institution and parents should instead send their children to the congregation's parochial school.[12]

The school superintendent deemed it a serious matter that the American public school must address. Wilson recommended that the public school offer special education to students with Norwegian parents, so that during a transition period they could receive instruction in their native language, preferably from a bilingual teacher. Bilingual teachers were the best means to integrate immigrant children into their parents' new country. In addition, Wilson pointed out that education in the public school needed to be improved by hiring more capable teachers with greater knowledge.[13]

Wilson's report exploded like a bomb, although several leading Norwegian-language newspapers in Minnesota welcomed it. Opposition to public schools among the Norwegian clergy and immigrants accordingly became a burning issue for Norwegian America, but first and foremost for the greater American society. To oppose the public school was unpatriotic; it demonstrated anti-Americanism.

In a letter to *Nordisk Folkeblad* [*Nordic People's Magazine*], Bernt Muus declared his strong commitment to religious education, confirming precisely what Wilson intended to demonstrate. In fact, Muus repeated one of the allegations that had shocked Wilson regarding the Norwegian American clergy, namely, that the American public school was a heathen institution. The public school didn't benefit Norwegian children, Muus believed. Rather, the American school was a center for dangerous, destructive forces.[14]

Wilson's response was sharp. He accused Pastor Muus of being intolerant, narrow-minded, and very hostile to American institutions. He declared that Muus was a foreign pastor, an aristocrat who traveled around as he pleased and who didn't have the support of his congregations. Pastor Muus was singled out as an enemy of society, a man who misused his authority as a pastor in the service of anti-Americanism. Muus was known as "a prominent opponent of cultural assimilation." These sentiments were only strengthened by the fact that Pastor and Mrs. Muus remained Norwegian citizens; they had never applied for US citizenship. Wilson concluded, "The reverend gentleman exhibits a spirit of the most narrow-minded bigotry and intolerance it has ever been my fortune to read, and I thank him for writing it. It shows for itself his *intensely* bitter hostility to American institutions, better than I can represent in words."[15]

Another of Muus's rebuttals was printed on May 12, 1870, in the *Red Wing Argus*, where he wrote, "I consider the common school an institution which according to its principles must work against the Kingdom of God, and furthermore, I consider it a poorly arranged institution, because the children learn there far less than they could and ought to learn." The editor of the *Red Wing Argus* decided it was necessary to preface his letter with an editorial titled "Education or Propagandism?"[16]

The reputation of pastors in Norwegian America was severely damaged after this debate, even though, unlike Muus, other key figures in the Synod knew to remain silent. But the debate on public schools resulted in a long aftermath with several results. At a meeting of the Synod clergy in 1873, H. A. Preus raised one hundred hypotheses about the American school; it certainly had many shortcomings. One year later, at a new Synod meeting, Pastor Muus pled the case for the Norwegian parochial schools, emphasizing that God's word must be at the core of all teaching. Christian parents certainly don't commit a sin by sending their children to the American school, but for every Christian it should be a social issue to work toward establishing their own schools.[17]

One editorial referred to the training Norwegian American youth received as being neither American nor Norwegian. The purpose of parochial schools was "to safeguard the spiritual life of the youth, and to shield them from possible filth and infection that might be of danger if they attended American institutions. They became spiritual quarantine stations against American infection."[18]

To what extent the public school debate contributed to the closure of Holden Academy before it had properly begun is not documented. Still, lessons learned from Holden Academy would serve Pastor Muus well in a new venture. Muus had been making good progress with a different school project, an academy that would eventually become a college named after Saint Olaf, Norway's legendary king. His daughter

St. Olaf's School first catalog, 1875.
Courtesy St. Olaf College

Birgitte later recounted that her father spoke of establishing St. Olaf when she was just six or seven years old, which would have been in 1866–67, even before Holden Academy was opened.

Muus recognized that the location of an academic institution was vital in its success, and the twenty-three miles that separated Holden from the nearest railroad line hindered its opportunity for growth. C. A. Rasmussen notes that Red Wing would have been a logical place for the establishment of a school, as it had a comparatively large Norwegian Lutheran population. "Pastor Muus in fact favored Red Wing. A good friend of his, the Rev. N. A. Quammen, favored Northfield. The two men agreed to ask both the cities concerned to submit bids for the location of the school which would be placed in the city submitting the best offer. Northfield won."[19]

William Benson notes that "a vigorous campaign was begun during the summer of 1874 to arouse the interest of the pastors and people in the movement toward the building of the institution." On November 6, 1874, the school was founded. Its articles of incorporation were signed by B. J. Muus, Harald Thorson, K. P. Hougen, O. O. Osmundson, and O. K. Finseth. The institution was originally styled "St. Olaf's School," and continued to be called so until 1889, when the articles of incorporation were amended by changing the corporate name to St. Olaf College. The charter shows that the original purpose was to make it a college, but Muus knew they were not yet prepared to do the work of a college, and therefore he insisted, contrary to the wishes of some of the other members, on the form then adopted. In 1877 the president of the Norwegian Synod, H. A. Preus, albeit perhaps with lukewarm enthusiasm, laid the cornerstone of St. Olaf's magnificent Main Building (later called Old Main) in Northfield.[20]

St. Olaf's School in Northfield in Rice County was intended for all confirmed youth—both male and female; for even young women should receive a high school education. In this way, Muus was a pioneer within his own synod. The school was more inclusive than anything so far attempted. It aimed to provide both religious and secular education, an idea that was quite new and revolutionary. In many ways, it directly addressed the ongoing debate of religious education verses the secular education that public school offered by seeking to provide both. However, the school cannot be understood as a school of the Synod. The Synod merely gave the permission to start a school and expressed its goodwill. It is, therefore, correct to say that St. Olaf College was started not by the church as a whole but by men of Northfield and the surrounding region in the interest of the church.[21]

In the new year of 1875, fifty students enrolled in the first term at St. Olaf's School, though only thirty-six were present on the first day of classes due to a heavy January snowstorm. The students ranged in age from fifteen to twenty-six years old and, remarkably, thirteen of them were young women. Thorbjørn Mohn, a graduate of Luther College, served as the principal in addition to professor. Upon the opening of the school, Principal Mohn stated, "the Christian religion is the first requisite for a nation's real prosperity."[22]

Professor Ingebrikt F. Grose, in the St. Olaf College history titled *Fifty Memorable Years,* notes that "in sum and substance the present investigations indicate that St. Olaf's School got its name and legal existence in Northfield in 1874 but in reality began its work in the Holden parsonage, Goodhue County, in 1869, the concrete manifestation of an idea which the Reverend Bernt Julius Muus had cherished almost to the consuming of his being since his coming to America in 1859."[23]

14

In Her Husband's Long Absence

....

"TODAY I RECEIVED YOUR LETTER," Oline Muus wrote to Peter Laurentius Larsen, commonly known as Laur. Larsen, her husband's former classmate, who had become a professor at Luther College. Oline
had a lot on her mind; the letter dated August 23, 1870, ended up being
four pages long. In even, beautiful penmanship, she wrote extensively
to ask the professor's advice on an important matter. But first she delivered greetings from her husband. Bernt Muus's last letter was dated July
26, when he had arrived in Hull, an English port city, after only ten days
on the Atlantic. On the journey from Chicago to Quebec, he had lost
his bag, as Larsen had probably heard. It had fallen off the pier, got an
unexpected soak—and on went the letter. Incidentally, in an earlier letter to her, Oline conveyed, Bernt had written that he might not return
home until the spring, that following his time in Norway, he would
travel to Denmark.[1]

Bernt had embarked on a long journey in the summer of 1870. He
was away for almost a year recruiting new pastors to the United States.
In the letter, Oline confided that couldn't say that she liked this news
very much, but naturally, if her husband could serve the church in this
way, then she was content. He needed to travel as long as he thought it
could benefit himself or others.[2]

Was Oline bitter about having to stay in Holden? She knew that several Synod pastors' wives had traveled to Norway with their husbands.
It had been more than ten years since Oline last saw her immediate

family. Her parents had since passed, but her siblings were alive and well. Oline would have liked to see her sister Pauline again, since the two had corresponded with each other all these years. But Oline's letter to Professor Larsen didn't indicate whether she was bitter about having to be at home with the children or having to take on all the responsibility for the parsonage. We would later learn from the complaint she filed against her husband that he wouldn't allow her to join him on his trip to Norway. Of herself and her family she wrote, "Thank God we are all healthy, and live a blessed and happy life." Then she came to the important issue and the reason for her letter.

After her husband had left, two members of the congregation, tradesmen by the names of Botolf Jahnsen and Vilhelm Hestemyr, started selling whiskey, and their business had already begun to bear disastrous fruits. She had tried unsuccessfully to urge several men in the congregation to warn the two against this type of business. She had taken the liberty the other day of going herself to Botolf. She'd told him that he must be careful not to bring sin and scandal down upon the congregation.

When she finished the third page of her letter, she wrote lengthwise on the paper, "With friendly greetings, Gratefully yours Oline Muus." On the fourth page, with several things struck through, but with the same even penmanship, was an account of the situation. The congregation had attempted to talk to Botolf about the sin and misery the whiskey trade brings to entire families. Botolf confessed that he had purchased only one barrel and promised not to buy any more. She doubted Botolf would keep his word, for "misuse" was his God. She intended to visit the other trader, Vilhelm Hestemyr, the following day. Halvor Huset from the congregation had agreed to accompany her. In her husband's long absence, Oline had taken her role as pastor's wife seriously. She acted with authority, energetically, and responsibly; she took initiative and worked hard for the congregation.

Barely three weeks later, on September 17, 1870, in a new letter to Professor Larsen, Oline was able to report that it was, for the time being, peaceful and calm at both places of business. She asked that Larsen not become impatient or angry with her, but she had to bother him once again with a question. This matter concerned a boy named Simon, who, with other boys from the congregation, had become a student at Luther College last fall. She didn't know Simon's last name, but he had a peculiar arm, so Larsen possibly knew the student to which she referred. Once again, Oline sent friendly greetings from her husband. He was still well; however, the climate in Norway wasn't agreeable to him. His last letter stated that he was in Ringsaker and would continue to travel north to his father's farm at Snåsa. He hadn't told her much about his stay in Christiania, mostly made up of short visits. Oline's letter contained both words struck out and ink blots, and occasionally the letters were large and thick. "In his letter, he doesn't mention his trip to Denmark," she wrote, "but talks a lot about coming home sometime this winter." She had barely begun writing a third page when she abruptly concluded by reproaching herself: "I have already taken up too much of your time. My kindest regards to your wife and children, gratefully yours, Oline Muus."[3]

Among the letters preserved from when her husband was traveling in Norway is a letter from Syvert L. Floren, a theology student at Concordia College (now Concordia Seminary) in St. Louis, Missouri. He was on familiar terms with the Muus family; Oline and Bernt were his confidants. Oline was enthusiastic about Syvert, not only because he was such a good preacher but also because they shared the same passion: music. Oline had found another musical friend in Holden: Just Christian Grønvold, the town's first doctor, who actually lived at the parsonage in the fall of 1870, for the second year in a row.[4]

Grønvold had studied science in Christiania and graduated with brilliant results. In 1865, age thirty-two, he immigrated to America and entered the Humboldt Medical School in St. Louis, aiming to establish a medical practice in Norwegian America. He ended up in Goodhue County, Minnesota's leading wheat producer and home to many prosperous farmers. Through the years the settlement had their own "doctors"—women who had "warm hands" or who were also knowledgeable about medicine. Mrs. Muus was often called upon because when she arrived in Holden in the fall of 1859, she brought with her a so-called family medicine chest, which was large and comprehensive.

Just Christian Grønvold, date unknown.
J. Christian Grønvold Papers, NAHA

In addition to instruments for making medications, it contained glass jars of ointments, medicines, and powders. It also included a handbook on health, a guide for laypeople on sickness and treatments. From her brother-in-law, who was a medical doctor, Oline had learned bloodletting, "glass cupping," and how to treat various illnesses. In her garden, she grew herbs and plants for her medicine chest, and she reportedly brought good results. When people in the settlement were sick, they came to Mrs. Muus for advice and to purchase medicine. And she cared for people beyond her immediate community, too. Many years later, Birgitte would tell of her mother visiting the local Dakota settlements to offer medical treatment such as bloodletting, though Oline seldom asked for anything in return for these services.[5]

Judging by photographs, Dr. Grønvold would have inspired trust and goodwill. Under his unruly, blond hair he had a high forehead and a confident and steady gaze. His small cleft chin was charming, and he had an aristocratic nose. Just, as his friends called him, was well liked. But Dr. Grønvold could also be quite stubborn and difficult to deal with. When he first arrived in Holden, Mrs. Muus, with the *Kolibrien* choir, was already a musical institution in town. Dr. Grønvold soon enriched the community with his own contributions, founding the Norway Singing Societies and Brass Band, whose repertoire included Norwegian and Scandinavian folk melodies.

For Bernt Muus, however, music was not a topic in his letters home during his 1870 journey to Norway. "My dear wife," his letters began, followed by detailed accounts of his travels, of relatives and friends, and of new acquaintances. In a letter dated August 15, he reported, among other things, that Oline's sisters Augusta and Pauline were for the most part unchanged (although Augusta had become quite heavy and gray), that Augusta's daughter was very excited to meet her uncle, and that he had met Grønvold's brother, a very likable man. What did Oline think when she read these details? Maybe she felt it was unfair that her husband wouldn't let her accompany him on his trip. After eleven years of marriage, the time for declarations of love and intimate confidences between them seemed to be over, based on the content of these letters.[6]

On October 25, Bernt wrote from his brother-in-law's residence in Christiania. Carl Pind was not very ambitious, Bernt reflected. Carl's planned immigration to America never came to pass, even though it would have been in his own best interest. The oldest son and heir to Tien had become a city dweller. Six years earlier, in 1864, when the court settled the estate of the district official Pind and his wife, Tien Farm had been lost and was taken over by strangers. Because Johan Christian Pind didn't have a will, it had been a complicated inheritance case, presenting the lawyer representing the heirs with a difficult job. Oline was kept abreast of all the family's misfortunes, as shown in a letter from her sister Pauline in the fall of 1864.[7]

By now, the inheritance had long since been settled, though Bernt didn't mention it in his letter to Oline. The inheritance from her parents had been paid and sent to the correct person. But who was that person? In accordance with Norwegian law, it was Bernt Muus, in his capacity as Oline Muus's husband. As Oline's guardian, he was also to manage her inheritance for the good of the family.

When Bernt wrote to his wife in mid-August, he was glad that everything was going so well at home and that she hadn't had too many difficulties. If she thought she had the time, she should take a trip to the city, he wrote. In her previous letter, she had told how illness ravaged the settlement, and he asked her to take good care of the children and herself. As he ended with a greeting to the children and "any others who might miss him," he wrote that he had begun to think of his return home. He had hoped a door might open for him in Norway, but he realized now that he must stay in America.[8]

15

The Church and Women's Emancipation

···

IN THE SUMMER OF 1870, *Kirkelig Maanedstidende* printed a short article about the Methodist Church that certainly sparked attention. The article noted that the Methodists had deleted from their marriage ceremony the word "obey" as part of the vow that a bride, according to Christian practice, had to make during the wedding service. The article commented that the word "obey," which governs the relationship between the spouses, had become outdated—not only for the Methodists but also for the vast majority of American churches. This shift was obviously due to women's rights reform. "Obey," *Kirkelig Maanedstidende* commented, is an unpleasant word, but it isn't evil. It doesn't mean a husband has the right to tyrannize his wife. "'Obey' must not be misused," the editors noted. "We won't defend in a single word, the tyranny some men exert over their wives." Nevertheless, to the editors, it was clear that a home without a master is a home without harmony and peace; it pleased the Lord to designate the husband as master. Sarah was obedient to her husband, Abraham; she called him master. The Bible is clear on this point, they contended: A woman shall be subservient to her husband. Just as the congregation is subservient to Christ, the wife shall be subservient to her husband in all things. Upon entering marriage, the woman must promise what God's word requires of her; she can't put human wisdom above God's demand. That only leads to misery and misfortune.[1]

For American biblical feminists, modernizing the Christian marriage ceremony was an old battle. When Elizabeth Cady agreed to marry her fiancé, Henry B. Stanton, in 1840, she did not agree to obey him. The religious ceremony took place without the word "obey" because she insisted the relationship between her and her husband be equal. The organized women's movement, of which Elizabeth Cady Stanton was one of the founders in 1848, set a new agenda for women's rights in church and in society. For the liberal women and men in old Europe, America had already become the land of the emancipated woman. But it certainly wasn't for Stanton and her fellow women. In their view, reforms and changes in the law that favored women advanced far too slowly.[2]

Still, a few victories had been won; among the most important was the legal reform that gave women the right to own property. A wife had the right to manage property and assets she brought to a marriage or received later, and she now had control over money that she herself earned. In 1848, New York introduced this legislative reform, with other states following soon thereafter. Minnesota, the state with the largest Norwegian immigrant population at the time, adopted this law in 1869. In the more progressive American states, laws granted a married woman the right to divorce if her husband abused her or her children or if he left home and didn't return after a certain number of years.[3]

The Seneca Falls declaration's demand that women should have equal rights with men to vote in both federal and state elections had not been met, so during the Civil War activists in the women's movement had created their own voting rights association. When women in Wyoming gained the right to vote in 1869 it was because one of the activists, Esther Morris, managed to convince legislators. She argued that women's voting rights would contribute to establishing law and order among the settler-colonists in the territory, a wilderness that hadn't yet acquired the status of a state. However, concern for women's rights wasn't what motivated the male legislators. By supporting woman suffrage, they could also perhaps deal with the gender imbalance in Wyoming; women's voting rights could make Wyoming an attractive place for respectable women to settle. One year later, in 1870,

Utah territory also granted women the right to vote, for the same reason as in Wyoming. All other women in America had to wait almost two generations before gaining suffrage, with the passage of the Nineteenth Amendment in 1920.[4]

In many local communities, on the other hand, women had been given the right to vote within their church and in school elections, and even to serve on local boards. In addition, women became visible in the workforce, as several states had opened up opportunities for women to study and graduate from colleges and universities. Helen Marr Ely was the first female graduate of the University of Minnesota in 1875. Compared to Norway and the rest of Europe, women's emancipation had come much further in America. Women were lawyers, journalists, doctors, and teachers and professors.[5]

But in Norwegian America the Lutheran church's beliefs were still firmly rooted in the old patriarchal order. Numerous articles in *Kirkelig Maanedstidende* maintained that anything else was evil. Although the articles were intended to be cautionary, readers gained insight into what was happening within churches in the larger American society. The Unitarian Church, the most radical of the Yankee churches, actually had a long tradition of female ministers. So did the Methodists. In 1872, the Synod paper announced in alarm that the Methodists counted seventy-six female reverends, referring to them as "Pastoresses." Among the Quakers, women were also not excluded from speaking in meetings. The paper had just published a lengthy article after a Quaker woman had spoken from the pulpit in a Presbyterian church. "As our readers are aware, there has been a movement brewing in this country for a long time, to secure, as they say, more rights for women" it stated, and continued, explaining that in order to attain these rights, many prominent women had spoken and written a great deal and that many eminent men had as well, including quite a few of the so-called popular pastors. Among the rights desired, continued *Kirkelig Maanedstidende*, is that marriage shall be dissolved as soon as one or both parties no longer wish to live together, that women shall have the right to vote, and that women shall be eligible to be elected to offices in both state and church.[6]

Kirkelig Maanedstidende mentioned all these details in connection with its article on the recent vehement debate about women's right to speak in church. In Brooklyn, New York, a Presbyterian minister, Dr. T. L. Cuyler, had invited a Quaker by the name of Sarah Smiley to preach during a church service. This news spread like wildfire around town. The president of the Brooklyn Presbyterian Church convened a meeting of the congregation to discuss the matter. At the meeting, which lasted two days, Dr. Cuyler defended himself and then stated that he was against women's rights to vote and easy divorce from one's spouse. But he also noted that he was well acquainted with the Quakers because he himself had preached to them. When he had invited Smiley to his own church, it was because he wanted to thank her for the trust the Quakers had placed in him. Smiley was one of Brooklyn's most accomplished Quaker preachers. A long and agonizing discussion ensued, with both supporters and opponents of Smiley using scriptures as a witness of truth. In the end, the congregation ruled, with only one opposing vote, that Smiley was not wanted as a preacher in their church.

The editors of the Synod paper commented that among the Presbyterians this branch of women's rights didn't have the brightest prospects. They pointed to how even a paper as liberal as the *New-York Observer* had praised the decision to prevent Smiley from preaching. And, according to *Kirkelig Maanedstidende,* the decision would have been approved by ninety-nine of a hundred of the Church's pastors and members. Satisfied, *Kirkelig Maanedstidende* concluded that women's emancipation, from woman suffrage to female pastors, had not yet infected the greater American society. It was not only within the Norwegian Synod and other European immigrant churches that women's emancipation faced powerful enemies. Christian orthodoxy was the same whether in the Norwegian, German, or American church; the woman's place was in the home as wife and mother.[7]

16

A Precocious Confirmand

....

AS THE POPULATION GREW LARGER and more clergy arrived, churches split into smaller congregations. In 1862, the churches in Goodhue County were divided into four districts: Zumbrota, Eastern (now Holden), Valdres (also spelled Valders, now Vang), and Tyske Grove (later Valley Grove and now Valley Grove Preservation Society). It was in the Tyske Grove congregation, on July 6, 1873, that a sixteen-year-old boy named Thorstein was confirmed. The son of Thomas Veblen, a prosperous farmer in neighboring Rice County, Thorstein was born into a large family.[1]

Pastor N. A. Quammen served as the pastor beginning in 1867. However, he must have been away traveling during Thorstein's confirmation, as it was none other than Pastor Muus who confirmed him. Thorstein would become one of the most influential Norwegian American academics, but one who notably took an American path, rather than a Norwegian one.

Thorstein Veblen was a hard worker and could easily pass the confirmation examination. During the catechism test, the congregation's youth had to answer verbatim from Luther's *Small Catechism*. Confirmands needed to know that the fourth commandment is the commandment to obey: "Thou shalt honor thy father and thy mother, that it may be well with thee, and thou mayest live long on the earth." And they had to know what the commandment meant: "We must fear and love God, not despise our parents; likewise those who have command

and rule over us, and not provoke them to anger, but honor, serve, obey, esteem, and love them." The fourth commandment was interpreted as a general commandment to obey, legitimizing the order of an authoritarian society. Children and servants, women and men must obey their masters, both the clergy and the secular authorities. There were many such explanations that Thorstein must have memorized, and he distinguished himself among the other confirmands.[2]

Written in the log notes on the day of Thorstein's confirmation are the biblical passages Pastor Muus chose: Ephesians 2:19–22 and John 17:24–. Both center on one's foundation. Muus was thoroughly impressed with Thorstein's religious foundation, specifically his aptitude and proficiency. Muus discussed with the boy's father the possibility of Thorstein studying theology. Exactly how his father responded isn't known, but if Thomas Veblen absolutely opposed anything, it was his son becoming a pastor. When Thomas, his wife, Kari, and their large brood of children moved from the Manitowoc forest in Wisconsin to the Valdres settlement in Rice County, Minnesota, in 1865, it was to live among relatives. Thomas held on to the old traditions: family and church were indispensable values.[3]

When Thorstein was confirmed by Pastor Muus, it had been twenty-six years since Thomas and Kari emigrated from Høre in Valdres to America, and in all these years they had been churchgoers. They were Lutherans, and the church where the service was conducted in their mother tongue by a Norwegian ordained pastor represented something constant and unchanging for life in their new country. Norwegian was the language of home and church; their English was developed as public school pupils.

The family's eldest son, Andrew, recounted in a reminiscence that pietism ruled in the home when he was growing up. His mother was strict, and everyone in the household observed Christian rules. Sunday was kept holy; all labor had to stop except what was strictly necessary, such as milking the cows and feeding the livestock. Before Sunday came, all meals had to be prepared and all the wood they needed had to be carried indoors.[4]

On Sundays, Andrew never saw his mother knit, even though on other days she always stood and walked with her knitting in her hands. The children had to observe the Sabbath as well; Andrew learned early on that it was a sin to play ball on Sundays. He wasn't even allowed to go outside and watch the other boys play. He had to remain indoors and sit perfectly still. Andrew would never forget what happened one Sunday when he was quite young and found a pocket knife. He had begun to whittle on a stick, and he was very proud when he showed the result to his mother's stepfather, who lived with them. The man said, "No, no, now what have you done?! Now the pastor is sure to come and carve out your tongue because you were whittling on a Sunday!" When Andrew recalled the episode decades later, he could still feel how afraid he was that the pastor would grasp his tongue, pull it out, and stick the knife in it.[5]

Thorstein Veblen, like his older brother, could recall the unusual atmosphere of his childhood home, where their mother watched over them all. She was more than pious; she was fanatical—in her son's words, "electrically religious." His father became a role model for Thorstein, who admired his industriousness, ingenuity, and wisdom. But Thomas was also a faithful and strict Lutheran; he didn't smoke and was temperate with alcohol. Throughout the years, Veblen senior subscribed to *Skandinaven [The Scandinavian]*, a Norwegian-language newspaper printed in Chicago that served as a voice for the low church movement in America, which allowed for a freer worship style with fewer procedures for rituals, liturgy, and the sacraments. Thomas was the very first in Rice County to subscribe to the newspaper, which initially appeared in 1866 and was in strong opposition to the Synod to which Pastor Muus belonged.[6]

In the fall of 1870, *Skandinaven* was sharply criticized in *Kirkelig Maanedstidende* for its position on the Franco-Prussian War. According to *Kirkelig Maanedstidende*, what *Skandinaven* wrote was clearly unchristian—that the German and French were at war with each other because they were each ruled by their own ambitious, vain, proud, and unscrupulous prince by the grace of God, and because they were brought up with the same idea that there was no authority other than that which is ordained by God. *Kirkelig Maanedstidende* alleged that

Skandinaven assailed the scriptures, advocating the abolition of an evil government, even by revolution and bloodshed. The paper quoted Romans 13:2, which its editors believed all readers of Luther's *Small Catechism* should know: "Therefore he that resisteth the power, withstandeth the ordinance of God: and they that withstand shall receive to themselves judgment." The paper quoted several other sources, including Erik Pontoppidan's classic catechism explanation *Truth unto Godliness*, question 165: "Are we then, for God's sake, obliged to obey even a heathen authority? St. Peter wanted the first Christians to be submissive to a heathen authority, saying, 'Be submissive to all human order, for the Lord's sake.'" It was highly appropriate, *Kirkelig Maanedstidende* maintained, to warn against the newspaper *Skandinaven* and its blasphemous statements.[7]

The story of the Veblen family is paradoxical: a mix of both convention regarding Norwegian state church rituals and opposition to the clergy's dominion over the laypeople. Though Pastor Muus strongly opposed the integration of Norwegian immigrants into the larger community, Thomas Veblen had applied for American citizenship for himself and his wife, Kari, and they were approved. Since all the Veblen children were born in the United States, they were American citizens. It is also worth noting that only Thorstein retained his Norwegian name. Each of his siblings eventually took or were given an English name.

As the Veblen children grew up and Thomas became a prosperous farmer, he made plans for them. He would pay for a higher education for both his daughters and his sons. It was a sign of the times that successful farmers wished to provide their children with an opportunity that they themselves had not had: namely, to become educated. For a son, owning his own farm was nothing to aspire to, even for the eldest, who in the old country would have inherited the family farm. Andrew didn't take over the farm; instead, he became a renowned professor of physics at the University of Iowa. Neither Thorstein nor his other brothers became farmers either.

In America, higher education wasn't a privilege reserved for the elite, as it was in Norway. America was the land of opportunity, and many religious communities invested precisely in the education of their youth. In the fall of 1874, seventeen-year-old Thorstein became a student at Carleton College in Northfield, Minnesota, joining his two brothers, Andrew and Orson, and sister Emily, who had begun in 1871, 1872, and 1873, respectively. Four additional siblings would follow suit.

Thorstein's older brother had plans to attend Luther College, but when he became ill practical considerations led him to Carleton. Carleton College was not free from religious affiliation: it was Anglo-American and founded by the Congregational Church. But it was free from the Norwegian clergy. Although St. Olaf College had not yet opened its doors when Thorstein's siblings began studying, it would have been an option for the younger siblings, including Thorstein. But the siblings followed each other, and in 1873 Thomas even built a house just off campus so that all of the siblings could live under the same roof. Emily, Thorstein's younger sister, is reputedly the first Norwegian woman to earn an undergraduate degree in the United States, from Carleton College, in 1881.[8]

Although the Veblens sought their education from a school without Norwegian roots, the family continued many interactions within Norwegian American communities. After graduating from Carleton, Andrew served on the Luther College faculty from 1877 to 1881. Here, the Muus and Veblen families were intertwined again as Nils, the second Muus child, lived with Andrew Veblen.[9]

Over time the Veblen siblings entered a variety of academic careers, but only Thorstein became a celebrity. His book *The Theory of the Leisure Class* (1899) sparked violent debate in the American public. As a sociologist and social economist, Thorstein Veblen, a second-generation Norwegian immigrant, became one of America's foremost social scientists. His research resulted in a series of books that influenced economic policy at the highest federal level. His contributions to American society would be commemorated when the Veblen Farmstead, near Nerstrand in Rice County, was placed on the list of National Historic Landmarks in 1981.[10]

Clergy Shortages and Deceitful Preachers

AT THE EXPENSE OF THE laypeople's democratic rights, President
H. A. Preus maintained order in the Norwegian Synod's congregations
by strengthening the power of the clergy. From the beginning, laypeople had represented their congregations in Synod meetings, but in
1876, this approach was changed into a hierarchical organization with
three districts presided over by Pastors J. B. Frich, Ulrik Vilhelm Koren,
and Bernt Muus. All business and representation in the Synod district
assemblies would be reserved for pastors and theologians. Thus, when
opponents disparagingly referred to the Norwegian Synod as a pastor's
church, there was more than a grain of truth in their criticism. Some
compared the districts to dioceses and their presidents to bishops. Pastor Muus, who had championed hierarchy within the Synod for years,
had been restored to favor, presumably because the Synod could not
manage without him. After all, his efforts to found new congregations
throughout Minnesota had borne abundant fruit.

The Synod had never been peaceful. From the beginning, according
to a commemorative book of 1903, the church had held a battle-ax in
one hand and a trowel in the other. No sooner than one adversary was
driven back, another appeared in its place. Although society wished
for peace to build up the walls of Zion, it constantly had to enter into
new struggles and troubles, the last possibly more difficult than the
first. The Synod's crusade to "renounce false doctrines" was persistent
and endless. Questions of doctrine—disputes over the right of laymen

to preach in public, over the observance of the Sabbath, over slavery, and over parochial education versus the public school—had all taken their toll on the Synod's congregations. And during the disputes over what was true or false doctrine, the clergy, with their theological competence, had assumed the role of experts. But the question of doctrine that created the greatest divisions, both among the laity and the clergy, was the so-called grace election controversy.[1]

The grace election controversy (or predestination controversy), which was just gaining momentum in 1876, has since been described as the most divisive debate in the Synod's history. And in this theological matter, Muus was seen as the main instigator spurring internal division. Joseph M. Shaw explains, "election or predestination means that God from eternity chooses who will be saved." Muus's stance and actions regarding the religious doctrine would later become pivotal.[2]

In the winter of 1874, the Norwegian Synod had grown to nearly 350 congregations, 500,000 members, and a total of 100 pastors and professors. Now, two decades after its founding, the Norwegian Synod began a new publication, *Evangelisk Luthersk Kirketidende [The Evangelical Lutheran Church Times]*, to succeed *Kirkelig Maanedstidende*, and increasing its frequency of communication to weekly. Still, the Synod lacked enough clergy. The shortage was precarious, *Evangelisk Luthersk Kirketidende* declared. The lack of pastors was caused by the continuous stream of Norwegian immigrants moving westward. In the older settlements, there were always a lot of young, unmarried people and families who didn't own houses or land. Over time, the landless traveled farther west, settled on the great prairies in western and northern Minnesota and in the Dakotas, and acquired their own land. And when a few families had established themselves in a new small settlement, others followed suit to build even more small settlements.[3]

As the new communities were spread over a vast area, it was difficult to organize congregations large enough to justify their existence. As *Evangelisk Luthersk Kirketidende* pointed out, a congregation that doesn't acquire its own Lutheran pastor is susceptible to being seduced by all kinds of religious sects and their so-called ministers. The paper cautioned that when a preacher forced his way into a new impressionable congregation, he was able to break them away. The Synod's lack of clergy led many Norwegian immigrants and brethren in faith into the hands of zealots or into the other Norwegian American Lutheran groups and caused the beloved Synod to lose members. Even in immigrant congregations that had their own Lutheran pastor, it was impossible for him to perform his ministry properly, the paper lamented. All day long the immigrants in the great plains fought for their daily livelihood. They were enterprising, but also restless. All their toil and struggle often dimmed any spiritual thoughts, and there was no place for the church in their lives, the paper asserted.[4]

The Norwegian Synod had strong competition from other religious communities. It was a battle for souls, as *Evangelisk Luthersk Kirketidende* testified in several articles. The Synod fell short in the rural areas as well as in the cities, and it wasn't only because of the lack of pastors. Although the Synod was the largest and wealthiest of the Norwegian Lutheran immigrant churches, it lacked the funds to really assert itself in the big cities, where many Norwegian immigrants lived. In New York, which after the Civil War had become the main port for immigrants, both Methodists and Baptists prospered, but the Norwegian Synod was struggling. It couldn't offer its fellow citizens anything but a simple hall in the city's run-down neighborhoods. Instead of seeking out the Norwegian Lutheran Church, the immigrants joined one of the big, beautiful American churches. There, everything was splendid. They could learn English and listen to the pastor preaching about many enjoyable topics. From the pulpit in the Norwegian immigrant churches, people heard the same old thing over and over again: sin and grace, law and the gospel.[5]

The report in *Evangelisk Luthersk Kirketidende* is remarkable for its self-critical tone. It wasn't that the Synod's clergy didn't defend the way they preached; they consistently raged on about America's superficial form of Christianity. "It's wrong to say that American pastors preach," *Evangelisk Luthersk Kirketidende* wrote in the spring of 1878, continuing: "No, you can't say that the American pastor preaches; he gives speeches, or he talks. He discusses topics such as electric lights, paper money, old maids, the President's policy on the southern states, telephones, microphones, measuring the depth of the Pacific Ocean." The conclusion: Americans had turned the church into a place for entertainment.[6]

Warnings of false prophets were also regularly published in *Evangelisk Luthersk Kirketidende*. One article in the winter of 1874 named, among others, the Dane H. P. Lang, who called himself a missionary and was allied with the Baptists. On his missionary campaigns to Wisconsin and Michigan, Lang had thrown himself like a ravenous wolf over the Norwegian immigrants. He mocked the Synod's pastors and branded their teachings as mere devilry. All kinds of "religious fanatics and false prophets" moved among the Norwegian immigrants, the paper wrote. Chicago, with its diverse population, was an arena for fanatics and false preachers—and, even worse, the infamous Danish pastor and writer Uffe Vilhelmsen Birkedal. He proclaimed that the Bible left room for Aryans, Pelagians, Rationalists, Baptists, Unitarians, Gnostics, and Manichaeans to claim the name of Christ's church. In addition, Birkedal alleged that one can produce a hundred different creeds from the Bible because the scriptures can support a hundred different interpretations. According to such speech, *Evangelisk Luthersk Kirketidende* commented, the word of God would contradict itself many times. But this kind of speech is nothing other than blasphemous, the paper concluded, finding support in Luther's interpretation of Paul's letter to the Galatians, which states that it is impossible for the scriptures to contradict themselves, although it's perceived that way by foolish, crude, and stubborn hypocrites.[7]

Competition from other churches and constant internal doctrinal conflict were thus the backdrop for the Synod's reorganization in 1876. During the 1860s, six congregations had resigned from the Synod in protest. In the 1870s, they were followed by several more. It wasn't unusual for a group of members to break out of a congregation; a large number of dissatisfied members in one of Pastor Muus's congregations left to join the Haugean church. The Synod was at war with enemies from within. In 1877, Synod leadership adopted five statements on divisions within the church. The third one states that he who causes or sustains a division in God's church by maintaining, defending, and spreading false doctrine is committing a double sin. He sins by falsifying the word of God and by dividing the unity of the church. The fifth statement asserted that all division was the work of the devil. Those who cause division, desecrate God's name, and ensure their own damnation don't serve God; they serve Satan.[8]

With the reorganization of 1876, Pastor Muus became the president of the Minnesota District and along with Pastors Koren and Frich advanced into the Synod's leadership. As a result, Pastor Muus was given increased authority to control the parishioners in his congregations and the clergy in his district. But even though the Synod had more than enough to deal with, the leaders managed to create conflict among themselves, over matters that were quite peripheral. At a clergy meeting in 1878, and in the parlance of the time, Pastor Muus asked why the Synod was not operating a mission among Negro communities in America, which he called "our own land." The answer he received was that Negro people were familiar with the gospel and those who wanted to be Christians were already in some church or other. It was impossible to operate such a mission because white Southerners would oppose it; therefore, Negro people had to have missionaries as well as pastors of their own race.[9]

Pastor Muus didn't agree with the Synod clergy. In a response published in *Evangelisk Luthersk Kirketidende* in the fall of 1878, he maintained that most Negro pastors were completely ignorant of the gospel and could not preach it to others. According to Muus, Negro pastors were no different from founders of other sects; they strove to influence feelings, to create "a kind of excitement." One thing he felt was certain: most Negro pastors were more ignorant than ordinary Methodist and Baptist preachers. The Negro pastors' sermons were an incoherent mixture of things that could excite the congregation, and the listeners themselves also had the idea that religion consists of exciting oneself. The goal was to enter such a state by means of amen, hallelujah, screaming and moaning, and jumping and throwing oneself on the floor.

Muus concluded that even though Negro people themselves believed they were Christian and had Christian pastors and congregations, they were heathens. The Catholic Church was also scrutinized. With malicious pleasure, Pastor Muus recorded that the Roman Church's mission in the South was met with indifference by Negro communities. On the other hand, the Congregational Church had prospered, so Muus criticized his own church for not having recognized this opportunity. "We Lutherans arrive too late as usual," Muus stated. The only excuse Synod pastors had was that many still had much to contend with in the religious life of the immigrants. The Norwegian Lutherans had not yet established order in their own church, through educational institutions and other essential ecclesiastical affairs.[10]

18

The Family Gathered

....

THE HOLDEN PARSONAGE was a hospitable place; visitors felt welcome there, wrote Pastor Ludvig M. Biørn, who for many years moved in the same circles as Bernt Muus. Biørn remembers Muus as a jovial and witty host, but he didn't say much about the pastor's wife. A parsonage at the time functioned almost as a hotel, where guests rarely paid for food and lodging. When the Synod's leadership held its annual meeting in Holden Church in 1874, almost fifty guests had to be hosted at the parsonage for four days. Usually entertaining at the parsonage was less demanding, as when Pastor Muus invited the Minnesota District representatives to meet there. During the course of a liturgical year, there were numerous banquets Oline Muus had to prepare and serve with the assistance of a maid and probably also hired kitchen help.[1]

Special responsibilities rested on the congregation's women, including the pastor's wife. During a Synod meeting in the spring of 1879, Pastor Muus used a biblical parable to explain women's role in the congregation. He referred to God's word, that he who gives a man a cup of cold water because he is a disciple shall not lose his reward. Women couldn't partake in the meetings to promote the Kingdom of God in the same manner as men. But women mustn't think that they can't serve the congregation; women can actually serve as much as men, namely, with their hospitality. A woman's hospitality was a Christian virtue. When a woman fulfills her duties to the congregation in Jesus's name, like the disciples, men can then work for the good of all, discuss the Kingdom of God, and spread it on earth.[2]

It's striking that Pastor Muus is not documented as having commented on women's contribution to the church's mission work. His own wife had, in fact, founded a missionary society, which she led. Norway had a strong tradition of missionary societies run by women. In the 1840s, Gustava Kielland, a pastor's wife from the Stavanger area, organized the women of her congregation to work for the mission to the non-Christians. The Mission Society was the first organized women's association in Norway. In America, women were active in Ladies' Aid Societies, which date back to the Civil War when helpers provided clothing and medicine for soldiers in the field. Ladies' Aid Societies were not missionary associations like those initiated by some women in the Synod's congregations. However, in the 1860s, the women's missionary organizations had little support, and Mrs. Muus's missionary society probably numbered no more than four or five members. Nevertheless, although there were only a handful of congregations in the Synod where small groups of women worked for the Church's cause, not insignificant amounts of money were collected over the years.[3]

A photograph from the summer of 1878 shows that the farmhouse at the parsonage in Holden was elegant. The wall around the main entrance was covered in large vines, either Virginia creeper or ivy, which spread across the first and second floors all the way up to the gable to form a large entryway. The original log house and the later lumber additions are clad with wood paneling and painted white. The windows are the checkered English type, with small windowpanes that can be lifted up to let fresh air into the rooms. The main entrance, which faces the farmyard, is located in the middle of the long side. On the roof are two chimneys, so likely both living rooms and bedrooms have fireplaces, woodstoves being essential for comfort during the long, harsh Minnesota winters.

In the winter of 1879–80, the Norwegian Kristofer Janson traveled extensively throughout the Midwest to Norwegian American settlements. In writing and speeches reflecting on his experiences, he was impressed by the communities he found. Here an ordinary farmer was much better off than at home in Norway. On the farms were neat, white-painted houses with porches and green shutters, spacious barns for grain and separate barns for animals, and expensive agricultural machines. A farmhouse's large living room was quite comfortable, with a sofa and armchairs, carpet lining the floor, and beautiful lamps hanging from the ceiling. There was also an organ, and when guests came to the farm, one of the daughters was happy to play for them. He noted that the most elegant farmhouses had carpets in every room, both on the first and second floors. Even the stairs up to the second floor, where the guest rooms were, was covered with carpet. Chandeliers hung from the ceiling in the guest rooms, and in a corner of one of the rooms was a fully stocked bookcase.[4]

Most of all, the Norwegian traveler was enthusiastic about the food he was served. For breakfast: slices of bread with the thickest sweet cream and apple porridge or jam. For dinner: soup and meat dishes, with coffee or tea and a considerable assortment of pudding and cakes afterward. America is—Janson declared—the land of cakes and sweets. He was served ice water and lemon water throughout the meal, and as a rule, an "extra dessert" of bread and cheese at the end. It is possible the food he encountered was only served to guests. Even if one arrived unannounced, a housewife could still dish up meals like those described in no time. And if he had come to the settlements when the Minnesota summer was at its hottest, he would see how comfortable the life of a farmer's wife was. Outdoors she had a summer kitchen that her husband had installed. Oline Muus had asked her husband for such a kitchen in vain. Indoors, it was warm enough already before one started cooking, generating more heat; with a summer kitchen outdoors, it would be more enjoyable to prepare meals.[5]

In the summer of 1878, Oline Muus gave birth to a son. She was now forty years old, and it had been three and a half years since she was last in childbirth. Harald, as the child was baptized, was the couple's sixth and final child. Just a few weeks after Harald was born, both parents and their children sat together in the farmyard; the entire family was to be immortalized with a photograph. The photographer was probably a professional, and he surely told the family members where and how

The Muus family outside of Holden parsonage, c. 1878.
Courtesy St. Olaf College

they were to stand or sit. With their farmhouse as the backdrop, the parents and children posed as a group right in front of the steps up to their front door with the grand entrance draped in vines. The family members formed a pyramid. Nils, the eldest son, stands at the highest point, and the mother and father sit at the outer edges. The pyramid, a harmonious figure, was a conventional way of depicting family, symbolizing connection and unity.

Remarkably, the Muus family was not united in one but in three groups on that summer day. Mother—Mamma, as the toddlers called her—sat to the left, with the newborn son, Harald, on her lap. She is conventionally dressed in a black dress with a white lace collar. Jens stands beside her; he had turned twelve in January and would soon be leaving to study at Luther College. Nils, the eldest son, stands a little way off. He was fifteen years old, already dressed in adult clothing, and would be confirmed at the beginning of September. He forms the middle group, together with older sister Birgitte, whose eighteenth birthday was around the corner. Oline was grateful to have her daughter as a helping hand at the parsonage, and when Birgitte wasn't there, she was missed. Birgitte sits dressed in a light summer dress with lace ruche, presumably homemade of American cotton. A straw hat sits on her lap. Little three-year-old Petter cuddles in beside her.

On the far right, in the third group, looms Pastor Muus, dressed in a bulky cloak. He sprawls casually, with one leg over the other, almost as if he doesn't have time to sit down. It is plain to see that forty-six-year-old Bernt Muus is the head of the household. His hair isn't as thick as it was in his earlier years, but he has grown an imposing, patriarchal beard. Six-year-old Paul, who stands close to his father's side, appears quite small and awkward.

Family portraits were often sent to friends and relatives on the other side of the ocean. Alternatively, they were preserved as a keepsake at home, either framed on the living room wall or placed in a leather-bound photograph album. A family portrait was a historical record in visual form. Parents and children could look back and say to each other, *look how strange we were when we sat there together.* The portrait acted as a symbol of the family gathered together, a memory of the family and where everyone in the inner circle belongs. Whether the Muus family portrait was framed or placed in an album isn't known. At some point, someone folded the photograph in half. It's still in one piece, but a deep crease runs between Pastor Muus and little Paul and the other two groups.

Church Discipline on the Agenda

WHEN ISSUE FIFTY-ONE OF *Evangelisk Luthersk Kirketidende* was printed on December 19, 1879, the newspaper felt compelled to report on a conflict that had already received much attention elsewhere. "From Goodhue County, in Pastor Muus's congregation, the following course of action has been made public," began a lengthy report. The article "A Couple Cautionary Examples" had in fact already been printed in *Luthersk Kirketidende [The Lutheran Church Times]*, the Norwegian Augustana Synod's paper. Why hadn't the report been sent first to the Norwegian Synod's paper? Perhaps the author, an anonymous member of Pastor Muus's congregation, didn't think the Synod publication would print the report. For Pastor Muus, consistently referred to as the "the pastor," was the accused.[1]

"Recently, (May 19, 1879) the treasurer was collecting money for the pastor's salary. But one member of the congregation thought the amount he was demanded to pay was way too steep," it stated. Furthermore, the report went on, this member of the congregation had refused to pay it; he offered instead a smaller, more manageable sum. Incidentally, it was merely a couple of dollars difference. But the treasurer wouldn't accept anything less than the stipulated amount and said he would report the incident to the pastor. Immediately afterward, the same member of the congregation met face-to-face with the pastor and insisted that the following Sunday he be allowed to go to the Lord's table. But Pastor Muus refused him communion because the parishioner wouldn't pay the set contribution to the pastor's wages.[2]

In other words, the pastor used church discipline as his personal means of power against a layman he thought was unwilling and obstinate. But the pastor certainly couldn't, at his own discretion, subject a member of the congregation to church discipline in this manner, could he? That would be in violation of the church bylaws. First the church council had to convene a meeting of the congregation to consider whether a member had committed a sin, and if a majority of the congregation supported this claim, then church discipline would take effect. In the end, Pastor Muus was accused of grossly abusing church discipline in this case.

The report stated that it wasn't the first time money issues caused conflict between the pastor and this member of the congregation. The previous winter, the two had also clashed. That time, it was the pastor himself who made the rounds in the congregation to collect the offering for Luther College's school fund. Each individual could determine the amount they would give. Nevertheless, the pastor expected this member of the congregation to commit to a larger sum, a total of $75. When the donor wouldn't contribute more than $50, the pastor said it was far too little and demanded $75. Finally, the donor pledged $60, and with that, he thought the matter was settled. But shortly after, the pastor again demanded the full $75. The parishioner had witnesses who could testify to having heard him pledge $60; if he didn't, he could be called a liar.

This member of Pastor Muus's church was upset, as were other members. The financial dispute resulted in the pastor banning the parishioner. It was rather strange, stated the report, that a Norwegian Synod pastor could demand such a substantial sum from the members of his church as he pleased. And it didn't end there. When members refused to contribute what he demanded, the pastor could coerce them into paying by denying them the benefits of the church.

These accusations made against Pastor Muus in the spring of 1879 were very serious. The parishioner had not only been refused communion for his ostensible stinginess, he had also been banned, which implies that he was excluded from worship services and meetings in his own congregation. The fact this report was printed in *Evangelisk Luthersk Kirketidende* sheds some light on the relationships within the Synod's leadership. But the report would not go unchallenged. In a brief response in the same issue, an anonymous "M," undoubtedly Pastor Muus, raged against the parishioner and his fellow conspirators in the congregation. "Which God is served by printing such lies?" he wrote, and added, "And when these men dare to print such things, which every reasonable man can see are lies, what does that tell us?" Then he answered, "Oh, you poor people, torn apart in grief."[3]

The report testified that at least one parishioner experienced Pastor Muus as a ruthless money collector. Yet it was also said that Pastor Muus showed great sympathy for parishioners who were in difficult circumstances. Once when he had collected an agreed-upon sum of money from a young man in his congregation, he returned the sum because he learned the family was in financial trouble.[4]

Pastor Muus may have acted contrary to the church's bylaws and abused the administration of church discipline. If so, he was in conflict with his own youthful ideals regarding the lay church, the free church. This case was of great importance within the Norwegian American Lutheran church. H. A. Preus, president of the Synod, convened a special conference in Goodhue County during the winter of 1879. There was only one matter on the agenda: church discipline. At the conference, not only pastors but also laypeople could decide to what extent the congregational meeting could discuss whether a church member should be placed under church discipline. And after the assembly's vote, it was decided that in cases of church discipline the congregation had the first and final say in the matter. Even the pastor (read: Pastor Muus) had to respect the outcome reached in a congregational meeting. That conclusion was certain, even though it wasn't stated explicitly or recorded in the special conference's printed account in *Evangelisk Luthersk Kirketidende*. But what was absolutely clear in the record was how a church discipline case should be handled. When a parishioner was guilty of sin, individual members of the congregation should discuss the matter with that person. According to the special conference,

Matthew 18:15–17 must be the guiding principle: "If your brother sins against you, go and tell him his fault, between you and him alone. If he listens to you, you have gained your brother. But if he does not listen, take one or two others along with you, that every word may be confirmed by the evidence of two or three witnesses."[5]

Such conversations were to be regarded as preliminary proceedings in a possible church disciplinary case. If a sinner was and remained irredeemable, the congregation had to use its authority. The minutes clearly state, "If he or she who has transgressed does not confess their sin and do penance, the congregational meeting must bring action against him or her." According to the scriptures, if the sin was so grievous that it couldn't be granted mercy, and "if he will not listen to them, tell it to the congregation. If he still doesn't listen to the congregation, then he shall be to you as a heathen and a publican." If the situation went this far, the congregation was fully entitled to place the parishioner in question under church discipline.[6]

A case of church discipline was much like a legal case, where the congregation assumed the role of the court. As it was written, the congregational meeting would consider the case against the member who has sinned and examine from testimony the truthfulness of the charges. If the accused confesses their sin during the meeting and promises to change, the matter is considered resolved. But if the sinner is unwavering and won't listen to the congregation's admonitions, they must be expelled from the church forever. During the special conference in Goodhue County in the winter of 1879, participants were concerned not with church expulsion but rather with the stages prior to it. With reference to the gospel of Paul, there was consensus that the congregation has one single motive to practice church discipline: namely, love and concern for the sinner's salvation.

The Synod's congregations had great power according to the constitution they adopted, and they acted upon it. A letter from a parishioner to schoolteacher J. M. Midbøe, which *Evangelisk Luthersk Kirketidende* printed in the fall of 1879, offers testimony. In this parishioner's congregation four farmers had applied for membership. They could each present a church certificate, issued by the pastor who had confirmed them at home in Norway. They also satisfied other admission criteria. They had lived within the geographical boundaries of the church for two or three years. They had been diligent churchgoers, and they had contributed money to the church's parochial school. But according to the letter writer there were questionable circumstances associated with these four farmers. They had not applied for admission earlier because they had not found the Synod's religious community to be uplifting. Two of the farmers admitted they had also visited the Methodists but hadn't thrived there. And when the four had to answer how they understood questions of doctrine, they were very unclear and confused justification with sanctification. The more the congregation learned about the four farmers, the more skeptical they became.[7]

The applications were considered during two lengthy congregational meetings before the male members finally voted on whether the four farmers would be allowed to become members of the church. The pastor had received their certificates in advance and read them aloud at the meeting. Next the pastor began a foundational conversation with them, asking if they recognized the Bible as their only rule and guide. Yes, the four applicants replied; one added that the scriptures cannot err. Then lay members continued the examination, and eventually the assembly could vote whether the four were worthy. At that point a layman stood up and said, "One can't vote for admission when the applicants show such a deplorably limited knowledge of the true faith." But during the vote, by raised hands, three of the four farmers, with their families, were approved by a majority. Still, there were those who hesitated. One parishioner followed up with a letter to Midbøe, voicing his concern and asking if Midbøe felt that these three deserved to be members of the congregation. Midbøe agreed with the parishioner; these three farmers should not have been approved, Midbøe explained in his letter to the newspaper.[8]

The account doesn't say whether the pastor agreed with the decision, only that he had to abide by the majority's decision. It resulted in three new donors to the Synod's most important social project, Luther College. In addition, there was Pastor Muus's own project: St. Olaf's School.

20

Hypochondria and Hysteria

WHEN OLINE MUUS READ her son's letter dated October 8, 1878, she must have been overwhelmed with fear and sorrow—and also resentment. Jens had fallen ill again. Despite his serious illness, his father had enrolled him at Luther College in Decorah, Iowa, where his older brother, Nils, was already a student. It was a long way from Holden, Minnesota, to Decorah, Iowa, at that time, but Pastor Muus was determined that his children, including his daughter, receive higher education. "Thank you very much for the welcome letter that I received from you today. I have now become worse again, to the point that I can't even go to class," wrote Jens. He had just gotten Nils to ask Professor Laur. Larsen if he could travel home. But Jens wasn't allowed. Instead, the professor said that he should stay and see if he didn't get better soon.

Jens's handwriting is not to be misunderstood. The letter is written in large, uneven letters with long spaces and dashes in between, and the margin slopes steeply outward. Jens was sick, but brave. The woman working for the housekeeper was very kind to him, he wrote. He was served eggs when he requested them, and in general she was friendly to him. He hadn't seen Diderikke Brandt, the headmaster's wife, whom many considered a surrogate mother, because he mostly stayed in his room, where he sat or lay in bed. He had "bad headaches, and sometimes had diarrhea."[1]

The letter from Oline's dear son Jens was heartbreaking. "I am so homesick, and I think that is the reason that I am so ill," he admitted. In the beginning, school had been fun. But when he became ill, he became homesick; he lay in bed longing for home until tears rolled down his cheeks. If Mother wrote back, he explained in the letter, she must tell him how everything was at home. She must greet Hilde Samson, if she was still looking after the little boys and the house. He asked his mother to greet everyone at home.

According to Jens's letter, in October 1878 Oline Muus wasn't at Holden parsonage. She, along with her daughter, Birgitte, was with a certain Mrs. Hoegh. What had happened at home at the parsonage? Did Oline and her daughter pay Hoegh a visit, or had something gone wrong? In fact, Oline wasn't completely well either; her health had been deteriorating for quite some time.

"I've only been in school for about 2 weeks, so I'm not quite sure how I like it," Jens wrote, continuing with a story about one of the teachers, Thrond Bothne, probably the strictest one they had. Sometimes he beat Hermann, Larsen's twelve-year-old son, almost to death, Jens wrote. Period. His mother had to understand that Jens was alone. He mentioned that he didn't see Nils very often. His older brother had room and board with Professor Andrew Veblen, who had been hired as a teacher at Luther College that fall. "God grant that you may soon be well again, dear Mother. Now I'm pretty tired so I have to quit for now. Best regards from your devoted son Jens."

The state of health in Holden and the neighboring settlements wasn't the best, as Dr. Just Grønvold discovered in 1869. After he established his medical practice in Goodhue County, he was not short of patients. In Holden, Grønvold had first lived with the Muuses and since 1873 had been their neighbor. The following year he married Eli Brandt, the niece and foster daughter of the headmaster of Luther College. Just Christian Grønvold was essentially married into the church where Bernt Muus was among the leaders. But in 1878, he was among those who withdrew from the Holden congregation. He had now joined Aspelund Church, which belonged to the Norwegian Synod's old archenemy—the Haugean Synod. Aspelund Church, which had always been a thorn in Pastor Muus's side, wasn't far from Holden. Nonetheless, Dr. Grønvold continued to be the Muuses' family doctor.

In his new homeland, Dr. Grønvold had made quite the career. He sat on the Minnesota State Board of Health, for which he prepared a research report: "The Effects of the Immigration on the Norwegian Immigrants" (1878). He asserted that the physical and mental constitution of a people is greatly influenced by their natural and climatic conditions. Conditions specific to every people characterize that people's way of life and culture. And when these conditions change, as they do when people move from one country to another, so do their lives, in a profound way. But before Grønvold explained what the migration itself had to say for public health, he gave a rather grandiloquent depiction of Norway and the Norwegian national character. Norway can be seen as a big mountain, he explained. There are dangerous coasts and fjords stretching far into steep valleys, and from time immemorial, Norwegians have loved the sea. Precisely because Norwegians love the sea and freedom, they are accustomed to adapting to new conditions. In other words, Norwegian immigrants were well equipped intellectually to manage the transition from Norway to America.[2]

Nevertheless, he continued, when immigrants become physically or mentally ill, there are particular causes. The newcomers had to work long and hard to survive. Dehydration as a result of drinking too little water while laboring in the scorching summer sun was exceedingly common. Also common were bloody diarrhea and cramps in the thighs and calves from drinking too much water when the workday ended. Further, newcomers often endured chronic gastritis. The causes were many, including the misuse of coffee and liquor. But first and foremost, American eating habits were to blame. For people who grew up eating porridge and gruel in Norway, a diet of pork and beef in large quantities was heavy fare. Often it was too heavily salted because the newcomers don't know how to properly prepare the food. And the immigrants didn't take time for a midday rest, as the Americans usually did, to aid digestion.

Grønvold believed stomach and gastrointestinal issues were the main cause of Norwegian immigrants' health problems. Furthermore, stomach discomfort and indigestion cause a whole series of ailments, whether of a mental or a physical nature or both. Nervous ailments stemming from the stomach and gastrointestinal tract can be divided into three main categories: hypochondria, hysteria, and neuralgia. According to medical science at the time, these conditions were distinct diagnoses, though they had a great deal in common. First, they were held up against a notion of normalcy. A doctor, someone with a keen understanding of medicine, was needed to examine each patient and his or her unhealthy condition. Since Grønvold did not describe hypochondria, hysteria, and neuralgia in detail in his report, it can be useful to compare the three diagnoses within the common medical understanding at the time.

The hypochondriac, one who imagines they are ill, is an ancient medical-historical notion. The disease develops when a patient pays excessive attention to their own body and bodily functions and at only the slightest sign of pain believes they are suffering from some serious illness. But hypochondria and hysteria, both diagnoses deriving from classical Greek medicine, were confusingly similar. Originally hysteria was a female disorder, the term for it coming from the Greek word *hystera*, for uterus. In antiquity, it was thought that the woman's symptoms were due to her uterus moving around her body. In the nineteenth century, hysteria was still diagnosed as a disorder of the uterus. At that time, hysteria was the most common diagnosis a woman received. Women between the ages of fifteen and forty were particularly susceptible, as during these years they menstruate, making them unpredictable and in many cases, according to medical expertise, causing abnormal conditions. In short, menstruation renders a woman the victim of an unpleasant force of nature, whether her period comes as it should or is absent without her being pregnant. The symptoms of hysteria were confusingly many, ranging from headaches, melancholy, and crying to cramps, insomnia, and loss of vision, and in the worst cases, epileptic seizures and paralysis.[3]

Grønvold claimed that hypochondria and hysteria were widespread among Norwegian American immigrants. When people went to see a doctor, it was often because they suffered from severe headaches, heart palpitations, or tremors. In addition, people complained about what they called nerve pain, and Grønvold pointed out that second to influenza and rheumatism the most common diagnosis was nerve pain, or neuralgia.

In his report, Grønvold described a startling finding: statistical evidence that hypochondria and hysteria were more prevalent in the Norwegian American immigrant population in Minnesota than in the population in Norway. His experience was that Norwegian American immigrants frequently commented that they did not feel as healthy as they used to in their homeland. They complained that work was strenuous in the new land and the air was heavy and unhealthy. In addition, Grønvold found statistical evidence that within the Norwegian American immigrant population women, more than men, were affected by nervous disorders. He explained that this prevalence was because the women were young when they married, had many children over a few years, and returned to work too soon after childbirth. In his report, Grønvold did not explicitly state that hysteria was the most common nervous disorder afflicting Norwegian American immigrant women, but that assessment was the subtext. Grønvold pointed out that women made up the largest share of patients at Minnesota's hospital for the insane, located in St. Peter, and most had immigrant backgrounds.[4]

Established in 1866, the St. Peter Asylum for the Insane, as the institution was first called, was a place that caused uneasiness. In Minnesota, there were certainly many men who, in a marital argument, might threaten their wife with sending her to St. Peter. The story of a minister's wife, Elizabeth Packard, whose husband committed her to an asylum, shows that this sort of scenario actually happened. In 1860, after many years of marriage, Mrs. Packard began to doubt the religious dogma her husband believed in, and consequently he had her confined to the Jacksonville Insane Asylum in Illinois. When after three years, with the help of her adult children, she was discharged, she filed a lawsuit against her husband. She wanted to be declared sane. The court ruled that Mrs. Packard was sane and that she could interpret the Bible differently from her husband.[5]

Kristofer Janson, ca. 1913.
From Kristofer Janson, *Hvad jeg har oplevet:*
Livserindringer (Christiania [Oslo]: Gyldendal, 1913)

21

The Norwegian American Elite

IN THE SUMMER OF 1879, Norwegian writer Kristofer Janson landed in New York and from there continued his journey to Norwegian America. He traveled to Chicago, Madison, Milwaukee, La Crosse, Eau Claire, and Minneapolis and visited new Norwegian settlements such as Holden, Valdres, and Urland. He gave lectures about Norway everywhere fellow countrymen had settled. Because people were anxious to hear news from the old country, they gladly paid for an entrance ticket. Janson was on a ten-month tour and planned to write a book about everything he experienced along the way. A significant amount of money could be made from such a tour. Whether by chance or not, the tour was also the beginning of a new chapter in Janson's life. Two years later, the book became a reality, a spectacular account of his journey, in which details about the Norwegian Synod, Pastor Bernt Muus, and Oline Muus filled many pages.

Janson loved America, the land of freedom and equality, the land of the republic and democracy. Yet, as a newcomer on American soil, he was overwhelmed. The culture and religious life were so immeasurably rich, women held so many important positions in society, and his emigrated compatriots had done so well in their new country. From one end to the other, with few exceptions, Janson applauded and praised what he saw and heard.

In the summer of 1879, Janson was still youthful and enthusiastic, though in two years he would turn forty. In photographs, he looks like an Old Testament prophet, a preacher through and through. His short and not-too-well-groomed hair and his patriarchal beard are black. Almost all of Janson is black, though his face is gentle. His eyes are dark brown and radiant, and he undoubtedly exerted an alluring charm on women. But the man was not to be trifled with; in the face of opponents, he was merciless, unyielding, and savage. Controversy and verbosity came naturally to Janson. He wrote as he spoke; whether enthusiastic or indignant, he appeared equally bold and unedited.

Janson came from an upper-class merchant family in Bergen and had a theological degree from the university in Christiania. He had never applied for a call to be a pastor. He wanted to become a writer, and he had early on earned state travel grants in support of his work and later a state artist's salary. He belonged to Norway's cultural elite, the national-liberal authors who felt solidarity with the common man, the left-wing movement, and women—first and foremost the women. Janson was familiar with John Stuart Mill; his book on women's subjugation had awakened Janson's sympathy. Just before leaving for America, Janson had published a thin little book, the play *En kvindeskjæbne* [*A Woman's Fate*], a flaming attack on the church and Christian family values. It would be strange if he hadn't brought a few copies with him on his tour.[1]

With fifty thousand inhabitants, Minneapolis was Minnesota's second-largest city and had several sizable enclaves of Scandinavian immigrants. Here, Janson naturally sought out and associated with the liberal intellectual elite. He became acquainted with angry young men who were writers, journalists, or academics and prominent Norwegian Americans. Among them was a man with the surname Jæger and the unusual given name Luth. In 1871, Luth Jæger had emigrated from the Arendal region in southern Norway to Wisconsin, where he studied at the university in Madison before embarking on a career in journalism. In 1879, as he approached his thirtieth birthday, he had been the editor of a Norwegian-language newspaper in Minneapolis for two years. *Budstikken* [*The Messenger*] was both liberal and independent. From the outset, the opposition newspaper had quickly become quite important in Norwegian America. It was the primary Norwegian-language press organ in Minnesota during the late 1800s.[2]

Luth Jæger, 1925.
Minneapolis Star and Tribune Photographs, courtesy Hennepin County Library

The publication was both loved and hated, not least because of its editor. Jæger was a writing editor and a master of the written word, whether expressing himself in arrogant, sardonic, and sarcastic terms or in sympathetic, moving prose. When Jæger had a cause, he used every means at his disposal. In this respect, he had learned a great deal from his colleagues in America, the birthplace of modern partisan journalism. In photographs, Jæger appears to be a refined man. He is well groomed and handsomely dressed, with a lean and energetic figure. With his large eyes and spectacles, he seems almost unabashedly bold. In addition, his American goatee lends him a mature man's patronizing authority as well as demanding respect. Jæger undoubtedly had a friend and a role model in Marcus Thrane, who was of the firm opinion that Norwegians in America had to become Norwegian Americans; a quick and thorough Americanization was necessary. Norwegian immigrants needed to take pride in mastering the English language just as well as their mother tongue. They had to adapt to an American lifestyle and customs, but without rejecting their Norwegian heritage. Jæger himself was a member of the Unitarian Church, which was at the forefront of religious and political liberalism. Through the church, he gained an extensive American network, in addition to his Norwegian and Scandinavian network in Minneapolis.

As editor of *Budstikken*, Luth Jæger addressed the Norwegian American public. In the late 1870s, barely a generation had passed since the Norwegian settlements in the "West," and later the "Midwest," had been established. Jæger practiced hyphenated nationalism. The ties to the old country were still strong; the possibility of transatlantic travel made the path between Norway and Norwegian America more feasible. Mass emigration from Norway after the American Civil War brought hundreds of thousands of Norwegians to America. Modern steamships in regular traffic ensured that a transatlantic voyage was no longer limited to a costly one-way ticket. Men who had emigrated from Norway thirty years ago could now visit the old country.

Touring around the Norwegian settlements, Kristofer Janson met individuals who had visited Norway—but who became so homesick that they returned to America as soon as they could. For Norwegian writers on a lecture tour and the Norwegian American cultural elite in Minneapolis, Norway, and Norwegian America, whether it lay west or east of the Atlantic Ocean, was the same project: a cultural-political project rooted in progress and liberalism. News in Norwegian America was also a news item in Norway, and occasionally, the opposite was also true.

In Minneapolis, Janson became good friends with another proud Norwegian American, the lawyer Andreas Ueland. Ueland and Jæger were also friends; they were the same age and had lived in America for the same amount of time. While Jæger had no family background worth mentioning, the opposite was true of Ueland. He was the son of Ole Gabriel Ueland, a farmer in Rogaland who, since the 1830s, had led the farmers' opposition in Parliament. In his final politically active years, he had joined together with Johan Sverdrup, the lawyer who led the tempestuous progressive liberal movement of the 1860s. Because Andreas Ueland couldn't inherit the family farm, he had immigrated to the land of opportunity following his father's death. From the very beginning, his objective was to become Norwegian American. America became his new home, and it was in the language of his new homeland that he wrote his memoir, *Recollections of an Immigrant*.[3]

In the early years, Ueland held many different jobs, including as lumberjack and farmhand, to save up enough money to study law and learn English so that he knew it as well as his mother tongue. After graduating from law school, he received his license and in 1877 established his own law office in Minneapolis. His career went amazingly well. In the Norwegian American settlements there were plenty of farmers who needed a bilingual lawyer, and Ueland gained a reputation for his ability to safeguard the interests of the Norwegian American immigrants within the larger American society.

In his first year as a lawyer, he earned $1,000 and could afford to move to a larger office. He was a bachelor and used much of his income to buy books, collecting both Norwegian and American literature. In the evenings, he was always going somewhere. He acquainted himself thoroughly with the different churches in Minneapolis and various organizations and cultural life.[4]

Andreas and Clara Ueland family, 1897.
MNHS collections

One photograph suggests that Andreas Ueland was an attractive man. Although he seems younger than his age, he instills respect. Both his hair and his clean-shaven face call attention to his boyish vigor. His broad and well-formed features would inspire a sculptor. Ueland would soon be something of a celebrity when, in 1880, he became both famous and notorious as Mrs. Muus's lawyer.

22

A Home in Deep Sorrow

....

NOVEMBER 6, 1878, BEGAN "bright and fair," but as the day went on it turned cold and threatening. The same can be said of the two life-altering events that took place for the Muuses that day.[1]

Bernt Muus was at St. Olaf's School in Northfield for the festive dedication of the Main, now known as Old Main. This event marked the transition of the school from downtown to its new location, called Manitou Heights. The event was many years in the making. It had been four years since Muus proposed his idea to the Synod and then wrote the articles of incorporation. He had so much to be proud of and celebrate on that November day.

But while Muus was giving his dedication speech, a messenger from Holden rode up with word that Muus's son Jens was dying. The news hit him hard, but it didn't come out of nowhere. Since the fall of 1878, the family at Holden parsonage had been severely tested by illness. Jens, a student at Luther College, had finally returned home, but he was in a miserable state. He had been infected with typhus, and in his condition, even Dr. Grønvold couldn't do anything. Typhus, which causes high fever, severe diarrhea, and intestinal bleeding, was often fatal. Muus finished his address with a prayer before he left for home.

Jens only lived to be twelve years old. Oline Muus would later refer to him as "our son who lies in the grave." Loss and grief can weld a family together or split it apart. In the Muus family, it seems as though the latter happened. The couple was incapable of comforting each other;

instead, each was left alone with their personal feelings of guilt, self-reproach, and bitterness.

Oline struggled with her own health after two separate accidents resulted in a broken leg. In July 1878, she had given birth to her son Harald. She was forty years old, and the delivery had certainly been exhausting. A few months later when Jens died, the parsonage became a house of mourning. A glimpse into the bleak atmosphere can be seen in three letters: two from her sister Pauline Henschien and one from a friend who signed with her first name only, Anna. "My dear, dear Sister! Finally, the time has come when I can write to you in peace and quiet, my dearest sister," Pauline began on February 5, 1879. The letter is written on mourning stationery, notable for its black edges alerting the recipient that the sender was grieving; her beloved husband had passed away. "You yourself, dear Oline, have recently been at your loved one's deathbed, so you know what this is like," her sister continued sympathetically.[2]

How was dear Oline doing? Pauline was worried; this was the third letter she had written since she had heard from Oline. Was Birgitte at home with Oline? Oline certainly couldn't manage without her daughter now that she was in such poor health. Did Oline think Birgitte might be allowed to travel to Norway next summer? It would be so nice to see her. Oline must promise to write soon.

Pauline had written three times to Oline without receiving a single reply. A great deal of time had passed since the sisters had been together—twenty years. Even though Pauline wrote openly of personal matters, perhaps this level of sharing was not reciprocated. Or was Oline so weighed down with grief that she couldn't express herself in a letter? It could be that she found it easier to confide in one of her revivalist friends, such as Anna in Sandefjord. In a letter dated March 28, 1879, Anna asked if Oline occasionally heard from her siblings.[3]

In the same note, Anna wrote that it was painful to receive Oline's most recent letter. On her knees she had prayed that God might give Oline strength, protect her, and grant her troubled, grieving heart peace. "You grieve over Jens's illness and death, and for a mother's heart this is only natural," she added. But her dear Oline must remember that

Letter from Pauline Henschien to Oline Muus written on mourning stationery.
Sven Oftedal Papers, courtesy Augsburg University

it is written: without God's will not even a sparrow can fall to the earth, much less a man who is redeemed with the blood of Christ. The Lord will help her understand God's word, and then she will also experience the healing power of the word of God.[4]

Anna wrote many words of comfort, and she repeated what Oline had written to her, "how good it was, that Jens longed to be with Jesus—yes, he probably wouldn't trade it for the happiest life on earth, and you wouldn't have wanted him to either." From the photographs Oline had sent, Anna could see how much Jens resembled his mother. "It must have been difficult to part from him," Anna wrote, "but you'll see that just as his life was a blessing to you, his death will be also." Anna thanked her for the small letter from Jens that Oline had enclosed; it was so proper and nicely written, one could see that he was a bright boy. She enclosed Jens's letter with her own to Oline, thanking her for the loan. When Oline told Anna that she wanted to come to Norway, Anna had been delighted at the thought of reuniting with her again. Now, nothing would come of it. Little Paul was sick and Harald hadn't yet turned one. Oline was indispensable at home, however much she needed rest and quiet.

In the midst of the grief over Jens, another misfortune came to the family at the Holden parsonage. Paul, who was only six years old and at school, became seriously ill. It began with a letter from the school reporting that Paul wasn't eating his lunch. Oline realized there was something seriously wrong when he came home early that evening and was in such bad shape that he vomited. At Dr. Grønvold's recommendation, Paul left school to be under his mother's care at home. Now, spring was approaching without any sign of improvement in Paul's condition.

How was Oline herself doing? Anna asked how her rheumatism was and whether she had any permanent damage from her broken leg. "I can well understand how difficult it is for you to manage without Birgitte at home, especially when illness strikes, but isn't she soon finished with school?" Anna asked. Birgitte was at St. Olaf's School, where Pastor Muus had enrolled his daughter.[5]

The grief of losing Jens had to be very difficult for Oline's husband as well, Anna wrote. During this difficult time, little Harald must be a consolation. Judging by his picture, he looked so healthy and handsome. Finally, Anna wanted to know how old Oline's son Paul was now, and whether Oline thought there was hope that he would recover. The words of comfort Anna couldn't fit on the last page of the letter she wrote in the margins on the first page: "Don't forget to pray for me, that I mustn't err, but fight the good fight, keep the faith, and finish the race." Her dear Oline must promise to write a few lines to her again. And with that, Anna had come to the end of her long letter.

That year marked two decades since Bernt and Oline Muus had arrived in America together. Perhaps the family at Holden parsonage had never faced greater trials than they did now. All the same, in the midst of this challenging situation, Oline did something unusual, even unheard of. She reached out to a lawyer in Minneapolis, and her husband was ostensibly aware of her request. The exact date of the first contact isn't known, but it was most likely in the latter half of 1879. Oline wished to inquire about her financial rights, specifically related to her inheritance from her parents, which Bernt had taken control of more than fifteen years earlier. This contact would be the beginning of a process that turned the family's life completely upside down and would influence the rest of both Oline and Bernt Muus's lives and the lives of their children.

The lawyer Oline contacted was none other than the progressive Andreas Ueland in Minneapolis, the son of the famous Norwegian politician. Perhaps Dr. Grønvold, who had often been called to the parsonage for the recent unhappy incidents, had connected her to Ueland; that is one speculation. It's possible Oline heard his name mentioned by the settlement's farmers or saw one of his ads in a newspaper. In any case, it seems almost inconceivable that Oline Muus, burdened with grief and worry and frail herself, had the energy to take this step. But she did.

She probably didn't say anything to her sister about the process she had initiated, since it isn't mentioned in Pauline's reply dated December 7, 1879. Oline had evidently told Pauline that her intended trip to Norway had to be abandoned because her son Paul was seriously ill.

"The little son you spoke of this summer with tuberculosis, how is he? Possibly the almighty Father has already delivered him from this wretched world?" her sister inquired. "Yes, my dear Oline, your trials are many and great," she continued compassionately. It could be that their trials served them when they believed in Jesus—if only they could keep their faith firm and alive. Pauline had recently been to Fet to look after their parents' grave site, "our" cemetery plot, as she called it. "The gravestones of father and mother had sunk and the picket fence around their graves had rotted," Pauline recalled. But she had made sure that the gravestones were reset, with evergreen shrubs planted beside them.[6]

At the end of the letter, she wrote a final greeting in the margin on the first page: "I hope the Lord grants you a merry Christmas and a happy New Year! Greet your children and be greeted yourself a thousand times, from your loving sister Pauline." The letter didn't include greetings to Oline's husband, though that was certainly just an oversight.

PART II

Family Trials

23

Battle on the Home Front

CHRISTMAS OF 1879 must have been quite strange in the Holden parsonage. The children surely suffered under the gloomy atmosphere, even though both parents tried to conceal what was brewing. If we're to believe what was later reported, the spouses were not communicating at all; they were not on speaking terms. The parsonage became the scene of a silent battle on the home front.

Without the outside world realizing it, the couple now stood on opposite sides of what would soon become a sensational legal conflict. In 1879, Oline Muus was forty-one and Bernt Muus forty-seven years old. The middle-aged spouses, with a long life together behind them, should have benefitted from the calmness and wisdom of their years. Instead, they inched even closer to a scandal. Both were authority figures and prominent in the community. The pastor and the pastor's wife were expected to have higher morals than ordinary people; they should be an example to follow. How was this expectation compatible with the conflict in which they now found themselves? For the time being, very few outside the parsonage's four walls were aware of the situation. But both Oline and Pastor Muus must have known that the conflict between them would sooner or later become public, with dramatic and unforeseen consequences for themselves, their family, and their congregation. Yet neither was willing to give in. They both stood their ground.

Few sources for this first phase of the conflict between the couple exist; thus, some of the chronology and details are uncertain. Most of the information we have about the beginning of their conflict comes from a document Oline wrote at a later date for the Holden congregation. This writing was very much a one-sided presentation, intended to put her in a good light, but several details have since been verified by other sources. Therefore, it's not unreasonable to use Oline's account as a starting point to try to reconstruct what happened when conflict arose between the Muuses in 1879.

If we're to believe Oline, the question of her inheritance from her parents had become increasingly troublesome for her. She desired greater financial independence from her husband. In order to provide for her family and manage the parsonage in a reasonable and refined manner, she needed more household money than Bernt was willing to give her. On several occasions she had asked her husband to allow her to manage her inheritance herself. Each time he refused. Finally, she presented him with an ultimatum: if he didn't allow her to manage her own money, she would contact a lawyer and bring the matter to court. Perhaps Oline already knew what rights a married woman had under Minnesota law.

Beginning in 1839, a series of state-level Married Women's Property Acts had placed married women on equal footing with unmarried women concerning the right to manage their own inheritance. When New York passed a Married Women's Property Law in 1848, it became the template for other states, with Minnesota following suit in 1869.[1]

According to Oline's account, Bernt consulted with a lawyer in Red Wing, Minnesota. The American lawyer, William C. Williston, was an adviser on inheritance and family finances. We don't know what kind of advice the pastor received, but apparently the conversation with the lawyer didn't make Bernt any less certain of his case. When Oline later reminded her husband of her ultimatum, he sent a clear message that he wasn't troubled by whatever she was planning. Whether she sued him or not was immaterial.[2]

Oline chose to carry out her threat. She sat down and wrote a letter to lawyer Andreas Ueland, in Minneapolis, asking if it really was correct that her paternal inheritance fell to her under American law. Yes, he replied. When a married woman receives an inheritance, it is by American law her private property. But how certain was Ueland in his reply? There's no doubt this legal case was a tough one to crack. Should the inheritance be determined by the law in the spouse's homeland, or by the law of where the two now lived? From the standpoint of Minnesota law, Oline obviously had a very good case. But the fact was that, even after living in America for twenty years, Oline and Bernt Muus were still Norwegian citizens. And if Norwegian marital laws were to be applied, Oline wouldn't be able to claim her inheritance as her own. In Norway, wives were legally dependent. She was under her husband's guardianship and couldn't legally claim her inheritance. The only recourse a married woman in her situation had in Norway was an appeal to Parliament, pleading for understanding. According to Norwegian law, a wife did not have any individual rights within marriage. When a woman married, all her possessions became the common property of the couple. The husband became his wife's guardian, and he administered and managed their property.

Which law was applicable in this case? That was the question. Although the couple lived under the same roof, mentally and in legal terms they were on opposite sides of the Atlantic—she in America, and he in Norway.

After Oline received her response from Attorney Ueland, it appears the case took another distinct turn. According to Oline's version of what led up to the lawsuit, she attempted to turn the dispute with her husband into an ecclesiastical matter. She took the issue of inheritance to the pastor. But not to her pastor, her own husband, with whom she was in conflict; he couldn't possibly act as her minister. Instead, she went to Marcus Olaus Bøckman, Holden's assistant pastor. Pastor Bøckman had immigrated to America in 1875, the year after he received his theology degree in Christiania. Within four years, he had gotten to know his superior and his superior's wife fairly well. Now, he inadvertently found himself at the center of the extraordinary conflict between the couple.

In principle, Oline followed good Lutheran Church practice—both Norwegian and American—by airing her problems to one of the congregation's clergy. A profound dispute between two members of the congregation was obviously a matter for the pastor. The pastor was a spiritual adviser, guide, and moral authority in the community. Members of the congregation sought counsel from the pastor in difficult situations, or the pastor himself contacted parishioners to provide personal comfort or to reprimand them. The pastor represented a key figure in the Lutheran community's moral life. He was also an important figure in modern Nordic fiction. In Bjørnstjerne Bjørnson's peasant tales from the 1850s, the pastor is portrayed as a true fellow human being and a respected authority; influenced by the ideas of national romanticism, it's a parsonage romance inside and out. But as literary naturalism gained ground, the pastor was demonized, as with Pastor Manders in Henrik Ibsen's family drama *Gjengangere [Ghosts]* in 1881. The theme is much the same in Kristofer Janson's play *En kvindeskjæbne* from 1879, although this work was neither widely read nor performed in any theater. In *En kvindeskjæbne*, the pastor, using the words of Paul, tries to pressure Martha, who has been abused for years by her husband, to remain married. Martha defies the pastor, takes her son with her, and leaves for good. But she doesn't file for divorce because she doesn't want to disclose the conditions of her private life to the world.[3]

When Oline Muus came to Pastor Bøckman, surely she brought Ueland's letter with her. What she apparently wanted to know was whether the letter gave her reason to call a congregational meeting. These gatherings were charged with handling personal cases that pertained to a member of the congregation—such as an inheritance dispute like this one. And if the congregation sided with her against Pastor Muus, the matter could be resolved in an amicable manner, with the congregation instructing Pastor Muus to give her the inheritance.

But young Bøckman said that she mustn't think about calling a congregational meeting. Either he thought it best for the congregation not to get involved with the Muuses' marital dispute or he tried in every possible way to keep the whole case under wraps. At the same time, he warned her not to go to court to claim her inheritance from her father's estate. Instead, he instructed her to try to reconcile with her husband. Oline listened to this counsel, but she knew trying to persuade Pastor

Muus to give in to her claim for her inheritance was useless. Only one way remained. "I finally found, however, that it was better to obey God than men, even my own husband," Oline later explained to the congregation in her letter. Now, taking up her pen once again, she wrote to her attorney in Minneapolis.[4]

In her second letter to Ueland, Oline requested that he take the matter to Pastor Muus in a courteous and precise manner. Ueland did so, writing a formal letter to the pastor explaining that applicable American law gave his wife the right to dispose of her paternal inheritance, and that he looked forward to Oline having her demands fulfilled. The pastor's response was neither formal nor friendly; it was downright "rude," Oline commented later. It was so short and aggressive in nature that even the lawyer felt a little offended by reading it, if we're to believe Oline's account. The pastor rejected the case completely. Nevertheless, a short time later Ueland traveled to Red Wing, where Pastor Muus was attending a pastoral conference, to talk to him and settle the matter in a quiet and reasonable manner. But this meeting didn't have any effect whatsoever.

Now, it was Ueland's turn to write a letter. He drafted a written account to Oline of his failed meeting with the pastor. The young attorney recommended that Oline file a formal lawsuit against her husband to recover her rightful inheritance. There was no alternative. Since Pastor Muus refused to settle and all attempts at dialogue had failed, the only possible way forward was through the court. According to Oline's later testimony, Ueland noted that by refusing conciliation, the pastor had only himself to blame for any detrimental consequences of a trial. The attorney advised Oline not to worry about what would happen next: "The publicity the case will receive, and which I know you've wanted to avoid for Mr. Muus's sake, needn't concern you." It was a very telling, almost ominous choice of words. In any case, Oline followed her attorney's advice. On December 26, 1879, she filed a civil lawsuit against her husband. It's not surprising that the atmosphere in the house was tense during the Christmas season. When the holiday celebrations officially ended on January 6, 1880, it wouldn't be long before news of the case between the spouses spread outside the parsonage.[5]

The Complaint with a Capital "C"

ON JANUARY 20, 1880, the front page of *Budstikken* reported a very unusual case to its Norwegian-language readership. Under the small heading "Oline Muus contra Bernt J. Muus" the newspaper announced Mrs. Oline Muus's lawsuit against her husband. Several days later, on January 26, 1880, the St. Paul *Pioneer Press* similarly reported the case, though its coverage had a scathingly vitriolic tone. Its headline read: "ANOTHER DIVORCE SUIT. A Prominent Clergyman of the Norwegian Lutheran Conference Charged with Incredible Meanness and Cruelty. A Wife Struggling for Her Liberty and Rightful Inheritance—Oline Muus versus Bernt J. Muus."[1]

Both articles explained that the complaint allegedly concerned a financial matter and that Mrs. Muus filed a civil suit to establish control of the inheritance left by her parents. The petition, filed by Attorney Ueland, was addressed to the Goodhue County District Court in Red Wing. The plaintiff and defendant had been married in Norway in the summer of 1859, emigrated in October of that year, and settled in Goodhue County. Since then, Pastor Muus, a clergyman in the Norwegian Synod, had served several congregations both within Goodhue County and elsewhere. The couple had five surviving children between the ages of nineteen and one and a half years old; one child had died. In the two decades between 1859 and 1879, Pastor Muus's income had averaged $1,500 a year. His fortune was over $25,000; these alleged assets included a sum which his wife now claimed. In 1860, Oline

Muus's mother passed away, followed two years later by her father, who had been a district official in Fet near Christiania. Their estate had been processed in the probate court and was settled in 1863.

In the same year, Mrs. Muus was bequeathed around $4,000 from the estate. However, her representative in Norway sent the funds to her husband, Pastor Muus, without her knowledge. She wasn't informed that the money had come into her husband's hands, and he had kept it ever since. The plaintiff hadn't given all or any part of this sum to her husband; her wish had always been to have it as her own separate estate. In addition to this inheritance, Mrs. Muus laid claim to ten percent annual interest on the amount, plus dividends on the interest on the money her husband had invested. Moreover, it was the plaintiff's wish, because circumstances forced her to do so, that her husband should account for this money, which he, as her guardian, had at his disposal.[2]

It was truly a strange case, affecting two of the most prominent figures in the region's Norwegian American community. But who could have leaked the details to one of the major local newspapers? No one knows for certain, but it's hard to imagine that Ueland, who had already several weeks earlier spoken quite emphatically about "the publicity the case will receive," wasn't involved in some way. The attorney had a flair for both politics and the law, and he certainly knew the value of having a case like this one lifted outside of the courtroom and into the public eye. One other detail suggested the lawyer's involvement. Along with the simple inheritance lawsuit against Pastor Muus, Ueland also drafted an appendix, a longer document providing moral and psychological justification for the financial case, which was attached to the lawsuit itself. The text explained how Pastor Muus treated his wife and children and the tyrannical conditions governing the parsonage in Holden, details reportedly contributed by Oline Muus herself. The appendix— or "The Complaint"—was quickly coined "Mrs. Muus's Complaint" by the Norwegian and Norwegian American press. The allegations in this document, the "Complaint" with a capital "C", later became the center of most of the media coverage of the spousal conflict. The provocative details in "The Complaint" boosted the already unique litigation between the two spouses to the top of the newspapers' front pages.

Budstikken reported that for quite some time, indeed for several years, it had been known in Pastor Muus's congregation and by others close to them that his family relationships were not as they should be. It had also been clear to everyone that his wife, Oline Muus, was the injured party. However, only recently had the status of the relationship been made public to the world, wrote *Budstikken* on January 20, 1880. The pastor and his wife were opposing parties in the same case. So far, the newspaper had withheld from its readers what it knew about the situation, but now that the necessary preliminary steps had been taken by the court, the case was public. Moreover, added *Budstikken*, justice required the public to be informed about the case. If Ueland, with the scandalous information included in "The Complaint," wished to create additional attention around the lawsuit he had submitted, he had already succeeded. Simply put, *Budstikken* became an extra defense on Oline's behalf, but with the public as a court. Everything suggests that *Budstikken* editor Luth Jæger and attorney Andreas Ueland had entered into some type of partnership. Playing "the woman's card," their ace of hearts, they would fight to win the public's support.[3]

While the inheritance law section of the lawsuit itself was prosaic and objective, the appendix was the opposite. "The Complaint" didn't spare any juicy details. It discussed what at the time was considered most sacred: the couple's private life. In the document, conditions in the parsonage that were exposed gave the naturalistic literature of the time a run for its money. Mrs. Muus's case was far from a parsonage romance.

"The Complaint" stated that Pastor Muus hadn't provided adequate support for his family for several years. The monthly household allowance Mrs. Muus received from her husband wasn't sufficient, so she had to earn money by teaching music and voice and by embroidering and sewing for others. But her ability to support herself had been reduced during the past three years when she had broken her leg twice. When she had been injured and limped and suffered from chronic illnesses, it was because her husband had "abused" her.

"The Complaint's" introduction gave the impression that Pastor Muus was a heartless, inadequate provider, but the word "abuse" presented an unambiguous picture of a malevolent man. He failed to provide sufficient support for his family and deliberately tormented his wife, both mentally and physically. "The Complaint" provided examples of Pastor Muus's "cruel and inhumane" treatment of Mrs. Muus, as well as the children. He had refused to send for a doctor when she broke her leg the first time, and she had to wait until the next day for medical treatment. When she broke her leg a second time, he refused to get her a crutch. Even the children hadn't been spared; they suffered from their father "treating them cruelly and inconsiderately in every respect." He had neglected his children, denied them necessary clothing, and acted heartlessly and ruthlessly.[4]

A troubling aspect of "The Complaint" was that the purported abuse was still ongoing. Mrs. Muus and her children were still subject to a head of family who didn't have their best interests at heart. She and her children lived at the parsonage at the risk of their own lives. Their health had already been destroyed, and she and her children lived in need and misery. The readers of the *Pioneer Press* and *Budstikken* had to ask themselves what would happen next. And soon, many others would read of the case in newspapers on both sides of the Atlantic.

25

A Psychological Puzzle

SEVERAL THINGS STOOD OUT about "The Complaint." Most importantly, it apparently had no practical significance as a legal document.
The question of inheritance under Minnesota law on which the lawsuit
was based was a formality; it could be settled entirely without regard to
the morality or conduct of the parties. The difficult question of which
laws were applicable to the couple also didn't concern their marital
relations or the husband's treatment of his wife and children. Attorney
Ueland's appendix was quite simply legally irrelevant. The lawyer must
have known that. So, why did he arrange to attach it to the lawsuit?

The most obvious answer is one already mentioned: he wanted to
win over the public and popular opinion, and in this way, put pressure
on the judicial system. It's often said that most cases are won outside
the courtroom. Regardless, Ueland wouldn't take the chance of missing the initiative in the public debate. Bringing Oline Muus's case to
the press allowed journalists to "create" the case as their own, comment
on it, and bring new elements to light. The press could argue about
and form an opinion on the case of *Muus v. Muus.* Ueland also knew
perfectly well that it was a very unusual case, with a clergyman as the
defendant and with women's rights at the center of the conflict. Little
else would engage the public more than this—everyone could see that
Muus v. Muus was a riveting case.

It hadn't been long since American society experienced how such a
dispute could cause an uproar. Several years before the conflict between

the Muuses hit the front pages, America was shaken by a case that was similar but even more volatile. *Tilton v. Beecher* was the scandal of the century, and it concerned double standards and adultery in a religious milieu. Henry Ward Beecher, the famous East Coast liberal pastor, was sued by a former associate who was also a member of his congregation. Plaintiff Theodore Tilton accused Beecher of seducing his wife, Elizabeth Tilton. The scandal was dealt with in three forums: in congregational meetings, in the courtroom, and of course, in the press. It generated enormous interest for a long time. Incidentally, it all ended well for Beecher. His wife supported him, and the charges against him gradually came to nothing when they couldn't be substantiated. For the Tiltons, on the other hand, things didn't go well. Ironically, Mr. Tilton himself was accused of adultery with Victoria Woodhull, a well-known woman's suffragist. When he was found guilty of the charges, his wife was granted a divorce.[1]

Ueland knew he could elicit public interest in the lawsuit he had filed. As in the case of *Tilton v. Beecher*, the question of divorce was an underlying element in the Muus case. In this area, American law also differed greatly from what Norwegians were accustomed to in their homeland. Kristofer Janson had observed during his travels that in no other country in the world were women treated with as much chivalry as in America. He delighted in how far America had come in regard to legal equality between a married woman and her husband. Norway, on the other hand, was utterly old-fashioned. There, the Bible was still regarded as a book of law that provided rules for everything, even for how a husband should treat his wife. According to Janson, a married woman was no more than a servant in Norway, subject to the whims and tyranny of her husband. And divorce was unthinkable, almost no matter how terrible the situation.[2]

The idea behind the old European marriage laws essentially was that a wife was to be subordinate to her husband. Seventeenth-century English Puritans brought these laws with them to America. But in the modern era, one by one the American states had freed married women from their husband's disgraceful guardianship. Janson was disturbed by the Norwegian marriage laws, which granted a wife the right to neither

separate property nor her own assets. American law also protected a
wife from a long and painful life under a tyrannical husband. Unlike in
Norway, spousal abuse was grounds for divorce in America. As Janson
witnessed during his travels in America in 1879–80, a married woman
abused by her husband could sue him and be granted separation and
divorce.[3]

In 1879, the year Oline hired Ueland as her lawyer, abuse as grounds
for divorce was the single greatest difference between American and
Norwegian divorce laws. It's worth noting that "The Complaint"
Ueland had added as an appendix to the lawsuit placed so much
emphasis on Pastor Muus's cruel and ruthless treatment of his wife and
children. Stamped on Mrs. Muus's husband was the word "abuse"—the
very word that could have a decisive influence when a judge considered
whether to grant separation and divorce.

Why didn't Mrs. Muus ask Attorney Ueland for assistance in filing
for divorce? That question was posed by one of the most important
local newspapers, the *Pioneer Press*, on January 26, 1880. The paper also
suggested a reason: "The reverend gentleman who is the subject of this
complaint occupies a most prominent position in the synod for the
Norwegian Evangelical Lutheran church of America or the 'Norwegian
Synod' . . . being president of the Minnesota district." Perhaps Pastor
Muus was too important a pillar of society for Mrs. Muus to dare leave
the marriage. As a solitary woman, the pastor's wife lacked courage and
strength to confront the most powerful forces in the Norwegian American community by herself.[4]

The truth was certainly something else entirely. Why hadn't Oline
filed for divorce? Among other things, a petition for divorce could
undermine her position as a pure and noble public figure, leaving the
impression that she was ruthless and vindictive. A divorce might also
have fatal consequences for her husband. Since a divorced man could
not serve as clergy, after an eventual divorce Pastor Muus would be
forced to "resign in acknowledgment," as it was called, under pressure from the church and his congregations. The case would imply not
only the end of their marriage but also the end of her husband's career.
Would Oline take the chance of appearing so aggressive?

Even more important were the practical circumstances. For Oline to petition for divorce concurrent with a lawsuit for her father's inheritance would be ill timed. Ueland must not have wanted the lawsuit for the disposition of her father's estate to come before the court at the same time that she filed for divorce. His first concern was settling the inheritance suit in her favor; then a petition for divorce could be filed. Ueland was thinking strategically. If everything went according to plan, when Oline filed for divorce she would already have her own money to live on, at a place other than the Holden parsonage. This interpretation could also explain why Ueland had attached "The Complaint" as an appendix to the lawsuit. If early on the general public was to view Pastor Muus as a heartless domestic tyrant and abusive husband, it would be much simpler to petition for divorce when the time came.

For its part, the *Pioneer Press* insisted that coercion was an explanation for the lack of divorce. The newspaper pointed out that Pastor Muus had "taken a most conspicuous part in all church controversies." He was as "noted for the FIERCENESS OF HIS TEMPER and violence of his denunciations as for his strict adherence to what the church organization to which he belongs considers doctrines of the most vital importance." On top of that, he exercised what the *Pioneer Press* termed a "remarkable influence" over his congregations. In practice, the newspaper asserted, he had completely browbeaten his Lutheran parishioners, even though many members of the church themselves were high-ranking members of society, owned valuable property, and elected representatives to the state legislature from their midst. The picture the *Pioneer Press* painted of Pastor Muus was quite demonic; his parishioners were "completely cowed into subjection, and presenting a strange and rather sorry spectacle of men apparently independent, but really obeying no will but that of their pastor's, daring hardly to entertain any thoughts but those that have been stamped with his sanction." Readers could only imagine how such a tyrant might treat his family behind closed doors.[5]

In the article, either the editor or a journalist noted that the pastor's wife was suffering and that members of the congregation had frequently shown her sympathy. Nonetheless, these same members were not "rallying to her support and using their moral or personal influence on her behalf. They have DONE ACTUALLY NOTHING." Here was an example of how the pastor's "remarkable influence" on members of the congregation was exhibited. None of the cowardly parishioners dared stand up against the tyrannical pastor, though it was clear to all that he was unfit to be either a husband or a pastor.[6]

The newspaper suggested that it was brave of Mrs. Muus to demand her inheritance. But she didn't dare claim more since she was tyrannized by her husband, just as the congregation was tyrannized by the pastor. According to the *Pioneer Press*: "It may seem strange that the plaintiff satisfies herself with suing for her money, but there is reason to think that she has hesitated in applying for a divorce on account of the scandal which such proceedings inevitably must cause in the religious body of which she is a member." All the same, the paper predicted the case would end in divorce—and stated that such an outcome "cannot but be fervently wished for."[7]

The *Pioneer Press*'s analysis of the case was based on assumptions and insinuations as well as prejudices and biases about both the Norwegian immigrant church and the Norwegian immigrant milieu. The newspaper's readers could visualize how women must suffer in such an environment. Mrs. Muus's case illustrated the subordinate position Norwegian immigrant women held within church, society, and the family—and how necessary it was to do something about the situation, for the good of these poor, suppressed women.

The article noted that "her complaint is at present a pycological [*sic*] enigma that may or may not be solved at some future time." It's a psychological puzzle indeed, for there's nothing to suggest that Pastor Muus used his income or wealth to his own personal advantage and neglected his family. After all, Bernt Muus was not a man tarnished by many vices. Indeed, the newspaper listed his many virtues: "he has always led a most frugal life, has no expensive habits whatever, is theoretically, at least, a thorough Christian, and is withal much thought of by his colleagues in the church for administrative ability, zeal and learning." Yet despite these attributes, it concluded, he may have treated his wife as claimed in "The Complaint."[8]

The psychological puzzle also contributed to the news media's fascination with the story. For an ambitious young lawyer, pursuing such a case must have been a gift. By the end of 1879, Andreas Ueland, the twenty-six-year-old who had recently established his legal practice in Minneapolis, had a dream case on his hands. Pastor Muus was more than an ordinary clergyman; he was a leader in America's largest Norwegian synod. Though the lawsuit was dry and formal, the cautious legal formulations could not conceal the underlying state of affairs. The court was presented with a transgressor and a lawbreaker, a husband who had stolen money belonging to his wife and then lied about it, a pastor who had violated several of his church's eternal commandments.

The case was also obviously politically attractive to the progressive Norwegian American lawyer. With Oline Muus's case, the big-city attorney was able to confront the Norwegian Synod. In Minneapolis, Ueland belonged to the elite Norwegian American opposition that fought for liberalism, democracy, and women's rights against religious orthodoxy and ecclesiastical authority. Now, he could also confront the conservative forces in Norwegian America in the courtroom, with a case that appealed broadly to the general public. Several of Ueland's cultural political allies, such as Marcus Thrane and Kristofer Janson, had long opposed conservative Christianity. It's not surprising that both Thrane and Janson came to be heavily engaged in what was happening both inside and outside the Holden parsonage. Before 1881 was over, the two had actually immortalized Mrs. Muus and Pastor Muus, respectively, in both operetta and prose.

26

Fifteen Days Before
the First Congregational Meeting

....

THE NEXT MAJOR EVENT played out in the church during morning service. On Sunday, February 1, the Holden parishioners witnessed a scene they would never forget. The sexton led the entrance hymn and the invocation, but when Pastor Muus was about to preach, he was in a pitiful state. A member of the congregation recalled that the pastor just stood there, overcome with emotion, weeping and sobbing. This Sunday he, who usually preached so vividly, could hardly read the sermon in front of him. Finally, he gave up and handed the manuscript over to the sexton. But even the sexton couldn't master his emotions. The church fell silent for a long time. No one said anything until Pastor Muus gathered himself enough to function. In the end, the pastor made it through the sermon as usual. But he wasn't finished. After the Sunday sermon, the pastor wished to read aloud from another document he had brought with him. It was an announcement to the congregation.[1]

"I have been accused before the court in the State of Minnesota of slanderous things," Pastor Muus began his statement. He didn't mention his wife by name but stated that libelous and untrue allegations were made against him. In this extraordinary situation he felt it was right to call a congregational meeting where the members of the Holden, Dale, and Urland churches would meet together. At the meeting the three congregations should "consider whether something ought to be done." What did Pastor Muus mean by this suggestion? And, by the sentence that followed: "one needed to decide how he wished the case to end"?[2]

Did the pastor want the congregation to confront his wife? In the records of his statements that Sunday Bernt Muus's purpose in calling the desired congregational meeting is unclear. Perhaps the pastor was deliberately ambivalent in his remarks. What clearly emerged from the announcement was that the congregations should evaluate his position as pastor. The question, as he put it, was "whether I should abstain from performing my pastoral duties until the Court has handed down its ruling." In accordance with Norwegian ecclesiastical law, which the Synod followed, a pastor couldn't perform ecclesiastical acts while he was under investigation. The congregation had little choice but to call the meeting the pastor requested.

News of the impending congregational meeting quickly spread. Two days later, on Tuesday, February 3, 1880, *Budstikken* printed an editorial commentary on the latest developments in the Muus case. It stated that some would reproach "us" for what "we" had published, that "we" had made public a private matter, but "we" couldn't accept such an opinion. It was, of course, Luth Jæger himself who wrote this article, although in the text he made himself a spokesperson for the great "we," the Norwegian American public.[3]

A further clarification of the case was necessary, according to editor Jæger. As long as the couple attempted to settle the differences between them and come to an agreement, the case concerned only the two of them; it would be inappropriate for the press to write about it. But the moment the matter moved beyond what Jæger called "the sanctuary of private life," it became public. *Budstikken*'s editor took on the social mission of the press. The Norwegian American public had a right to know "what was going on." For "one" couldn't let only narrow circles know that something was wrong. Idle gossip didn't benefit anyone.[4]

Because the case was unique, it concerned the general public to a great extent, Jæger asserted. The marital conflict involved one of the most powerful and celebrated leaders in the Norwegian American church. Pastor Muus was too central a figure to claim protection from the public. Because Pastor Muus had to appear in court and defend himself against his own wife's claims, he must also expect the press's attention. According to Jæger, the nature of "The Complaint" also strengthened the claim that the general public had a right to know about the relationship between the spouses.[5]

Budstikken's editor took it for granted that "The Complaint" was true and complete. On the surface, "The Complaint" was a lawsuit regarding inheritance, but essentially it was a defense for the protection of the disadvantaged party. In this case, Oline Muus was undeniably the underdog, in need of protection. The law in the matter was perhaps weak, Jæger admitted in passing, though without going into more detail regarding the points to which he referred. Yet there was only one consideration "we," the press, must take into account: that she, as "the presumably oppressed and mistreated woman," was seeking her rights. She didn't even claim damages, only what she thought belonged to her. She had been forced to act in self-defense. The newspaper editor must have been well aware of the associations readers had with the word "self-defense," depicting a lonely woman in a great house with the domestic tyrant, the pastor.[6]

Then Jæger speculated: What would happen at the upcoming congregational meeting? Budstikken's editor wasn't in doubt. Pastor Muus would receive the full support of his congregation and the Church, for the Synod ruled that the wife should submit blindly to her husband, and religion and women's rights were at the heart of the case. The congregation would stand by its pastor through thick and thin and put Mrs. Muus under church discipline, Jæger guaranteed his readers. Jæger explained that church discipline was a spiritual torture device. Against "this whole apparatus of spiritual torture," Mrs. Muus, as a woman and a pastor's wife, was in reality defenseless, and for this very reason, she required the public's protection. Bernt Muus was the villain wearing a pastor's vestments and would be defended by his followers. Only the press and the public could save the defenseless victim. Fifteen days before the congregational meeting, Budstikken had taken the role of judge in the case and announced the verdict.

Later, when the agenda for the congregational meeting was sent out, all it said was that the three congregations would meet to determine whether they still wished to have Pastor Muus continue as their pastor. The meeting notice didn't contain anything to suggest that there would be any discussion about a church discipline case against Mrs. Muus. *Budstikken* mentioned the summons the day before the actual meeting, but without commentary. Possibly the moderate formulations from the congregation were experienced as a small disappointment for editor Jæger—possibly even for lawyer Ueland. Perhaps the inseparable progressive friends were both interested in the tone of the accusations against Mrs. Muus being as harsh as possible so that the conflicts in the case would be wholly visible. At any rate, the days leading up to the gathering were full of planning and consultation, with secret meetings everywhere. While Pastor Muus and the church council deliberated in church, Mrs. Muus was in regular correspondence with Ueland. Despite the editor's predictions, no one could quite be sure what would happen at the congregational meeting. Both parties undoubtedly wanted to be well prepared.[7]

A Scandal Within the Scandal

NEWSPAPER HEADLINES leading up to the first round of congregational meetings didn't mince words: "A Prominent Clergyman of the Norwegian Lutheran Conference Charged with Incredible Meanness and Cruelty"; "A Wife Struggling for her Liberty and Rightful Inheritance—Oline Muns versus Bernt J. Muns [sic]"; "Goodhue County Scandal"; "Mr. Muus's Muss"; "GOODHUE County has a first-class scandal."[1]

The Norwegian-language press in America was equally engaged in the case. *Verdens Gang [The Course of the World]* in Chicago on February 3, 1880, wrote that the marriage conflict between Bernt and Oline Muus was Bernt's "scandal case." In the Norwegian Synod, the newspaper reported, Pastor Muus had a very eminent position and for years had been "one of the most aggressive and fiercest in the public squabbles and scandalous newspapers." Thus, he was well known among the Scandinavians in America, and now his name was tied to a scandalous case that would be followed with great interest. If the outcome showed that the charges against him could be proven, the *Verdens Gang* editor thought it would undoubtedly help diminish the influence pastors had among Norwegians in America. The case was of such a character and Pastor Muus's position was such that his synod shouldn't allow the matter to fade away or attempt to cover it up. If Pastor Muus was found guilty, it was in the Synod's best interests that he be treated in the same way as a less-distinguished person apprehended in obvious sins.[2]

On February 17, the day before the meeting, *Budstikken* printed a new editorial note in which Luth Jæger repeated his contention that the congregational meeting intended to put Mrs. Muus under church discipline. The case could end with the poor woman being expelled from the congregation: "In the congregational meeting, which is a religious court, and which has also sided with Pastor Muus, Mrs. Muus is without protection." For Jæger, there was only one fair solution: Mrs. Muus had to be allowed to prepare her defense, summon and question witnesses, and choose a man to plead her case, just as in a secular court of law. Otherwise, the entire process would be invalid. If so, she would simply have to object. The congregation mustn't be allowed to interrogate her, demand evidence, or judge the case concerning her and the pastor's private affairs without a legitimate process. With that, editor Jæger attempted to set his own agenda for the congregational meeting.[3]

Budstikken vigilantly followed the events both within and outside Holden Church. The paper must have incurred a great deal of expense in connection with the case as the discussions surrounding the couple dragged on. The meeting on February 18 became the first in a series that took place over six months. All the meetings were thoroughly discussed in the newspaper, with extensive and in-depth reports from the negotiations. In order for *Budstikken* to cover the matter properly, it sent its own reporter to Holden. The reporter was obviously a very patient man: his articles were miles long, and no detail was seemingly too small to be mentioned. The articles were unsigned, but everyone must have known the author: Erik L. Petersen, one of the eccentrics in the Goodhue County Norwegian American immigrant community. As a young man he had left Norway, converted to Catholicism, and made a vow of obedience as a monk. While he lived in an Italian monastery, he had begun to write poetry, but without success. When he left Europe, Catholicism, and monastic life, Petersen ended up among his fellow countrymen in Norwegian America. He made a living as a reporter for *Budstikken* in Faribault, a town near Holden. For a time, he had been a member of the Episcopal Church, the foremost Yankee church. If Petersen was still a believer, he was certainly a stranger to the Norwegian Synod's kind of Christianity.

Most Americans at the time probably didn't hold Norwegian immigrants in very high esteem, but neither were they ranked lower than other European immigrants. Norwegians perhaps were rated slightly higher than the Irish and the Italians, the major Catholic immigrant groups. In the 1850s, Americans had battled a popular anti-immigration movement with the eloquent name of the "Know Nothings." In 1880, this movement was still alive and well. Newspaper editors were always on the lookout for anything that could be perceived as anti-Americanism. Not only Catholic immigrants but immigrants in general were suspect. Would they respect American laws and institutions, send their children to American schools, and learn English? Would they become American citizens?

The America to which Bernt and Oline had arrived in 1859 was a country that made demands on the immigrants who established themselves there. Immigrants were expected to assimilate, to undergo a process of Americanization, to acquire American values and an American way of life. When the Muus case aroused widespread attention, it wasn't only because Ueland conducted it as a scandalous case in the press or because it involved a prominent clergyman. The worst thing about the case from the viewpoint of American society at large was that it concerned an immigrant group that opposed Americanization and isolated themselves. The Norwegian immigrant church was accused by both Yankees and liberal Norwegian Americans of being as faithful to authority as Catholics were to their priests. Both Norwegian American Lutherans and Catholics represented an internal threat to American society, as they were first and foremost obedient to an authority outside of the United States.

This perception brought about a tremendous uproar. On February 14, 1880, the editor of the *Pioneer Press* reported that a congregational meeting was to take place and would be attended by as many as fourteen Norwegian Lutheran pastors. They were to discuss the case of the "inhumane treatment" by the "reverend discipliner." Readers of the *Pioneer Press* were encouraged to believe that the leadership of the Norwegian Lutheran Church was similar to that of the Catholic Church: note that prejudiced people called Pastor Muus "Pope." The article further stated that "every Lutheran in the county stood up valiantly for their beloved leader and shepherd, as was, of course, expected." The American editor trusted people's judgment: "I find that numbers of Norwegians are beginning to think that, after all, their pastor may be slightly to blame."[4]

However, coverage in other newspapers was much less marked by scandal and much more impartial. Petersen's writing in *Budstikken* was thorough. His reports appeared to be more like lengthy, detailed minutes without commentary, which in retrospect provide unique insight into the extraordinary congregational deliberations. For Jæger, the congregational meetings perhaps read more like parodies, a series of tragicomic scenes of people's narrow-mindedness and religious arrogance. But *Budstikken* covered the meetings in Holden with a seriousness and an insight that stood in interesting contrast to the newspaper's campaign against the Synod in other contexts.

Some days later, a local English-language newspaper, the *Red Wing Argus*, printed an explosive editorial. The congregation wished to decide the case that was basically a theological disagreement between husband and wife in a closed and arbitrary private trial. Mrs. Muus had relied on the idea that in America "an accusation was not the same as a conviction, and that the country's Supreme Court allows the defendant a full and proper trial before an impartial jury."[5]

Later, another local English-language newspaper, the *Goodhue County Republican*, would sharply reprimand the pastor who had suspiciously resisted assimilation and integration: "Let no man, though he refused for twenty years to become a citizen of the United States, attempt to obstruct the course of civil justice here, by vexatious church proceedings." It was a scandal in the midst of the scandal that Pastor Muus had never applied for American citizenship. The newspaper wisely didn't mention that Mrs. Muus was also still a Norwegian citizen. Pastor Muus was the villain. He didn't respect the law and justice in the country where he had lived for two decades. The congregation for its part would use its own court and disregard the civil legal system. In essence, both the pastor and the Norwegian immigrant church were deeply anti-American.[6]

28

Out of Control

··

THE BITTER COLD, sharp northwest wind and poor driving conditions were not enough to intimidate people from making the journey to Holden Church on February 18, 1880, for the first congregational meeting to discuss the case. From the first to the last row, the church was filled with an expectant crowd, wrote the *Budstikken* reporter. Erik Petersen recognized several of the clergymen besides Pastor Muus, including Pastors Thorvald August Hansen, Marcus Bøckman, and L. M. Biørn. Professor Thorbjørn Mohn, principal of St. Olaf's School, was in attendance as well. *Budstikken's* reporter speculated that up to one thousand people were packed into the large wooden church at Holden. Mrs. Muus was among only three women there. Men from the three neighboring congregations, men who came from far away, and even those who didn't attend church at all sat on the women's side of the church.[1]

The meeting began with a hymn. Afterward, Pastor Hansen read from the book of Romans, where Paul writes to his brethren about the law that rules over men and about the married woman who by law is bound to her husband as long as he lives. In conclusion, Pastor Hansen read: "So now it is no more I that do it, but sin which dwelleth in me. For I know that in me, that is, in my flesh, dwelleth no good thing: for to will is present with me, but to do that which is good *is* not. For the good which I would I do not: but the evil which I would not, that I practice. But if what I would not, that I do, it is no more I that do it, but sin which dwelleth in me." These well-chosen, admonishing words reminded the assembled that everyone, women as well as men, must acknowledge their human weaknesses.[2]

Thorvald August Hansen received a call as Pastor Muus's assistant pastor in 1879. He arrived at Holden with his wife, Kristine. He had a theological degree from Christiania and was only thirty years old. But when he began the monumental meeting in Holden Church, he had recently become pastor at the Urland and Vang churches, Pastor Muus's formerly yoked congregations. Both Hansen and his wife had been in close contact with the Muuses during the months they had lived in the parish. Perhaps Kristine Hansen was one of the women who accompanied Oline Muus to church that day. Another possible companion was Dr. Grønvold's wife, Eli Grønvold. As the parsonage's nearest neighbor for several years, the doctor and the doctor's wife had had ample opportunity to get to know Oline, and although the Grønvolds were members of the Haugean Synod's Aspelund congregation, it wasn't forbidden for them to attend this meeting. The doctor himself was apparently not in attendance; the presence of such a prominent man would certainly have been commented on by *Budstikken*'s reporter.[3]

When Pastor Hansen finished reciting the Lord's Prayer, Pastor Muus stepped forward. He stood in front of the altar, at a long table that for the occasion was placed in the chancel. The meeting's agenda was unclear; no one knew quite what to expect. Even who would serve as meeting chairperson turned out to be a difficult question. Since the matter concerned Pastor Muus's own person, his congregations, and the Synod, he had first requested Pastor H. A. Preus, president of the Synod, to attend the meeting and conduct the proceedings. But Preus had sent a telegram saying that he wasn't available. Professor Laur. Larsen, whom Preus had suggested in his place, was also unavailable. It seems Synod leadership had determined that Pastor Muus had to manage on his own. The case was so embarrassing that the Synod didn't wish to be officially involved. The cursory manner in which the Synod's newspaper covered the matter strengthens that impression.

For a while it seemed that Peder Langemo, one of the settlement's earliest arrivals, would get the job. But then Pastor Bøckman, whom

Oline had secretly confided in a few months earlier about the conflict over the inheritance, appeared. He had been in the church for a
short time at the beginning of the meeting, then had left, but now he
had returned, *Budstikken*'s correspondent recorded. Pastor Bøckman
explained that he hadn't felt well and wasn't in any shape to chair the
meeting. Perhaps he also had his own reasons for wanting a less prominent role. But the voting members of those assembled ignored his
objections, and against his will Pastor Bøckman was chosen to conduct
the historic meeting.

Now the agenda could be set. But what was the agenda? There was
disagreement here as well. Were the men of the congregation supposed
to discuss and consider "The Complaint" made by Mrs. Muus against
the pastor? Or should they simply determine whether they wanted Pastor Muus to continue as their pastor? Ole Huset, a farmer and member
of the church council, immediately took the floor. He firmly believed
the meeting must address both issues. If the congregation wanted to
know more about "The Complaint," he had a copy with him. Evidently
some had come to the meeting well prepared. A majority vote was in
favor that "The Complaint" be read aloud at the meeting. Professor
Mohn volunteered to read "The Complaint." His English was excellent;
"The Complaint" needed to be read aloud.

But this decision didn't conclude the case. Several laymen, including the settlement's former religion teacher Ole Solberg, wanted an
even more thorough treatment of "The Complaint." Solberg insisted
the document had to be translated into Norwegian and read out point
by point because many parishioners couldn't fully understand the original English document. Then, the congregation could determine if that
which was claimed in the text was actually true. Langemo disagreed;
a complaint that was so dubious couldn't be debated. The meeting's
task was to decide whether to suspend Pastor Muus at this time, not to
go into some sort of investigation of the case in full. Several speakers
agreed with Langemo, and there were many different opinions.

After voting, they reached a compromise. A majority of the congregation wanted Pastor Muus to remain as their pastor until the information
in "The Complaint" could be proven. Then for the first time the meeting

got out of hand. The meeting's chair, Pastor Bøckman, obviously did what he could to keep "The Complaint" off the agenda. He pointed out that since "The Complaint" wasn't directed against the congregation, it couldn't become a matter for the congregation either. Pastor Muus stood up and reprimanded the young chairman sternly. Muus explained that he experienced "The Complaint" as defamatory; he had already made that clear when he announced the meeting. He couldn't live with these accusations remaining uncontested within the congregation. Careful not to refer to his wife by name, he insisted that "The Complaint" was the congregation's responsibility to discuss, and now that it had been made public, it was also appropriate to address it in the meeting.[4]

After all, Pastor Muus pointed out, the congregation couldn't know whether the plaintiff could corroborate her charges with proof. The civil court's eventual judgment in the case was not relevant in this context and did not concern his congregation. Instead, the congregation had to hear "The Complaint"; it had to be read in Norwegian, and the congregation then had to investigate if it was true. "The congregation owed him and itself in such a case to demand serious evidence for the charges brought against him," Petersen reported that Muus concluded. It was a powerful speech from the offended pastor.

Pastor Muus's remarks immediately gained new support in the congregation. Religion teacher Solberg considered it a Christian duty to deal with "The Complaint" and believed certain points would probably be withdrawn before it came to trial. Another religion teacher, Nils Raabølle, also wasn't in doubt: the accusations against Pastor Muus must be proven according to God's word. The only proper court in this matter was the congregation. By submitting family affairs before a secular court, Mrs. Muus had acted contrary to good church practice: with her case, she had bypassed the congregation. Interestingly, there was only one point the speakers fully agreed was beyond the authority of the meeting: the central point of the legal case, the question of money. Mrs. Muus's claim to her inheritance didn't concern the congregation, Solberg believed. It was a matter for the court. However, what concerned the congregation very much was the defamatory accusations of "The Complaint." No one present objected to Solberg's characterization.[5]

29

Who Was the Complainant?

PASTOR BØCKMAN BEGAN THE DAY feeling ill. How did he feel after the first round of discussions? He had played the role of Oline Muus's confidant early on. His efforts to prevent "The Complaint" from being discussed in the congregational meeting brought Bøckman into direct conflict with his immediate supervisor, Pastor Muus. So far, the meeting hadn't confirmed the predictions of *Budstikken* and the other newspapers, who believed everything had already been decided and that the pastor, the congregation, and the Synod would join forces to stop the troublesome Mrs. Muus. Instead, it had become clear that the Synod leadership was trying to keep the difficult conflict at arm's length. Among both the clergy and the parishioners there was obviously disagreement on how best to resolve the matter. As long as Pastor Bøckman could make sure "The Complaint" didn't come up for detailed consideration, the congregational gathering also could avoid becoming a meeting about Mrs. Muus's credibility, her claims, and her personality. But how long could that last? Pastor Muus's speech had turned the tide. It appeared the majority now wanted to consider "The Complaint," point by point, in the overflowing church.

Pastor Bøckman took the floor. He had some private information to share, presumably from Mrs. Muus. His remarks sent the meeting in a dramatic new direction. According to *Budstikken*'s account, Bøckman doubted "it was really Mrs. Muus who had lodged the Complaint." Was "The Complaint" written by the pastor's wife herself, or was it composed by someone else—and perhaps even sent to the court and the press without her consent? Bøckman now encouraged the assembly to ask Mrs. Muus to submit her case directly to the congregation, a reasonable way to clarify the question of authorship. If Mrs. Muus hadn't lodged "The Complaint," she couldn't submit it to the congregation, and then the congregation would no longer have to deal with the defamatory allegations concerning the pastor's private life.[1]

Pastor Bøckman, Oline's confidant, had suddenly sown doubts about one of the most important grounds for the meeting. Ole Solberg exclaimed that he hoped "The Complaint" didn't come from Mrs. Muus, because many, including himself, knew the accusations were false and would declare they were lies. Accordingly, he wished to withdraw his proposal to discuss "The Complaint" point by point and instead agreed to Peder Langemo's earlier motion—to refuse to consider "The Complaint" because it was so vague. But Nils Raabølle, the parochial schoolteacher, was unwavering. If the congregation refused to investigate "The Complaint," it would be tantamount to asking Pastor Muus to leave his ministry. Everyone could see how unreasonable that course of action was. It didn't make any sense to demand the pastor's resignation because someone lied about him.

Again, the congregation's opinion was not at all unanimous; not everyone stood behind their pastor. As *Budstikken* and the American newspapers had pointed out, it was unreasonable for such a case to be handled without the accused being allowed to speak or without a systematic judicial examination of the allegations. And the relationship between the spiritual and the legal aspects of the conflict was obviously unresolved. One by one, members of the congregation rose up and spoke seriously about difficult and complicated questions. Anyone who had something to say had to be heard; every matter was important; and each one was discussed at great length. People listened to the arguments and were willing to be swayed by clear-minded and persuasive speeches. Motions were brought forth and voted on; the meeting was run according to democratic rules of order. Proponents who lost a vote had to bow to the majority. Although the meeting was connected to a conservative and closed religious tradition, it was also a democratic institution where a united effort was made to resolve problems the congregation had never previously faced.

Following Pastor Bøckman's startling information, most of those who spoke considered "The Complaint" to be dead—except for parishioner Andreas Rygh, who maintained that once an accusation had been made in public in this manner the congregation was obliged to review it. Moreover, Rygh thought Mrs. Muus must be allowed to speak. This last point appeared to be close to a provocation. Women didn't have the right to speak in church. But should an exception be made in this unique case? Should Oline Muus be permitted to speak on her own behalf in front of the congregation?

But Pastor Bøckman was adamant. He reiterated that the meeting hadn't been convened in order to discuss "The Complaint." Nor, as he put it, in all fairness could she be required to produce evidence then and there. Bøckman was again countered by a parishioner, Gudmund K. Norsving, a forty-three-year-old farmer and a member of the church council. The meeting's purpose was, as Norsving understood it, to defend Pastor Muus, and consequently the matter had to be investigated. But then Pastor Hansen also spoke. He could confirm Pastor Bøckman's presumption that it wasn't Mrs. Muus who had written "The Complaint": she had told him she had nothing to do with creating the appendix. In addition, the young pastor insisted that attorney Andreas Ueland be allowed to attend the congregational meeting in order to plead Mrs. Muus's case.

The meeting's conflicts weren't just between the clergy and the parishioners; there was also disagreement within the groups and along different dividing lines. The next speakers supported Langemo's and Solberg's motion to disregard the "vague" complaint. So did Nils Ottun, the congregation's secretary and meeting secretary. The thirty-eight-year-old Ottun, who, like Langemo and Solberg, owned a farm near the parsonage, was pleased to hear that Mrs. Muus hadn't written "The Complaint." Accordingly, there was no longer "anything criminal" about the matter, and the only thing the meeting could take a position on was the question of whether Pastor Muus should be suspended.

After several new verbal rounds, the congregational meeting finally proceeded to vote on Langemo's motion: that Pastor Muus could continue in his position for the time being, without considering the substance of "The Complaint." Pastor Muus won an overwhelming victory: of the three hundred voting members from the three congregations, only one man voted against it. No matter what one might think of what had happened or how it should have been resolved, there was no doubt the pastor had strong support among his congregants.[2]

And yet they hadn't come to the end of their deliberations. Apparently, it was never too late for an extra round. The teacher Raabølle rose and asked if the assembled didn't wish to encourage the couple to a meeting in their own congregation. In this way, the spouses could negotiate with each other in the presence of their congregation and hopefully be reconciled. The motion immediately received a great deal of support. A new speaker suggested that only those who belonged to the Synod be permitted to attend this meeting. His motion was voted down. Could it be that the congregation was sympathetic to Mrs. Muus and her desire for public awareness of the matter? Pastor Bøckman offered a reminder that the pastor's wife had wished Ueland be present and able to speak on her behalf. Perhaps this arrangement could be considered for the next meeting.

The protests to Bøckman's proposal were relentless. One by one, parishioners came forward to insist that lawyers participating in a congregational meeting served no purpose. As the farmer Ottun put it, "It would be deplorable if a lawyer's presence was required, for only the word of God was necessary." Raabølle agreed. However, he had another, surprising solution to suggest: couldn't Mrs. Muus speak on her own behalf at the next meeting? Then, the spouses could actually speak to each other directly. Another difficult round of discussion followed. Norsving felt that the lawyer could be present—but only if Mrs. Muus first withdrew her allegations. Ottun disagreed. The purpose of the next meeting was to negotiate as Christians and let God's word be the prosecutor. Finally, a vote was taken on the motion that Ueland be present and allowed to speak. It was rejected—but only by three votes. On this point, the congregation was divided almost evenly.[3]

Then Pastor Muus, who had long remained silent, asked to speak. He couldn't accept the congregation's resolution on a meeting between him and Mrs. Muus. He didn't understand the intent of such a meeting, and he didn't want anything to do with it. What was there to discuss if it wasn't even certain that "The Complaint" was written by his spouse? The meeting went back and forth, considering whether the congregation could really defy Pastor Muus's wishes so directly. At this point Bernt Muus's former assistant pastor, Pastor Hansen, stabbed him in the back. He offered to elaborate on what he had said earlier, that Mrs. Muus had told him she had nothing to do with the creation of "The Complaint." He affirmed it shouldn't be understood that the pastor's wife believed "The Complaint" wasn't true. As Pastor Hansen rather ambiguously put it, it was only the representation of her troubles as presented in "The Complaint" that wasn't reliable. This last testimony caused Pastor Muus to explode; the accusations against him still hadn't been withdrawn? Now the two pastors opposed each other directly; everyone could see what was at stake between them. Pastor Hansen replied that he could only repeat what he had already said, that Mrs. Muus would not be held accountable for what the lawyer had written. After five long hours, the meeting adjourned.

Afterward Bøckman penned a letter to Synod president H. A. Preus, seemingly seeking the support of his superior. He gave a detailed account of the meeting and the case from his perspective and why he ruled as he did. He requested a favor on behalf of Oline: to please write to her. He closed his letter with the words, "God have mercy on the Muus family."[4]

30

Like a Bolt of Thunder

WHEN THE FIRST CONGREGATIONAL meeting was over, confusion reigned. What had just happened? What was at the center of the case? Was it rejected, or just ignored for now? What should they do next? Although the congregational meeting had voted unanimously to allow Pastor Muus to continue in his position for the time being, the rest was unclear. And the fog wouldn't lift in the ensuing weeks. From the sidelines, the press and especially *Budstikken*'s editor Luth Jæger continued the case against Pastor Muus, his congregation, and the Synod. But the way *Budstikken* covered the marital conflict wasn't unchallenged.

On February 26, 1880, church council member Gudmund Norsving wrote a long letter to the editor, which was printed on March 9. It was with great sorrow and distress that the congregation, and likely all reasonable people both within and outside the Synod, had read *Budstikken*'s account of "The Complaint," the pious layman began rather cautiously—before turning to attack mode. Like *Budstikken*'s editor, Norsving also spoke on behalf of the larger "we": "We and all those who have been close to Pastor Muus and know his great devotion and sincere willingness to do his pastoral work diligently are filled with indignation at such an unprecedented and outrageous attempt to tarnish the reputation of a servant of the Lord."[1]

Within the congregation, few knew that something wasn't quite right between the couple. Consequently, the reporting in *Budstikken* struck "like a thunderbolt on a clear day." Although perhaps not a very clear day, because Norsving added that from the beginning one was inclined to believe "The Complaint" contained "a little truth." But since then no information had come to light to prove Mrs. Muus's accusations— quite the contrary.[2]

"The Complaint," Norsving pointed out, was initially due to a "family dispute" regarding an inheritance. Mrs. Muus must bear responsibility that this disagreement had escalated into a full public debate on life in the parsonage. Norsving more than implied that she lacked evidence to justify the claim against her husband. Or, as he put it, Oline Muus, in order to have grounds for her claim, has searched for such grounds. He believed she had "made mountains out of molehills."[3]

It's striking that Norsving didn't write a word about the pastor's wife and her work within the congregation outside the conflict. After all, he had been a neighbor to the parsonage and belonged to the same congregation for two decades. Yet Oline was portrayed only as a liar and a troublemaker. Point by point, Norsving considered "The Complaint" and its allegations. First, it was difficult to understand that the fifteen-dollar household allowance was insufficient. Further perplexing to Norsving was the allegation that Pastor Muus forbade her to shop on credit at the surrounding stores. Norsving had actually investigated a little on his own. He had talked to the merchants, who could inform him that Pastor Muus knew well that his wife shopped at these places from time to time. The pastor himself settled up afterward; he paid the bills in cash. Norsving also wished to correct the information about Mrs. Muus's first broken leg, which happened in Faribault. The year wasn't 1877, but 1876, he corrected, and it wasn't true that Pastor Muus had denied her medical treatment. Nor was it true that he had refused to get her a crutch when she broke her leg the second time.

The rest of "The Complaint," according to Norsving, was written in "somewhat vague terms"; it wasn't very concrete. In the newspaper, this farmer with an education limited to the public school back in Norway behaved more like an experienced defender for Pastor Muus. Norsving knew well that Mrs. Muus was plagued by illness, but he cast doubt on whether her husband could be blamed for her conditions. In what way had her health and that of their two children been harmed? Was it the result of inadequate nutrition and clothing as well as poor housing, as "The Complaint" suggested? The congregation paid Pastor Muus an annual salary of $1,500. Besides, he had assets valued at approximately $25,000, Norsving estimated. In addition, the pastor had a hundred acres of land with a parsonage, located in the middle of a large settlement of wealthy farmers. The Muus family couldn't possibly be suffering from any need; the farm yielded enough agricultural products to be self-sufficient.

Later, it became public knowledge that Pastor Muus couldn't account for his own income or assets. Norsving, on the other hand, knew the pastor had begun to build wealth in 1863, the year he had received Oline's inheritance from her father. At that time, according to Norsving, the price of gold was high, so when converted into US dollars, paper money, it was a large sum for Pastor Muus to begin with. And with an interest rate of ten percent over seventeen years, Pastor Muus's wealth had grown significantly. Part of the interest was used to pay for household expenses at the parsonage. Norsving had received this information from Mrs. Muus a few years earlier, for it was the case that the pastor's income wasn't always sufficient.[4]

Norsving accordingly believed Mrs. Muus had more household money at her disposal than she stated in "The Complaint." On the whole, the family's living conditions had to be far better than she described. Against her depiction of the deplorable state of the parsonage, Norsving painted the picture of a prosperous farm. In his eagerness to defend the pastor, he ended up criticizing him. Some parishioners believed the couple lived far too extravagantly—at parishioners' expense. It was well known that Pastor Muus had always kept a large house of servants and expensive tutors, and he could also afford to pay tuition for his children. Not everyone in the congregation was so privileged. To put the pastor in a slightly more favorable light, Norsving added that Muus had given "considerable sums" to St. Olaf's School.[5]

All in all, he concluded, "The Complaint" was far too outrageous for any reasonable person to put their trust in it. Nor was "The Complaint" confirmed by witnesses under oath, which consequently didn't inspire confidence. No one in the congregation could judge the credibility of

these allegations. And why hadn't Mrs. Muus gone to the congregation
with her initial complaint? Naturally, the congregation took pride in
providing for the pastor's family. Norsving maintained that if the congregation erred in any matter concerning the pastor's financial situation, it would be corrected. If it should turn out, against all assumptions, that Mrs. Muus had cause for her discontent, the congregation
would give it due consideration.

Before closing the letter, Norsving criticized *Budstikken*, which had
publicized the case before the other party, Pastor Muus, had an opportunity to respond. The newspaper appeared to believe Mrs. Muus was
the aggrieved party and the only one entitled to the public's protection,
but that couldn't be the case. If the public had been more than willing to
believe the charges against Pastor Muus, perhaps it was because he was
known in ecclesiastical disputes as a hard and uncompromising man.
Norsving wrote, "For our part, we will also admit that the pastor has
spoken carelessly, and in our opinion, expressed himself both harshly if
not unjustifiably, both in speech and writing." But still it wasn't fair to
judge Pastor Muus in this matter on the basis of his conduct otherwise.[6]

31

Personal Punishment

....

CHURCH COUNCILMAN Gudmund Norsving valiantly attempted to refute "The Complaint" as unreliable and false. But this view wouldn't be echoed in the American press, and certainly not in *Budstikken*. In editorial commentary Luth Jæger denied that the newspaper had sided with Mrs. Muus in her capacity as aggressor. *Budstikken* had only made readers aware of how vulnerable her position was. She couldn't rely on the support, sympathy, or help of her community. He wondered: was Mrs. Muus surrounded by people who wished her well? Jæger embarked on a long, hypothetical commentary about the congregation, where her brothers were without influence and her sisters weren't considered. There was no reason to believe the parishioners, the clergy, or the Synod were impartial. Jæger reiterated that the general public had the right to insight into the nature of the circumstances and the difficult position in which Mrs. Muus found herself.[1]

The greatest possible publicity was her only protection, Jæger asserted. For how had the congregation where she remained a member treated her? Time and again Bible-spouting parishioners spent hours using all their powers of persuasion to get her to admit her sin—which was only that she had stood up and claimed her legal right from her husband. *Budstikken* followed up with a sensational report. The newspaper revealed that Oline Muus had already been subjected to church discipline from her husband, the pastor, almost ten times without public knowledge. The pastor had denied his own wife communion, the very sacrament of salvation and forgiveness, in a grotesque blending of marital conflict and religious discipline. In this way, the pastor's wife's exclusion from the congregation had already begun. How shameful and how painful it must have been for Oline Muus to be excluded from the comforting fellowship of communion, *Budstikken* reported.

These details hadn't been published anywhere before. The only possible source for them was Mrs. Muus herself—or someone very close to her, such as attorney Andreas Ueland. If the information was true, it was difficult to avoid the impression that Pastor Muus had grossly abused his clerical authority over his wife. But why hadn't these details come out earlier? Was it really possible to trust the newspaper's reporting? The author of the same article also claimed to be well informed that Pastor Muus's congregation had already held secret meetings about Mrs. Muus. According to the newspaper, this information came from "a man close to Pastor Muus." Had *Budstikken* established direct contact with any of the colleagues who had distanced themselves from the pastor during the first congregational meeting, such as Marcus Bøckman or August Hansen? The way Jæger spoke about the Synod clergy didn't otherwise indicate that he had allies among them: "Now, as far as the clergy's impartiality is concerned, it's quite significant that at least one of them who, on the question of whether the wife is really her husband's slave, gave the comforting answer that he couldn't follow her."[2]

On March 2, the conversation in *Budstikken* took another spectacular turn. A whole new debater came into print: Oline Muus herself. The pastor's wife contacted *Budstikken* directly. Her piece titled "To the Holden Congregation" was an open letter. "Since the current process between me and my husband has been so widely deliberated, caused so much outrage, and brought so much misjudgement to both him and me, especially in the congregation, I would like to make the following statement," she began.[3]

The explanation concerned itself mostly with the question of public knowledge about the case. The pastor's wife explained that she had found herself in a situation where she was compelled to take the necessary steps to gain control over money she had inherited from her father, which was now in her husband's possession. She had sincerely hoped her efforts would succeed without the case being made public or anyone other than the civil court interfering. She had told her lawyer not to bring before the court any more information about her unhappy family circumstances than was strictly necessary in order to get the case settled as quietly as possible: "No one regrets more than I that the case has been talked about so much, but attorney Ueland and I have taken every possible precaution to amicably gain possession of this inheritance."[4]

At the congregational meeting in February, confusion had arisen about Oline's participation or lack thereof in "The Complaint." In *Budstikken,* she now wrote to clarify that "The Complaint," which she sadly had seen made public, had been drawn up in her absence. She hadn't had the opportunity to read it until it had already been sent to the court. Therefore, "The Complaint's" depiction of family relations wasn't correct, nor could it be proven on all counts. But she added: "in essence the content is true."[5]

Oline Muus was giving her community an explanation, albeit a very ambiguous one. She thanked the congregation, which for so many years had shown her so much goodwill. In a postscript she wrote that she had been summoned to another congregational meeting on March 10. She would attend, but only if her demands were met: a man from outside the Synod whose impartiality she could trust had to write the meeting minutes, and those minutes should be read out so that she could check if errors had crept in, and she should have the opportunity to correct any mistakes. If her demands were denied, she wouldn't attend the meeting. With that, the premises had been laid for even more heated discussions within the congregation.

The actual call to the meeting was printed in the same issue. According to *Budstikken*'s assessment, the most startling point of the meeting summons was that Mrs. Muus's obedience as a wife was now an item on the agenda. During an evening meeting at the church, Pastor Muus had "decided" that the congregational meeting on March 10 would address their marital relationship. Mrs. Muus's understanding of the commandment that a wife should be obedient to her husband was to be discussed, in addition to her involvement in "The Complaint" brought before the court in her name. Pastor Muus also intended to attend the meeting, the summons said. The meeting summons's author, Pastor Bøckman, closed again with the words "The Lord have mercy on you and your house."[6]

32

Under Church Discipline?

....

ON WEDNESDAY, MARCH 10, Holden Church was again jam-packed with spectators for the second round of congregational meetings. Already by ten in the morning, nearly eight hundred people, including many curious onlookers, had arrived. For outsiders, it was a unique opportunity to witness the congregation's judicial process firsthand. Mrs. Muus was to be subjected to the "apparatus of spiritual torture," as *Budstikken* had called it. Pastor Bøckman began by reading from Paul's first epistle to the Corinthians. This time Bøckman was evidently composed, since *Budstikken*'s reporter didn't remark on the chairman's state of mind.[1]

The scripture Bøckman had chosen was timely: "Love suffereth long, *and* is kind; love envieth not; love vaunteth not itself, is not puffed up, doth not behave itself unseemly, seeketh not its own, is not provoked, taketh not account of evil; rejoiceth not in unrighteousness, but rejoiceth with the truth; beareth all things, believeth all things, hopeth all things, endureth all things." The reading continued, and after a while the congregation heard: "When I was a child, I spoke as a child, I thought as a child, I judged as a child; but when I became a man, I put away childish things. For now we see in a mirror, in a riddle; but then we shall see from the aspect of aspect; now I know in part, but then I shall know fully, even as I am also fully known." Would the Muus case remain a mystery? Or would the matter be disclosed in its full truth? Finally, Bøckman spoke the last famous words of the chapter: "But now abideth faith, hope, love, these three; and the greatest of these is love."[2]

When the meeting began Pastor Muus presumably stood at the long table in the chancel where he gave a brief statement. Since the previous meeting, at the congregation's request, he and his wife had been negotiating with each other in the presence of witnesses. He had asked two church members, Hans Westermo (sometimes spelled Westermoe) and William Rønningen, to attend the negotiations in order to follow the "rule of God's word," the pastor explained: "Against an elder receive not an accusation, but before two or three witnesses." With the two witnesses present, Pastor Muus had asked Mrs. Muus if a wife was obliged to obey her husband in everything, even when contrary to God's word. Her answer was clear: No. In the presence of witnesses, Oline Muus declared she didn't believe she was obligated to absolute submission to her husband.

Could everyone see what had happened? With her response Mrs. Muus had obviously committed a sin. She broke the fourth commandment; she contradicted the word of God, the very religious doctrine that the wife should obey her husband. This transgression demanded the third degree of Church discipline, the most serious form. The meeting between the spouses ended without reconciliation, so Nils Raabølle's vision of an amicable solution to the conflict didn't become a reality. Instead, the pastor now insisted on church discipline against his wife; this would be the subject of the meeting. Following the congregation's rules, he asserted, there was no other choice.

Pastor Muus took the initiative in this second congregational meeting, steering the day's proceedings. Since the previous meeting the pastor had also apparently changed his strategy. When the congregation was last gathered in Holden Church, the pastor had repeatedly insisted that "The Complaint" be discussed in that forum. Only by the widest possible consideration of the allegations could the accusations finally be repudiated and the pastor's honor restored. But in the introduction on March 10, the pastor did not seem to be at all concerned with "The Complaint." Instead of a far-reaching and uncontrollable plenary discussion about life at the parsonage and the pastor's relationship with his wife, Bernt Muus wanted the second congregational meeting to concentrate on a fundamental matter of church doctrine and his wife's violation of it. Had Oline really refused to recognize the fourth commandment? Pastor Muus proposed that this matter was the only one the congregation had to determine and pass judgment on.

When the pastor had finished, the meeting chair, Pastor Bøckman, asked if Mrs. Muus was present. The question caused a stir in the congregation, and when there was no answer, people must have stretched their necks, glanced here and there. Bøckman repeated the question, but still no one answered. Then, he asked if anyone had heard why Mrs. Muus wasn't in attendance. He still didn't get an answer. The assembled would have to choose two men to fetch her. It wasn't possible to consider a church discipline case without the accused being present.

The task eventually fell on Peder Langemo and a man named Nils Nordby. But before the two men left, there was a lengthy exchange of words. Langemo wondered: what if Mrs. Muus set conditions for appearing? Andreas Rygh, who had previously spoken on Oline's behalf, felt she should be accommodated as much as possible. Nils Ottun agreed. When at the last meeting Mrs. Muus was denied the opportunity to have someone speak on her behalf, it was because the meeting had gone on for so long, the members of the congregation were tired, and they found her conditions very presumptuous. Now the case was different, Ottun believed. Abraham Simpson, a neighboring farmer, also thought it was normal in cases of church discipline for the person concerned to be present. But he added that the congregation wasn't obligated to comply with conditions demanded by a person under church discipline. Pastor Bøckman agreed with Simpson, but pointed out the extraordinary circumstances. If the congregation accepted Mrs. Muus's terms, she might agree to appear.[3]

Back at the parsonage, Mrs. Muus was dressed and waiting. Langemo and Nordby obviously didn't need to use their persuasive gifts, for shortly afterward the two returned to the church with Mrs. Muus. Without saying anything, the pastor's wife approached meeting chair Bøckman and presented him with a letter to read aloud. Consequently, everyone in the congregation heard that Mrs. Muus believed she had good reasons for not attending the meeting. First, the congregation didn't accept the demands she had made in order to appear. Second, the congregation's requirement that she had to prove everything written in "The Complaint" was meaningless. Third, she had been kept on tenterhooks under church discipline long enough. And fourth, the congregation obviously intended to have her expelled from the church. On these grounds, Mrs. Muus understood that her presence wasn't necessary; the congregational meeting could take place without her, for there was no lack of witnesses.

But now Mrs. Muus was present in the church. Whether she sat in one of the front or back pews isn't known. Still, we know something for sure: she remained silent. At the same time her words filled the entire church. Pastor Bøckman gave voice to her carefully written words; thus the whole congregation could hear the pastor's wife swear that she would never consent to the Synod's doctrine on marriage. No one need be in any doubt about her position. If the congregation so desired, Oline would be happy to state her own belief concerning the marriage doctrine.

This theological announcement was followed by a list of conditions that must be met for the pastor's wife to remain at the meeting. Again, Mrs. Muus demanded that attorney Andreas Ueland be allowed to attend and speak and that her spokesman be from outside the Synod. In addition, the meeting must be open to everyone. If she had committed a sin, let everyone hear and see what evil she had done. If she hadn't committed a sin, then let everyone hear that she was innocent.

Oline had been busy in advance of the meeting. She had carefully prepared. Now as Bøckman stood there in the sanctuary with the completed document, it must have burned in his hands. Mrs. Muus explicitly requested the meeting chair read the entire long document aloud. It contained her personal signature and was dated Holden parsonage, February 1880. Perhaps Ueland had once again come from Minneapolis to Holden to help her write her defense and to instill courage in her. The lawyer knew he wouldn't be admitted to the meeting, so he wasn't at the parsonage when the two men from the church came to get her.

Pastor Bøckman took the floor to disclose that he already knew the content of the document. He said it saddened him greatly that Mrs. Muus didn't agree with the Synod's doctrine on marriage. He expressed surprise that the pastor's wife felt the congregation had her on tenterhooks because there was uncertainty as to whether Mrs. Muus was really under church discipline. The chairman was also unaware that the congregation planned to expel her from the Synod. In any case, Bøckman believed the only right thing to do was to allow the pastor's wife to have a voice. He straightened his back and prepared to read aloud.[4]

Just as Bøckman was about to begin, a voice came from the audience. Peder Langemo asked for the floor. The longtime parishioner believed Mrs. Muus had misunderstood the purpose of the meeting. It was supposed to discuss the doctrine on God's word, not prove or discuss "The Complaint." Langemo was fully in line with Pastor Muus's new strategy from earlier in the day. He was supported by Nils Ottun. Two parishioners had now stood up for the pastor. Pastor Bøckman, on the other hand, was unsure whether it was right or possible to put Mrs. Muus under church discipline now. First the congregation had to decide whether she had the right to complain about her husband or not. If she didn't have that right, then the congregation would have grounds to hold her accountable. But it was too early to decide at this time. Bøckman felt the meeting should be presented with Mrs. Muus's defense in its entirety before the deliberations could continue.

Suddenly, Pastor Muus lost his temper. His strategy was about to fail, and he needed to speak clearly. The congregation absolutely didn't need to hear the statement. In Pastor Muus's view, Pastor Bøckman had confused two different matters. Mrs. Muus accused her husband: that was one thing—and it was irrelevant to the case concerning church discipline. Something completely different was that he, Pastor Muus, in front of the congregation had accused his wife of denying God's word. This last point was the church discipline case the congregation was to determine—and nothing else. By refusing to obey the congregation, Mrs. Muus exposed her soul to eternal damnation. Church discipline, Pastor Muus explained, was an act of love that God had imposed upon the congregation. Again, discussion flared up and opinions opposed one another. In the end, a vote was the only way forward. The result was striking: despite Pastor Muus's fierce attempt to persuade the parishioners, a majority decided that the new defense must be read aloud. Mrs. Muus's statement, at just under six thousand words in length, was directed at the Holden congregation and was read aloud in its entirety.

33

The Big Defense Speech

"WHEN I ADDRESS THE CONGREGATION, it's to clarify something that has not only shaken the congregation, but has also caused me much grief and offended me a great deal," Mrs. Muus began her defense. In keeping with classical rhetorical instruction, she was careful to present herself as a morally credible person, a person with a convincing ethos. She noted that the congregation had to understand it was difficult for a wife to sue her own husband. As a woman in an assembly of men, she couldn't expect to be understood; yet she attempted to connect with the audience and their feelings. Before the congregation judged her actions as brazen obstinance, she asked each individual to consider what she had to endure during the last twenty long years.[1]

Oline Muus couldn't have hoped to gain support solely by using pathos, the appeal to emotions. In the audience sat many married men; it was doubtful how receptive they were to her sentimental rhetoric. More solid theological arguments were needed. Mrs. Muus revealed that she was ready to leave the congregation voluntarily. She simply couldn't accept the doctrine of marriage upheld by both the congregation and the Synod. The defense's main argument was concerned with the commandment of obedience. Although she had come to a different understanding of marriage than her husband, she attempted to convince the congregation that hers was both morally defensible and correct according to the Bible. "If God had created women to be a husband's blind instrument and servant in all things, surely he wouldn't have given her independent spiritual faculties and powers," she wrote. She pointed out how abominable and impossible it would be for a wife to deny herself every right to independence as a human being.[2]

Clearly, Oline was well informed of the current biblical criticism. In addition, the mindset, argumentation, and certain fashionable keywords testify that she was quite familiar with John Stuart Mill's *The Subjection of Women*. Her lawyer, to put it mildly, was opposed to Lutheran orthodoxy, and he may have helped her develop the argument. Even Martin Luther had believed that man stands only in obedience to his God, and therefore, it must be obvious that a husband can't demand blind obedience from his wife.

Mrs. Muus vehemently castigated the Synod, which regarded women's submissiveness as a sacred commandment, implying that a husband had the right to exercise despotic dominion over his wife and children, who were to be regarded as slaves or docile creatures. But, Oline continued in her defense, it is both erroneous and unchristian to interpret the commandment as such. A wife is destined by God not only to be her husband's helper but also to be his equal. No one can deny that these are God's own words, she argued.

Mrs. Muus pleaded her case with biblical criticism's breadth and theological argumentation. Her defense made a strong impression on the assembly. That these words were put forth by a woman who was, in addition, a pastor's wife only strengthened their impact. Following the theological argumentation, Oline wished to clarify why she had gone to court to gain control over her own assets. It wasn't because she was inspired by women's rights—she wanted nothing to do with that assertion; it was due instead to her inner need. The document Pastor Bøckman read aloud stated: "I've had to endure many difficulties, until my patience was finally at an end. And out of an inner compulsion I had to choose to stand independent of the tyrannical pettiness that I have suffered for over twenty years."[3]

Point by point, with words increasingly more emotionally charged, she elaborated on her case against her husband. Her defense had turned into an attack; "The Complaint" had been joined by a new complaint, even more comprehensive and detailed. "Tyrannical pettiness" was the phrase she used, and she supplied many examples. Her husband had a dresser made for himself, and God help her if she dared to use it. She had to store her own and the children's clothing in large boxes in the farm storage building. In the parsonage, the family had lacked a great deal, everything from furniture and clocks to a sewing machine and bedding. Because her husband refused to light more than one stove in the winter, her health was deteriorating. She had never starved, but the family hadn't had sufficient food. Her husband had long refused to give her a household allowance, and for the past ten to twelve years, she had received only fifteen dollars a month. She had to take on work knitting and sewing for others to provide her family with needed food and clothing.

Rarely had she been allowed to go anywhere. In the past twenty years, she had only been to Decorah, Iowa, twice. Decorah was considered the capital of the Synod, where the pastor's wife from Holden could also have enjoyed entertainment and fellowship with other influential and faithful women. Mrs. Muus had not had many "pleasure trips," as she called them, except for one or two to the nearest towns. When she once asked her husband if she could travel to Norway, partly for the sake of her health and partly to visit relatives, he refused. He thought she would ruin him, and that both she and other wives who demanded such unreasonable things should be sent to the asylum at St. Peter. She told about one son who lay in the grave and another who would never recover because they both had been treated thoughtlessly by their father.[4]

She never forgot what her husband said to her when she came home after breaking her leg in two places. When she asked him to send for the doctor, he replied that she had to anoint herself with patience until the doctor arrived. Her defense thoroughly described subsequent stories about the night of her accident and her deteriorating health. The tale of what had happened when she had raised the issue of her father's inheritance with her husband and then when she sought advice with Andreas Ueland was also explained in detail; these descriptions are the only source of the conflict's first phase.

At the statement, "As you may all be aware, I have suffered the superfluous persecution of preliminary church discipline, and likely now stand among you as a member of the congregation for the last time, with only my excommunication remaining," it was impossible for the assembly not to notice her emotion. "Why am I now standing here in this position in the congregation?" Bøckman read from the chancel. "Because I, broken down in health and strength, found it necessary in a cold winter in a house in bad condition, to get a rug for the living room and a fire in our bedroom.... And what wife, who has seen better days, and whose wealth in addition totals several thousand dollars would put up with it?" Her only goal was to ensure that in the future the family would have sufficient food and clothing, material goods, and a warm home. Yet, when she asked for justice, she was seen as a criminal and brought before the congregational tribunal.[5]

The defense read like a convincing staged monologue. Oline held the audience's attention in the palm of her hand. After this climax she returned to her arguments against the Synod's marriage doctrine. Pastor Muus and Pastor Bøckman had declared that the Lord in His wisdom has ordained it so that there can be no disagreement between husband and wife. For in marriage there is but one absolute and unconditional will in all things, and that is the will of the husband. Oline had been taught that a wife should obey her husband in all things—even in attire and desires. This understanding implied that she had to strip herself of her personality and her individual being. Rhetorically she asked, "Must it not then first be necessary to get used to not thinking and having independent ideas?"[6]

Gradually, she built toward a new crescendo, touching on an especially sensitive point for the Synod: its view of slavery. Although the overwhelming majority of Norwegian Americans were antislavery, during the Civil War the Norwegian Synod had concluded that slavery was not a sin, noting that the Old Testament states that slavery is not a sin; therefore, it could be justified. But as Odd Lovoll points out, the "statement was intended to be a compromise. The full text of their declaration shows clearly that the ministers expressed themselves against slavery. But the clergy's compulsion to find a strict Biblical basis for doctrine hindered them from taking a clear and unequivocal position against slavery as an institution."[7]

When Oline called attention to this proclamation, which had stirred intensely strong reactions—from the larger American community, within parts of Norwegian America, and in Norway—she reminded the public that the majority of Norwegian immigrants were Republicans and abolitionists and that the Norwegian Synod didn't represent the majority view in the northern states. The Haugean church, for example, upon its founding in 1846, had agreed that slavery was a sin.

In her defense, Mrs. Muus likened a wife's position with that of a slave, following the pattern of the American biblical feminists' account in the Seneca Falls declaration of 1848 and John Stuart Mill's incendiary book in 1869. "One doesn't have the right to exercise absolute power over his neighbor," she stated, "and thus act in place of God!" She reminded the assembly that when slavery was discussed Pastor Muus had maintained that it was an absolute necessity. The slave relationship also applied to the family: "For if Pastor Muus had no slaves, at least he had his wife and children." His opinion on the matter was heartfelt and sincere, and he had proved it to her from the first moment she came into his house.

Oline Muus believed the relationship between a slave and her master should be quite different from a wife's relationship to her husband, for a slave is a servant of his master, while a wife is a support to her husband—and his equal. God first commanded how a husband should relate to his wife and then how the wife should relate to her husband. The mutual relationship between the spouses explains how this commandment is to be understood. If a husband fulfills his obligations, it would be a joy for a Christian wife to be submissive in love to her husband. If, on the other hand, a husband is a domestic tyrant, it is impossible for the wife to be submissive to him in all things.

Oline Muus didn't mince her words when she once again described the conditions in the parsonage. Pastor Muus had attempted "to kill the love, respect, and obedience which is a mother's best and greatest joy to find in her children." He had told the children that they had a faithless mother, and they had been instructed not to accept clothing from her, "clothing that [she found] it necessary to give to the children, because their father doesn't always realize that these clothes are needed." They weren't even allowed to receive small gifts from their mother. But, Oline asked rhetorically, is it right that children should only obey their father and not their mother? Moreover, she revealed that Pastor Muus had abused his clerical position, and in the most grievous manner. In her letter, Oline confirmed the shocking accusations previously reported in *Budstikken*: Pastor Muus had on several occasions denied her participation in communion because she had allegedly sinned. Among other things, he believed she had sinned when she forgot to empty the washbasin and cups before going to bed, and the water froze in the washbasin, causing it to burst overnight. For the slightest housewifely misdemeanor, her husband had punished her by denying communion.

Even as she outlined her husband's sins and weaknesses, she also had to do some serious soul-searching. She wasn't free from sin; she was both thoughtless and impetuous, which had often caused offense and misunderstanding. She had much for which to pray forgiveness. But she had tried to maintain a good relationship with her husband and for the longest time attempted to be patient with him. As a wife she had been more than patient, and her forbearance was precisely why the "scandal" had not been made public earlier. After twenty years of "abuse"—not until the end did she use that strong word—it was comforting for her to know that she had truth and justice in the most essential details on her side. She had been treated unfairly. She acted out of weakness, not out of intentional ill will. In this case, her husband was the guilty party. He was authoritarian, and he ruled over her with strong judgment, iron will, and an icy heart.[8]

Oline concluded her defense with a small legal consideration. After the February 18 meeting, she had been encouraged by several members of the congregation to prove everything she had said about her husband; otherwise, they would consider her a liar. But, she asked, could any of the farmers here legally prove all the unpleasantness and sins they committed against each other, husband and wife, parents and children at home? She couldn't in any case prove what had happened between her and her husband, for when she had sinned against him, he hadn't immediately called witnesses. And when he had sinned against her she hadn't immediately called witnesses either. On the contrary, the spouses had tried to avoid witnesses as much as possible. But now, by placing her under church discipline and accusing her of lying, the congregation had forced her to give this account. The congregation was responsible for this new public scrutiny and had to answer for the consequences of her statement.

"Differences in character, opinions, and inclinations are an exceedingly harmful thing in marriage," Oline concluded. "A very small seed can grow into weeds over many years. It's difficult to say where and when the first shoot sprang up, and who is to blame." She was attempting to explain why her marriage had become the way it was. She needed to double her efforts to seek her God genuinely and sincerely, and she asked the congregation to judge her gently or, rather, to leave the judgment to Him whose judgment was infallible. She ended her letter thus: "I now have nothing more to add. I have, as far as I am able, accounted for the complaint against my husband. And I can't accept any responsibility if misunderstandings or inaccurate representations of my accounts to Attorney Ueland have crept in. Oline Muus, Holden parsonage, February 1880."[9]

34

The Money Question

....

IT HAD TAKEN PASTOR BØCKMAN half an hour to read the defense from beginning to end. But churchgoers were accustomed to the pastor's lengthy sermons and to long-winded and time-consuming discussions in meetings. Still, they had never heard a statement like the one read aloud in Holden Church on March 10. What happened just after Pastor Bøckman read Oline Muus's statement isn't documented in *Budstikken*'s report. Perhaps everyone was silent. Maybe the meeting took a break?

When the discussion resumed, chairman Bøckman approached Mrs. Muus directly. Hadn't she considered it her duty to appear when the congregation summoned her? To this query she replied yes, and apparently said nothing more. She remained at the meeting. With the defense, her second complaint, she had given the assembled yet another matter they needed to address. She had repeatedly been reproached for not having presented her complaint to the congregation from the outset. Now, she had finally turned directly to the community to which she belonged.[1]

Andreas Rygh, who had previously defended Mrs. Muus, asked to speak and offered a constructive suggestion. He proposed that Pastor Ludvig M. Biørn, the former army chaplain in the Norwegian American regiment and a close friend of the couple, be given the role of Mrs. Muus's spokesman. The congregation adopted his recommendation and thus the men of Holden Church accommodated Mrs. Muus. A congregant who was placed under church discipline would normally have to answer for themselves. But Oline received special treatment, either because she was the pastor's wife or because the case was completely without precedent. Biørn was a pastor in the Synod and on paper one of Bernt Muus's allies. However, on this day he was an acceptable advocate and spokesman—at least to the men of the congregation.

Oline insisted on having a spokesman because otherwise it would be difficult to secure the right to speak in front of the assembly, though perhaps she also saw her own limitations. She wasn't trained to speak in public meetings, assemblies of men. Indeed, women never spoke in public meetings, and not only within her social milieu. There were few female lecturers, even among the liberal cultural elite in Norway or Norwegian America. An exception was women's rights pioneer Aasta Hansteen, who would later become interested in Oline Muus's case. Hansteen was a public orator, and for that very reason, she was also depicted by cartoonists as a man with a mustache and wild gestures. The cartoon emphasized the common belief that a woman who spoke in public wasn't a real woman. Now, with a spokesman in place, Mrs. Muus was able to speak while at the same time preserving her femininity.[2]

With a spokesman secured for Mrs. Muus, the church discipline case could begin. But first the congregation needed to be reminded of the true doctrine on marriage. As meeting leader, Bøckman saw it as his duty to reprimand Mrs. Muus. Marriage, he expounded, is more than a matter of personal will; it is a union established by God. He referred to the gospel of Paul and explained that if a wife's obedience to her husband doesn't come from natural love, then obedience applies as God's law. In fact, it is a wife's distinct duty to be submissive to her husband. Even an unreasonable and bitter man is entitled to his wife's obedience, Bøckman specified. You can just as well call her a slave, Bøckman maintained, because she is in a relationship similar to that of a slave to their master. The pastor might come to regret his last assertion.[3]

Furthermore, the pastor continued, obedience must be a wife's cherished duty, and if this duty was objectionable to her, then she was herself abhorrent before God. The congregation was accustomed to hearing this kind of preaching. Parochial schoolteacher Nils Raabølle

Ludvig Marinius Biørn, date unknown.
Photograph collection, NAHA

immediately got up and gave Bøckman his endorsement. But the meeting's proceedings indicate that the marriage doctrine was not uncontroversial in Holden.

Mrs. Muus's spokesman, Pastor Biørn, began to plead her case. His formulations seem thoughtful; one could almost believe they had been prepared in advance. The pastor commented that he had understood her thus: a wife is obligated to obey her spouse as long as he fulfills his duty as a Christian husband. Submissiveness cannot apply as a principle but as a relative concept. He would—until proven otherwise—regard Mrs. Muus as both a Christian and an honorable woman, implying that Pastors Bøckman and Muus did not.

Pastor Muus spoke next. In this theological debate he was among his equals. Pastor Muus wanted to know if his colleague Biørn meant that if a governmental authority freed a woman from God's required duty then she was exempt from fulfilling this duty. Biørn replied no, with a longer commentary in which he subtly brought up Mrs. Muus's money question by setting the commandment of obedience into a historical context. In primitive societies, where there is no governmental authority, the husband controls all property. In developed societies such as their own, on the other hand, the government must safeguard the rights of both men and women. The government can't favor the husband, and the husband mustn't be allowed to manage the couple's property rights—even if it is for his wife's sake.

Thus, the meeting came to address the question of Mrs. Muus's assets, albeit indirectly, which according to the verdict reached on February 18 was irrelevant to the congregation. Suddenly women's civil rights were on the agenda, and Pastor Bøckman fell into the trap. He didn't agree with Biørn, he said. A wife must obey her husband in all that he demands of her, otherwise how would a household function? There must always be one master, or every society would be consumed by discord. Nils Ottun agreed. One could only imagine what society would be like if Pastor Biørn's understanding was translated into real life.

For example, woman's suffrage would create confusion in the family when a wife had to fulfill her civic duty, to participate in election campaigns, and so on. Ottun also reportedly stated that no woman should exercise a right given to her by law if it was contrary to the word of God. With that, the long and dramatic discussions of Wednesday, March 10, 1880, were concluded. Two days had been set aside to address Mrs. Muus's case. The meeting would continue the following day.

35

A Christian Husband?

··

THE PROCEEDINGS BEGAN on the morning of March 11, 1880, with heated debate. Mrs. Muus's new complaint hadn't been included in the meeting's minutes. When the pastor's wife left the meeting on Thursday evening, she had taken her defense letter with her. She had delivered the document to the secretary afterward, but he had managed to copy only part of it. A serious democratic body like the congregational meeting couldn't live with such inaccuracy. Several speakers insisted that the congregation must be satisfied that the secretary's transcript was correct, and it must be read aloud before it could be approved. The process took a considerable amount of time.[1]

Afterward, Pastor Bøckman asked to be relieved of his duties as meeting chair, excusing himself as "indisposed." Reliable Peder Langemo took over, but he also failed to prevent further discussions of the meeting's minutes. Pastor Muus was the most tenacious of the speakers. He launched a frontal attack on his own congregation because it hadn't begun the church discipline case long ago. One of their members—meaning Mrs. Muus—was accused of denying God's word, but the congregation didn't seem to want to determine whether her action was a sin. Instead of beginning the proceedings on church discipline, the congregation had allowed him to be verbally abused for half an hour. If the congregation wasn't even able to resolve questions of obedience and disobedience, it would be best for the meeting to adjourn. According to Pastor Muus, the teachings had to be the guide;

if old married couples couldn't agree on the word of God—that a wife should be submissive to her husband—"they might as well pack up and quit." Those words were unusually harsh, even for Bernt Muus.

On the other hand, Mrs. Muus's spokesman, Pastor Biørn, couldn't see that there was any case for church discipline at all. The vehement way Pastor Muus expressed himself was "remarkable," Biørn noted. The congregation surely felt that it couldn't deal with the church discipline case without first investigating the long-standing "disparities" between the married couple.

Not surprisingly, Nils Raabølle wanted to begin the church discipline case immediately. Meeting chair Langemo also wanted to start there. How could Pastor Biørn doubt that the congregation had a case of church discipline? Langemo himself, speaking on behalf of the congregation, had an instinctive feeling that both parties, Mrs. Muus as well as Pastor Muus, had sinned. Even the most loyal of the congregation's parishioners insisted on taking small stabs at Pastor Muus.

However, before the church discipline case came up, Raabølle unleashed another round on the previous day's theological topic. He claimed that Biørn wasn't taking the doctrine of marriage seriously when he said that under certain circumstances governmental authorities could relieve a woman from the duties imposed upon her by God's word. As Raabølle stated, every Christian woman is obliged to hold the word of God above all else, even if the government exempts her from it. Pastor Biørn responded that he was loyal to the Synod's view of the marriage doctrine, but as spokesman for Mrs. Muus, he had tried to familiarize himself with her thinking and portray it in the best possible light. After all, she was under church discipline. Moreover, it was church discipline in the third degree, taken up in front of the entire congregation.

As to what the case concerned, Pastor Biørn continued, "If Mrs. Muus had lived through everything that she stated in her defense, it wasn't strange if her mind had been shrouded and dulled." If the pastor's wife had lost her spiritual balance, it was Pastor Muus's fault. Biørn had learned at a recent pastoral conference in Red Wing what Pastor Muus meant when he said a wife must obey her husband "in all things."

There, Muus had explained that "in all things" must be understood as "to the fullest extent." Pastor Biørn distanced himself from this interpretation. No Christian husband can demand such all-encompassing obedience from his wife that she loses her identity as an independent being. Biørn concluded that Pastor Muus's demand for absolute obedience was in opposition to ordinary humanity.[2]

Again, the atmosphere in the meeting was beginning to turn against Pastor Muus, as several statements testified. People showed sympathy and compassion for Mrs. Muus. More importantly, she was believed, including by parishioner John Lilleskov, who pointed out that in marriage love must rule; love is everything. The Bible commanded a husband to love his wife, even as Christ so loved the Church and sacrificed Himself for it. If there's love in marriage, one doesn't question who is right in all things. Lilleskov continued, in some respects a wife is equal to her husband, for a husband can't rule over his wife, and if he exercises his authority in love, that authority isn't in all things. Rasmus Villum found it strange that when a wife was mistreated by her husband to the point that her health was at stake, she wasn't allowed to refuse him obedience. Villum was immediately and sharply rebuked by Pastor Muus, but the parishioner stood firm. He knew what rights the congregation's democracy gave him.

Before the meeting adjourned the chairman posed a question directly to Mrs. Muus for the second time. He asked if the testimonies had affected her in any way, to which she replied no. Pastor Muus also offered a final outburst. He would decline any further exhortations to reconcile with his wife. He prayed that God would preserve him from ever having to come to terms with the doctrine Biørn presented. Even though God's word was difficult to understand, Muus said ironically, the congregation needed to arrive at an understanding of it. Once again, he criticized the assembled for not preventing "The Complaint" from being read. Nils Ottun replied bluntly: Now that the congregation finally knew what Mrs. Muus complained about, it could deal with the case.[3]

But which case? A motion from Ottun won support from the assembly. At the next meeting in Holden Church, the congregation should first and foremost address the allegations made by Mrs. Muus against her husband. If there was time, the church discipline case against Mrs. Muus could be revisited. In addition, the congregation should ask Synod leadership—President H. A. Preus and District Presidents Koren and J. B. Frich—to attend the meeting. Ottun's motion received a majority in the final vote. Pastor Muus must have been even more furious than before. In practice, much would be up to the Synod's leaders when the proceedings resumed. They were men, and they came from the outside.

36

In the Backwoods

....

FIVE DAYS LATER, on March 16, 1880, *Budstikken* printed its report of the first day of the March meeting. It was front-page news. The newspaper correspondent in Faribault, Erik L. Petersen, had once again done his job. The article was so long that it had to be divided over two days. Nearly three months had passed since Mrs. Muus's case had been first published in the St. Paul *Pioneer Press* and *Budstikken,* and attorney Andreas Ueland must have been more than satisfied with how his client's case had been covered in the press thus far. Both Norwegian as well as mainstream American newspapers defended Mrs. Muus. The accusations against her husband were presented as facts by editors and reporters. And her new complaint, offered to the congregation at the March 10 meeting, was more disturbing than ever. Both directly and between the lines, people could read that Pastor Muus was a domestic tyrant—a cold, thoughtless man who ruled over his wife and children with an iron fist. The press's version of *Muus v. Muus* was repeated with incessant new embellishments, and Mrs. Muus's credibility was consistently strengthened. Was it possible to shake the press's portrayal? Church council member Gudmund Norsving hadn't completely given up.[1]

On March 30, Norsving's letter to the editor was published on the front page of *Budstikken.* He wished to defend his congregation from allegations and suspicion. The congregation had not made this case a public scandal. The congregation had the right to investigate whether

187

Mrs. Muus's allegations were true, but until the charges were proven, Pastor Muus must be treated as innocent. And the members of the congregation were neither stupid nor isolationist. As Norsving put it, "If we don't understand that such things are wrong, it isn't because we close ourselves off." Norsving objected to the press's accusation that the congregation excluded anyone from the meetings. The only thing the members didn't want was to be educated on Christianity by a lawyer. Obviously, newspaper reporters had access to the meetings: the discussions were summarized and the congregation was berated in *Budstikken* and the *Pioneer Press*. "We don't live in the backwoods either," Norsving exclaimed, "where one can take care of oneself, without anyone in the outside world becoming aware of us until now." He explained: "We admit that the case in question is of extraordinary public interest. There's no point in complaining about the press's interference, now that it's already occurred. But we can't see that the congregation bears any responsibility for it. Nor that the congregation has earned the treatment it's received in certain newspapers. Therefore, we have with wounded pride and damaged self-respect, ventured to come forward in protest."[2]

Budstikken's response was printed in the same issue as Norsving's letter and was as uncompromising as ever. Administering church discipline is naturally a Christian congregation's right, editor Luth Jæger wrote sarcastically, but in this case, it was practiced in a manner that was anything other than Christian: "Not for one hour at a time, but for three hours at a time, the person concerned, often ill and in constant pain, has been so treated, and not love, but threats and fear of the divine law have been the means of persuasion. It wasn't a crime in human terms that she was guilty of." Mrs. Muus's view on obedience, opposed by both her husband and the majority in the congregation, isn't a crime in civil society. Her view, Jæger added, is even shared by Christians.[3]

"We don't live in the backwoods?" *Budstikken's* editor quoted Norsving's letter and then stated ironically: "No, the powerful Norwegian-American settlements in Goodhue County aren't in the backwoods anymore. But it isn't their fault that they're no longer there." For the editor, it was a mystery how the Norwegian American Lutherans had been able to live isolated for so long, completely outside the wider society. Jæger considered the relationship between congregation and clergy enigmatic. To him, it was a relief that the Muus case had come up; otherwise, the Norwegian American settlements would still be living in isolation.

Budstikken, as usual, had the last word. Should the conservative forces in the Holden congregation wish to respond in more detail, they would have to choose a different venue. The next attempt was printed in the Synod's own paper, *Evangelisk Luthersk Kirketidende*. The individual who expressed himself there was none other than the man at the center of the battle, Pastor Muus himself.

He offered a theological reflection on the marriage doctrine and an attempt at self-defense on behalf of the Synod. Had Pastor Bøckman, during the March 10 and 11 meetings, really said that a wife's position toward her husband is like a slave's position in relation to her master? Pastor Muus defended his colleague. On the question of whether a wife should be submissive to her husband in all things, except that which is contrary to God's word, Bøckman had noted similarities between a wife's relationship to her husband and a slave's relationship to her master. "Slave woman. With this word, the church's enemies amuse themselves especially at this time," noted Pastor Muus. "But they falsely stated that Pastor Bøckman, in a congregation meeting in Holden, said that a wife is a slave." Pastor Muus's appeal didn't get much support. A little later Pastor Bøckman found it timely to make a statement himself. He claimed in *Evangelisk Luthersk Kirketidende* that he hadn't used the word "slave woman" but rather one of the meeting attendees had, to ridicule the Bible's teaching on a wife's submissiveness to her husband. He dismissed the accusation while at the same time criticizing his opponents.[4]

Mrs. Muus had forged an effective weapon for herself by using the words "slave woman," "slave," and "slavery" in her letter of defense. In 1880, it was only fifteen years since the northern states had forced the Confederacy into a humiliating peace agreement. America was many countries, but one of them, Yankee America, the land of the victor, was above all others. The Synod's viewpoint on slavery made it even more suspect in the eyes of the majority, strengthening its reputation as un-American.

Both *Budstikken* and the local English-language newspapers knew how to light a fire under the wider community's prejudices against Norwegian immigrants. When Norwegian Lutherans were not assimilated, integrated, or Americanized, it was because they were under the control of the church. The clergy of the Norwegian Synod were held accountable for the fact that Norwegians in America remained Norwegian. "[T]he relations existing between American citizens born in this country and the Norwegian immigrants are in a special sense, exceedingly thin," wrote the *Goodhue County Republican* editor on April 29, 1880, in an article entitled "The Letter Killeth." By subjecting Mrs. Muus to church discipline and judging her case, the congregation and the clergy countermanded the secular court. Instead of sending children to the public school, Norwegian Americans founded their own church schools where teaching took place in Norwegian. Moreover, the Norwegian American Lutherans had shown their anti-Americanism by siding with the South and supporting slavery. "No religious body has more consistently carried out these views than the Norwegian Evangelical Lutheran Synod," the *Goodhue County Republican* asserted. The sharp commentary begins by stating that "our Norwegian fellow citizens perform certain political duties in a very creditable manner, and have earned and deserved the gratitude of the Republican party for their staunch fidelity to its policy, from the very first day of its birth; but, on the whole they hold aloof from the distinctive American element, and place themselves in a position of distrust which repels by its mere existence."[5]

The Red Wing newspaper *Advance* had come to the same conclusion a month earlier. On March 24, the newspaper characterized the members of the Holden congregation as a pack of oppressed beings who have neither principles nor will beyond what "their master" asserts. "The majority in the congregation," the *Advance* wrote ironically, "are empty bottles filled with Muus."[6]

Analysis of the Muus case was not limited to criticizing the defendant and the plaintiff. Their allies were harshly scrutinized as well. The editor of the *Advance* specifically pointed to Peder (in the article referred to as "Pere") Langemo as "one of Mr. Muus' admirers and tools," characterizing him as "one of the head men of the crow corner, of the west part of Holden."[7]

Herman Amberg Preus, date unknown.
Courtesy Evangelical Lutheran Synod Archives

37

The Leadership Takes the Case

....

IN ADDITION TO PENNING A LETTER to the congregation, Oline Muus sought input from the Synod's foremost authority, namely, Herman Amberg Preus. The fifty-five-year-old Preus was a theological expert; for nearly two decades he had been president of the Norwegian Synod. Judging by his photograph, he was large and imposing, his face rough-hewn and beardless, his gaze steady. He looked more like a military officer than a clergyman. His indomitable drive had not diminished over the years; with youthful energy he carried on his work as Synod president and pastor. He and his wife, Linka, had been married for nearly thirty years, and the couple had served as pastor and pastor's wife in Spring Prairie, Wisconsin, for just as long. As posterity has come to know them through Linka Preus's diaries and letters, in their time they must have been seen as an ideal couple.

Throughout all his years in America, Preus had the solid support of Ulrik Vilhelm Koren. Koren was more outgoing and lively than Preus, and he had gained clerical authority and esteem. A photograph testifies that at fifty-four his hair and beard had become gray, but he was by no means lacking in vigor. A cartoonist portraying Pastor Koren would undoubtedly have made a point of his large, protruding ears and bushy beard. Koren was a good listener and spoke well. He had served as the Synod's vice president for five years and was now president of the Iowa District. He was the most powerful man in the Synod after Preus.

It is unclear the type of relationship Oline had with Preus or Koren.

They were obviously close colleagues with Bernt Muus, and it was becoming clear that they had had their fill of the quarrelsome pastor. But would that be enough for them to take a public stand on one side? A series of letters Oline wrote outlines her attempts to solicit their support.

In the first missive, dated April 15, 1880, Oline wrote that she had received many anonymous letters saying that "The Complaint" contained lies. She boldly accused Preus: "You dear chairman of the Norwegian Synod, and many of your brothers in Christ have *spread defamatory accusations against me of the worst kind*." Oline wrote that it was not only Preus who was damaging her reputation, it was also the rest of the Norwegian Synod. Oline pressured Preus to travel to Holden to investigate the case. If he didn't, she threatened to contact a president from another denomination. Oline demanded that Preus prove every word he had said about her.[1]

Oline received a reply written on April 19, in which Preus denied spreading rumors. But the letter wasn't enough to stop her from continuing to use her pen to argue her case, feeling she had not really been heard and that Synod leadership was brushing her off. She continued to write more letters.[2]

In a follow-up a couple of days later, on April 19, Oline stressed that Preus was the one who had spread ugly lies about her all the way to Norway. Oline unapologetically questioned Preus: "Is it you who have brought these rumors out in the world without knowing if it was the truth or lie what was said about me, have you done a great sin against me?" When she confirmed the instigator of these lies, she planned to expose his name and position publicly. Throughout this letter Oline uses male pronouns when referring to the gossiper. Most likely she was trying to intimidate Preus or other members of the Synod, who she believed to have been the instigator(s) of falsehoods against her.[3]

The sharpest letter from Oline to Preus is dated April 20, 1880, in which she stated that she had received three letters and that "my enemies won't be at peace until they have trampled me in the mud." She again requested that Preus come to Holden as soon as possible to get to the bottom of the matter, and further that "I won't accept being treated

Ulrik Vilhelm Koren, date unknown.
Luther College

like the dog of the Norwegian Synod any longer." A woman expressing herself in this way to someone of such authority must have been interpreted as both brazen and shocking. But her words aptly describe the dehumanizing treatment she was experiencing, suggesting that she did not want to be perceived as a woman kept on a leash, forced to always obey her master's orders. Her letter conveys that the Synod leadership saw her as nothing but a misbehaving dog who needed a muzzle and a restraint. At the end of this letter, Oline warned Preus that if she didn't get a response within eight days, she would call a congregational meeting and withdraw from the church.[4]

On May 4, 1880, Oline replied to Pastor Preus. The stationary was small, and her handwriting was large, straight, and even. The day before she had received a letter from Preus through her spokesman, Pastor Biørn. The letter read as an order to appear before the entire congregation to provide proof of the vile accusations she had made against her husband. In reply, Oline again clarified her terms and pointed out that the congregation had set other conditions. In any case, she was willing to attend the meeting, where others would no doubt be encouraged to prove the accusations they had flung against her, both in America and in Norway. She believed that if her husband had behaved like a man and lived like a Christian with his wife, he would have avoided this ugly matter altogether. Now, he had to put up with the consequences and be thankful things hadn't gotten significantly worse.[5]

On the next two pages, Oline gave Preus detailed examples of what her husband required of her, while asking rhetorically if she was obligated to obey him. The examples she listed were clearly of such a nature that they couldn't be made public. But because Preus was the Synod president, Oline felt he should be informed about them. Here, Oline raised new allegations against her husband, ones even more provocative and bizarre than before. He had, on more than one occasion, ordered her to go and muck out the stables. He commanded that everyone in the household should eat the same food as him: namely, cultured milk and bread for breakfast and fried pork for dinner. Her husband also had what she called "peculiarities." Among other things, he ordered her to wear short dresses like a little girl because he fancied such attire. Her

letter maintained that she in no way felt obliged to be made a spectacle among people just to satisfy her husband's tastes. But, what people
couldn't know, she confided in the letter, was that when only her husband was present, she wore the little girl's dresses to please him. When
her husband thought he could not afford to buy coffee, she had to make
it out of wheat. She also wasn't allowed to buy a "milk cupboard" and
had to put the milk pails on the floor in the basement. Imagine, she
had to endure such conditions when she and her husband together had
several thousand dollars in assets.

In short, she could list hundreds and hundreds of such instances.
But she neither could nor would obey her husband's commands. And
if for that reason she was expelled from the Synod, then she was genuinely willing to be thrown out at any time, and as soon as possible.
She added an ironic note: "I think the honorable Synod will fire a shot
that sooner or later it will regret." If the pastors and Synod leadership
didn't want to stand as hypocrites before God, Oline asserted, then
they must be content for their wives to obey their reasonable orders
and not their unreasonable and sinful commands. The Synod's leadership and pastors could ask their wives about this matter, but they had
to know their wives were in the right. "Don't come with commands to
us wives," Oline wrote to Preus and the Synod. Before this church discipline case continued, she advised them all to carefully consider what
they were doing. The clergy and Synod leaders must know that the sin
and shame brought upon her would rest twice as heavily upon them. It
was a warning, a prediction, and an appeal all in one.

At the bottom of the fifth and final page of her letter, Oline noted
that now that she had given her opinion on the situation, she left it to
them to decide what to do. As long as the ecclesiastical process was
ongoing and the civil lawsuit hadn't been decided, Oline had to remain
at the parsonage. If things got too bad there, she had a friend in Østen
Hanson, the pastor in Aspelund, the Haugean church. It was just a
matter of walking to the Hansons', and he would comfort her as best
he could. Hanson also reportedly tried to talk to Pastor Muus, but to
no avail. No sources reveal how Pastor Preus reacted upon receiving
Oline's letter.[6]

A "Spectacle" at the Parsonage

ON MAY 13, SIX WEEKS AFTER the second round of congregational meetings, spring plowing and planting were complete, and the farmers could with clear consciences set aside two days to participate in the third congregational meeting in the Muus case. Although Oline Muus asserted herself through her letters, once in Holden Church she was to remain voiceless.

She had won a silent victory in that the president of the Synod, H. A. Preus, had finally accepted the invitation to attend. Likewise, the Synod's district president Ulrik Koren of Iowa and Pastor Frich, another Synod leader, had also arrived. Finally, the Holden congregation would benefit from outside experts and the highest authority. Why Synod leadership hadn't intervened before is difficult to answer. Were they supporting Mrs. Muus because they wished to control the course of the meeting, to make certain they would not be publicly identified as initiators of the rumors against Oline Muus?

Even before the meeting began, parishioner Ole Gjesme repeated an earlier suggestion: Those who didn't belong to the Synod shouldn't be allowed to attend the meeting. Once again there were clearly more than a few outsiders in attendance at Holden Church. The clergy was very well represented; a total of seven pastors were present. And Mrs. Muus was there; she may have been the only woman in the assembly and was required to remain silent.[1]

There were no objections to Preus leading the meeting. But when the congregation reelected Pastor Biørn as Mrs. Muus's spokesman, Pastor Muus took the floor to protest: A church member under church discipline didn't require a spokesman. If she had sinned, she would have to explain herself to the congregation.

Preus disagreed. After all, the congregation wanted to be helpful to this church member because, naturally, a woman wouldn't want to speak in a public meeting. Preus's first act was to rebuke Pastor Muus and instead show understanding for Mrs. Muus. This pattern would repeat itself several times during the meeting. The Synod hadn't sided unequivocally with Pastor Muus, as *Budstikken* claimed. Perhaps Preus wished, first and foremost, to clear up the matter, to put an end to it. But the church leadership's position concerning Pastor Muus appeared to be a deliberate choice of church politics.

Clearing up the matter was easier said than done. Everyone knew how stubborn Pastor Muus was. In addition, the congregation followed its free church rules faithfully. Even the Synod's president had to respect the congregation's practices. As the meeting chair, Preus had to call for an initial discussion of Gjesme's proposal that the meeting should be closed to the public. Many people signed up to speak, including the strict conservative advocate Nils Raabølle, who agreed that only members of the Synod should be allowed in the meeting. Raabølle felt there had been unpleasant pressure in the previous meetings. It wasn't easy to speak confidentially and sincerely with all kinds of people around you. Ole Solberg agreed: The congregation must be master in its own house. But Pastor Bøckman had misgivings. It might be true that the public meetings had caused harm to both the parties involved and to the congregation, but was the damage so great that the doors had to be closed going forward? And what would be the consequences of excluding outsiders? He declared that the meeting should continue to be open to the public.

The Synod shared this view. According to the powerful Pastor Koren, it would be risky if the doors were suddenly closed. When he first had the floor, he added a startling strong criticism of the congregation. Did the congregation really have the right to bring a case of church discipline against Mrs. Muus? And had she really sinned against

the word of God? Koren couldn't at the outset consider this case to be
one for church discipline. The congregation instead had created what
he deemed "a public scandal." It must have been surprising to most of
those present: District President Koren seemed to support Mrs. Muus.

According to Synod leadership the congregation should have left
the matter to a committee. Both parties, Mrs. and Pastor Muus, should
have been represented by men belonging to the Synod and chosen by
the spouses themselves. This arrangement would have been the correct way to proceed. The committee should have investigated the matter and written a report to the congregation. Afterward, they should
have discussed the matter to determine what the consequences for the
two parties might be. Then the relationship between the spouses would
be investigated internally, out of the public eye. But this setup presupposed that the congregation had had the courage to intervene before
Mrs. Muus decided to go to civil court. That hadn't happened. Pastor
Bøckman was especially responsible for how the situation played out.
Mrs. Muus had shown him attorney Andreas Ueland's reply, and he had
advised her not to present it to the congregation.

Despite the Synod's desire for a committee to handle the case, the
meeting had begun and wouldn't be stopped. After a majority had
decided to keep the meeting open to the public, the actual deliberation
could begin. Initially, Pastor Koren stated he would start at the beginning, by examining what Mrs. Muus's complaint against her husband
actually contained. The meeting's purpose was to take a position on
"The Complaint," to refute it or confirm it. The congregation shouldn't
judge the matter; the goal was to find the reasons for "this deep misery."[2]

But which of Mrs. Muus's complaints was the congregation to deliberate? She had offered at least two. Immediately, this question became
too much for the meeting's chair; Preus was unable to control the
assembly. Hands were constantly in the air. Pastor Muus, Pastor Biørn,
and several others repeatedly expressed and elaborated on their opinions. Chairman Preus's attempts to sort out the confusing amount of
information and viewpoints seemed hopeless. Finally, the majority
concluded that the meeting had not one but two complaints from the
pastor's wife to consider.

In addition, Pastor Biørn had spoken so well on Mrs. Muus's behalf during this discussion that Chairman Preus was even more confused. Should the assembly consider Mrs. Muus or Pastor Muus as the accused? Pastor Biørn couldn't decide that question, as each party was both accuser and accused. The majority of the congregation reached the same conclusion. Accordingly, Mrs. Muus's spokesman had won a great victory almost before the meeting began. Was Pastor Muus a Christian husband? Pastor Biørn suggested the matter be investigated further, and the congregation agreed with him. After that, Biørn could begin to read aloud to the congregation from "The Complaint," with the shocking passages about how Mrs. Muus's husband had behaved at the parsonage regarding her broken leg.

A Doctor, a Horse, and a Crutch

NOW HOLDEN CHURCH TRULY RESEMBLED a courtroom, with pastors as lawyers and parishioners as witnesses and jurors. Mrs. Muus's accounts of the doctor, the horse, and the crutch could be corroborated by several men present at the meeting. Bernt Muus acted as his own defender, while Pastor Biørn acted in defense of the pastor's wife. First, Pastor Biørn told the congregation what Mrs. Muus claimed had happened with her husband when she'd broken her leg twice. The crutch incident came after Oline broke her leg for the second time, during a trip to Faribault. Oline asked her husband to have a neighboring carpenter make a light and comfortable crutch for her. She had previously borrowed a similar crutch from the Heyerdahl Pharmacy in La Crosse, Wisconsin. But the answer was no. Instead, her husband had said that the farmhand could go into the woods and chop down an aspen branch for her to use. Pastor Muus hadn't said anything about possibly getting her something better eventually.[1]

The next story was an even worse example of how ruthlessly Pastor Muus treated his wife. "The account of the doctor and the horse that is told now, is supposedly a misunderstanding. What was happening outside or around me at the time, I only know from what others have told me," Biørn read from Oline's complaint to the congregation. But one thing she remembered clearly: the answer her husband gave when she fervently begged him to fetch the doctor straightaway. She knew there were good doctors nearby in both Cannon Falls and Zumbrota. But Pastor Muus said that since it was soon night, he didn't want to send his farmhand and his horses to get the doctor. His wife should "anoint herself with patience" until the doctor arrived, meaning their family doctor, Just Grønvold, who was visiting a patient out of town.

Biørn concluded his reading with Mrs. Muus's rhetorical question: "Would even an honorable heathen have treated his wife so cruelly?" Farmer Abraham Simpson was called to testify on Oline's behalf. Simpson could confirm that Mrs. Muus's story was true; he was the one who had brought Mrs. Muus home from Faribault after she broke her leg. By the time they arrived at the parsonage it had become dark, and Pastor Muus said they would have to wait until the next morning to fetch a doctor. Simpson had heard what the pastor said to Mrs. Muus: "She had to anoint herself with patience until the doctor came."[2]

As a shrewd defense attorney, Biørn turned to the jury—the members of the congregation. He asked every person to consider how Pastor Muus's words to his wife sounded, for the words were heartless. Even though she was in pain, her husband refused to send for a doctor. Any other husband whose wife was in such a state would have done as she pleaded, even if the doctor couldn't arrive until the next day.

Biørn had barely completed his defense before Pastor Muus asked to speak. He demanded that Mrs. Muus declare to the congregation that what Pastor Biørn said was true. When asked by Chairman Preus if the case was as stated, Oline replied yes, that was how it happened. Spokesman Biørn was at the ready with clarifications. When it was said that Pastor Muus had subjected his wife to cruel and inhumane treatment, it had to be understood as psychological more than physical abuse. Other than that, the facts were clear: Pastor Muus hadn't sent for a doctor. He had forbidden the farmhand and the neighbor from fetching a doctor.

Pastor Muus, already angry, grew furious. The fact was that Mrs. Muus had filed a complaint with the court. When she said he had refused to send for the doctor, it was a lie and slander. He wanted to know who had included the lies in "The Complaint": was it the lawyer or Mrs. Muus? Biørn replied that he knew nothing other than that "The

Complaint" had been submitted to the court without Mrs. Muus having seen or signed it.[3]

Pastor Muus, during one of his angry rebuttals, asked what kind of
Christianity was in a person like Mrs. Muus. He drew a picture of his
wife as a notorious liar, perhaps not quite normal either. For those who
read the minutes, it's difficult to avoid the impression that Bernt Muus's
conduct during the meeting backfired. In the church that day, the pastor appeared in no way to be an exemplary husband. The congregation
was accustomed to their pastor not sparing any harsh or austere words,
but during this meeting he was even more intense.

But then he broke off, explaining that he had something to confess. It must have become silent in the church. The wording in the
minutes is both strangely convoluted and vague. That may be the secretary's fault, or perhaps Pastor Muus was unusually unclear. It seems
the pastor implied there were important things he could have said but
that he withheld out of a consideration for decency. He had pondered
"whether his conscience would permit him to take certain matters up
in public." There were certain things which, for his own sake and that of
Mrs. Muus and the children and their possible descendants, shouldn't
be known to the outside world. He had concluded that, even though it
affected him, it was best to remain silent, an easier choice since it had
consequences only for himself.[4]

He had presented a noble thought. For the time being, Pastor Muus
did not elaborate on what he meant by "certain things." Instead, he gave
his version of what had happened after his wife's accident in Faribault.
She was not well when she arrived home, and many people showed her
compassion. He couldn't vouch for the grievances outlined in her complaint. He simply didn't remember, as he hadn't kept a diary; everything was too vague for him to comment. The skeptics in the meeting
must have registered that Pastor Muus used the world's oldest excuse
to avoid saying any more about the matter. Concerning the story of the
horse and the doctor, he couldn't remember if the neighbor had defied
him or if any neighbor had gone to fetch Dr. Grønvold. In all likelihood, what was said wasn't true, Pastor Muus declared. But, shock-
ingly enough, at the same time he admitted that he hadn't taken care

of his wife—strangers had. He couldn't recall, despite his best efforts, if she had asked him to send for a doctor in Cannon Falls or Zumbrota. He believed it to be something she had thought up later. Likewise, he couldn't remember saying that she should anoint herself with patience. When she came home, he thought he might dare approach her, to speak with her. And in jest he may have used the phrase "anoint herself with patience." But if so, she would need to prove it.

The pastor became more clear when he reached the main point of his defense: his wife's mental state. She had received the care at home that was available. He couldn't approach his wife himself; once again there were "certain reasons" that must remain unsaid. Someone other than Pastor Muus provided Mrs. Muus the care that was at hand. Beyond that, Pastor Muus reminded Mrs. Muus that she had received more medical care than is common in the countryside, more than she could have received in a city, and more than she would have received in a hospital. Doctor Grønvold came to the parsonage often, frequently visiting her several times a day.

40

In Loving Jest

....

When Pastor Muus had finished, Chairman Preus requested clarification on one particular point. How might the phrase "anoint oneself with patience" be understood? The congregation immersed themselves in interpreting what he meant. Parishioner Ole Apeland claimed the expression was common and mustn't be understood as malicious. Pastor Biørn had previously described the expression as heartless; now he stated that not only was the phrase vulgar, from a pastor's mouth it was unseemly. He reminded the congregation that Mrs. Muus was willing to swear on her honor that the words were spoken as she claimed. Preus was sympathetic. He admitted that the phrase "anoint oneself with patience" could be used in various circumstances: the words could be said coldly and harshly, but also in jest.[1]

Pastor Muus took the floor again, and this time he made a confession that really captured everyone's attention. In the past two or three years, he hadn't spoken to Mrs. Muus more than was absolutely necessary. He wasn't going to speculate why that might be. For the third time, he made vague insinuations about his wife: she was neither talkative nor of sound mind; it wasn't appropriate for him to explain why. However, he couldn't recall using the phrase "anoint oneself with patience." But if Mrs. Muus swore that he had said it, he wouldn't object. He also couldn't remember Mrs. Muus asking for messengers to be sent to Cannon Falls or Zumbrota. He returned to a previous point: Was there any truth in a person like Oline Muus? An honorable person would have been ashamed to bring such a scandal down upon their house as she had.

However, the meeting chair didn't give up the pursuit for a common understanding of the disputed words. Pastor Koren took the floor to interpret the phrase with the best intentions, and in doing so, for the first time during the meeting, he defended Pastor Muus. Koren could imagine how, under similar circumstances, he might have comforted his wife with these words spoken in loving jest. He even showed the congregation with gestures and body language how he might have said as much in a loving, playful manner while he stroked Pastor Preus, who was sitting in front of him, on the head. It was theatrical. But when a member of the audience began to applaud, Koren reprimanded him sharply. According to *Budstikken*, the man had clapped his hands in admiration of the performance.

Time after time, Chairman Preus tried to conclude and get the congregation to determine whether Pastor Muus had sinned and neglected his wife or whether Mrs. Muus had sinned and made false accusations. But there was no end to the discussion. When Pastor Biørn, on behalf of Mrs. Muus, declared that he wished to present a new piece of evidence in the case, the chairman was forced into yet another round. First, Pastor Biørn gave a little moralizing recommendation to Pastor Muus. It would be an infinite blessing to Pastor Muus, his household, and the wider community if this matter could teach him to watch his mouth. Pastor Muus's greatest downfall was that he constantly spoke heartlessly.

Then the spokesman continued his attack. Biørn claimed he could prove that Pastor Muus had said the words "anoint yourself with patience" just as Mrs. Muus said he did. Pastor Hansen's wife could testify. She didn't have the right to speak, but Biørn explained that he had brought a written statement from Kristine Hansen, which he would now read aloud. But before he could begin, he was interrupted by Pastor Muus acting as his own defense attorney. "No heathen court would bring in such testimony," Muus proclaimed. An affidavit couldn't be used as evidence when cross-examination wasn't possible.[2]

The meeting chair agreed with Pastor Muus. The statement wasn't allowed to be read aloud. The following day, the congregation's own pastor, Pastor Muus, was scheduled to conduct his cross-examination of witnesses. The account of the doctor and the horse wasn't over. Nevertheless, on May 13 the congregation meeting held a vote on Pastor Koren's motion. Was Pastor Muus guilty of cruel treatment of his wife when he didn't send for the doctor that night? The preliminary verdict was surprisingly unfavorable for the pastor's wife: fifty-seven members believed Mrs. Muus's accusation to be false, while only six members believed it was true.

After the vote, the account of the crutch continued. Pastor Biørn again read aloud from Oline's written defense, about how Pastor Muus had refused her plea for a crutch and said she had to get by with an aspen branch. It was a tasteless expression, spoken coldly and heartlessly, Biørn insisted. He himself had ample opportunities to get used to that kind of speech from Pastor Muus, so he knew the story wasn't improbable. Oline Muus's account could be confirmed by a witness, Johannes J. Kvam, who had worked as a farmhand for Pastor Muus and was present at the meeting.

With that, testimony under oath regarding the aspen branch could begin. Kvam was the first to be called forward. Oddly enough, it was Pastor Muus who questioned the witness. "What is an aspen branch?" Pastor Muus asked his former farmhand, whom he consistently called by his first name. "It's a long stick," Kvam replied, similar to the pole used for drying grain sheaves. Kvam recounted that the pastor had told him to go into the woods, cut down a branch, and make a crutch. He also said that Dr. Grønvold had a carpenter make a good crutch, according to the doctor's own drawing. When Pastor Muus asked where the money came from, Kvam replied that the doctor supplied the materials and paint.

It now became known that Dr. Grønvold had paid for Mrs. Muus's crutch. Things were looking even worse for her husband. Pastor Muus didn't offer commentary on his former farmhand's testimony. He remarked that it wasn't until later, when his wife was recovering, that she had asked about a crutch. He then replied that he didn't have a crutch like the one she asked for, and there was a crutch in the house that he had used earlier. He didn't have anything more to say. The congregation was nearing the end of the proceedings for May 13.[3]

When they began again the following morning, it was difficult to say how much progress had been made. The story of the crutch wasn't over, although the discussion had gone until six in the evening the day before. The tale of the doctor and the horse also demanded a new discussion. And, as the meeting commenced, the minutes from the previous day immediately caused an uproar. Pastor Muus couldn't accept the following wording in the minutes: "When Mrs. Muus arrived home, she was of course carried in." Pastor Muus doubted that he had personally done so, because for certain reasons he was very reluctant to approach her more than absolutely necessary. Pastor Muus insisted he would have never said this. Pastor Biørn stood by his word: the record was correct; that was precisely the account Pastor Muus gave the day before.[4]

However, Pastor Muus insisted on a longer addition to the minutes: "Then I distinctly recall that I went over to Dr. Grønvold's house myself, to find out from his wife, where I might find him. I specifically recall that when I arrived, it was getting dark. I only heard that the doctor was at the Swedish settlement." Pastor Muus remembered far more details on the morning of May 14 than he had the previous day. He now stated that he had inquired about Dr. Grønvold's whereabouts himself. Muus had good reasons for not sending for the doctor because, as he requested the addendum to read: "If a farmhand had been sent to the Swedish settlement, it would have been pitch dark before he got there to look for the doctor. I reminded Mrs. Muus that I had hired people and wouldn't order them to go on such an errand. I don't recall Mrs. Muus asking to send to Cannon Falls or Zumbrota for a doctor. If she did, she would need to provide proof. The doctor didn't touch her broken leg those first few days." Besides, Pastor Muus added, "I didn't know of a doctor in Zumbrota or Cannon Falls with whom I wished to entrust the treatment of Mrs. Muus. Except for Dr. Tibbitts in Cannon Falls, who the congregation probably knows you can't depend on. The doctors I knew and trusted lived in Red Wing, a full twenty-seven miles away. It wasn't reasonable to believe that if a doctor were summoned from that far away that he would arrive before Dr. Grønvold. And if another doctor had come before Dr. Grønvold, he could, as far as I know, do nothing more than give her strong medicine."[5]

41

False Accusation

PASTOR KOREN, WHO HAD TAKEN OVER as meeting chair following Pastor Preus the day before, requested the congregation adopt the
corrections to yesterday's meeting minutes, which would be added as
an appendix. Secretary Nils Ottun apologized for the shortcomings
in the minutes by admitting that he had started writing them at three
that morning. Chairman Koren expressed appreciation, remarking that
Ottun was not a "fast writer." Other speakers also complained about
the minutes of the previous day, that they were misquoted or that their
contributions were omitted. This included Botulf Lie, whom Pastor
Biørn noted was missing from the record. "If anyone in my household
had been in the same condition as Mrs. Muus, whether wife or servant,
yes, even if there had been an Irishman, I would have sent for a doctor,"
Lie had said. With this statement, Lie implied that he would take action
even for someone outside of his religious community, as an Irishman
equated a Catholic. After this comment, Pastor Muus lectured Lie on
the meaning of the word "gossip": When one couldn't furnish proof for
one's hateful assertions, that was gossip.[1]

But Pastor Biørn's opinion was that circumstantial evidence was
the only thing one could furnish for Mrs. Muus's two complaints.
This case concerned family matters, and the assembly must know that
Pastor Muus and his wife were refined people. If there was something
wrong between them, they wouldn't cause a commotion or uproar in
the moment, and so one could only show proof of what had probably

happened. Biørn maintained that it was widely known that Pastor Muus spoke abrasively and that there was a document stating that on another occasion he had used an expression similar to "anoint yourself with patience." Biørn pointed out that he had wanted to present documentation, Mrs. Hansen's testimony, to corroborate Pastor Muus's conduct. But Pastor Muus had refused to allow it and accused Biørn of spreading rumors.[2]

Finally, the congregation could approve the minutes of the previous day's meeting. Chairman Koren encouraged members to come forward and testify about the circumstances surrounding fetching the doctor so that the truth would come out. The assembly also determined that the witnesses should be cross-examined—by Pastor Muus himself. It was a bizarre arrangement. As if in a court of law, Pastor Muus acted as if he were a lawyer and cross-examined witnesses under oath. He started with religion schoolteacher Ole Solberg, who stated that he knew the farmhand went east to get Dr. Grønvold and claimed that Muus had described the direction the doctor was believed to have traveled.

MUUS: Was that before or after Mrs. Muus had arrived home?

SOLBERG: Before.

MUUS: He traveled east and fast?

SOLBERG: Yes.

MUUS: Solberg didn't see him return, as long as he was in the parsonage?

SOLBERG: No.

MUUS: Can Solberg recall if others were present?

SOLBERG: Ole H. Huset, Pastor Bøckman, Karl Heggernäs, and the farmhand, named Jacob.

Then it was Ole Huset's turn. "What could Huset recall from the parsonage at the time?" Muus asked. "Did anyone leave to fetch the doctor after learning that he wasn't at home?" "Yes," answered Huset. He didn't remember who told him, but he assumed it was Solberg. Then, Pastor Muus continued his cross-examination of Abraham Simpson, Pastor Bøckman, and, once again, Ole Huset.

After a thorough and demanding round of questions regarding the fetching of the doctor, it was Pastor Muus's turn to be cross-examined by Mrs. Muus's spokesman. A note that two doctors in Faribault had written about how they had treated Mrs. Muus quickly became important to the discussion. Biørn explained that the note for Dr. Grønvold had arrived at the parsonage with the man who helped carry Mrs. Muus from the wagon into the house. The man gave the note to Nils, Mrs. Muus's son. Nils went to the doctor's house, where he handed the note to the doctor's male guest named Janson. They had believed that Janson had ridden after Dr. Grønvold to give him the note, but he didn't return until three in the afternoon the following day. The doctor had arrived home two hours earlier. Biørn summed up: Had Pastor Muus done everything in his power to summon the doctor? It was known that Muus had sent a farmhand after the doctor, but the farmhand's whereabouts were presently unknown. That evening when Mrs. Muus requested a new messenger to fetch the doctor, her husband said no. He wouldn't send his farmhands out on "a fool's errand."[3]

Biørn was interrupted by Pastor Muus, who unusually enough admitted a mistake. He said that in fact he could have asked the farmhand to fetch the doctor. After claiming that victory, Biørn continued tirelessly: Muus did "nothing positive" to send for the doctor. Instead, it was Mrs. Muus who had to send a messenger, Janson, the doctor's guest, who took the note with him. And Janson didn't go to the parsonage to ask Pastor Muus to lend him his horses. Janson went to a neighbor, and it was in fact the neighbor—not Janson—who went after the doctor. According to Biørn, the inevitable conclusion was that the doctor's guest and the neighbor had done more for Mrs. Muus than Pastor Muus had done.

Chairman Koren agreed entirely with Biørn—and again took sides against Pastor Muus. Nevertheless, Koren had something to say regarding the note, and on this point, he defended the pastor. What had happened leading up to fetching the doctor that actually caused harm? He advanced an imaginary hypothesis, with the Synod's marriage doctrine as the premise: If Mrs. Muus had been patient and obeyed those she should obey, things would have gone better. The note wouldn't have gone astray with Janson but would instead have remained there until the doctor's return. If Mrs. Muus had listened to her husband, Dr. Grønvold would have known at once how she had been treated in Faribault. But Grønvold didn't have this information because when he finally came to the parsonage to treat Mrs. Muus, the note wasn't there. The note didn't reach him until later, so Mrs. Muus, by acting on her own, had hindered Dr. Grønvold from giving her the best treatment.

It was a strange intellectual maneuver: Koren was clear that Pastor Muus hadn't done enough for his spouse when she needed it. In that respect, Pastor Muus was guilty. But if Mrs. Muus had simply followed the Synod's teachings and done as her husband said—in spite of his obvious sins and lack of empathy—the result would still have been better. Who should be blamed in retrospect: the heartless pastor or the disobedient pastor's wife? The congregation must have been completely bewildered.

Pastor Bøckman added his name to the list of speakers. As the pastor's wife's former confidant and the unfortunate leader of the first congregational meeting, what he had to say would be crucial to how the rest of the meeting proceeded. Bøckman took the floor to make a confession. He had to admit that he had long been silent on what he knew about Mrs. Muus. He hadn't said anything for her sake, but he couldn't in good conscience remain silent any longer. Bøckman declared that Oline Muus lied about her husband not trying to fetch the doctor.

According to Bøckman, Mrs. Muus had long ago learned that Pastor Muus had in fact ordered someone to find the doctor. Yet, in court, she had come up with quite a different story. On January 17 or 18, after the clergy meeting in Red Wing, Bøckman was at the Holden parsonage. In the presence of the couple's eldest son, Nils, Bøckman had asked Mrs. Muus about getting the doctor. When Bøckman asked Nils if his mother's account was true, Nils said no, his father had indeed tried to contact a doctor. This statement caused Mrs. Muus, who sat there listening to her son's account, to exclaim, "I didn't know this before. You should have told me this before, and not after the fact."

Immediately after her lawsuit and Complaint had been sent to the court, Mrs. Muus heard that her husband had done the right thing and sent someone after the doctor. But she failed to remove this serious point from "The Complaint"; it remained, even though she knew it wasn't true. Mrs. Muus had not only lied, she had falsely accused her husband.

Bøckman now turned and confronted Mrs. Muus directly on this point. He asked Oline if what Nils had told them both in January was true. Mrs. Muus admitted that it was. Confessing in the meeting was the same as admitting that she had lied when she wrote in "The Complaint" that her husband hadn't sent for the doctor. Pastor Bøckman declared to the assembly that Mrs. Muus acknowledged that, on this point, "The Complaint" was false.

A collective sigh of relief must have gone through the congregation. Mrs. Muus's spokesman, Pastor Biørn, said nothing. Pastor Muus said nothing. After the meeting chairman Koren composed himself, he turned to Mrs. Muus once more and asked her to ponder what the inevitable conclusion might be after she had admitted that Bøckman's account was true. If she had been made aware in January that she had made a false accusation and hadn't withdrawn it then, Koren left it to her to consider how serious this infraction was.

42

The Question of Blame

FOLLOWING THIS DRAMATIC REVELATION, Pastor Koren decided a forty-five-minute break was in order. He took the opportunity to talk to Pastor Preus and the other clergymen, including Pastor Muus. When the meeting began again, the chairman invited Mrs. Muus to make a confession regarding this serious detail. Oline Muus had been caught in a lie. Koren asked the congregation to consider how they should handle the situation.

When the Holden congregation adjourned the meeting several hours later, at 5:30 in the evening on May 14, Koren's summary was clear. Instead of focusing on the revelations that had come to light and how they influenced the case, he returned to the procedural point he had formulated the previous day: A reasonable examination of the relationship between Mrs. Muus and Pastor Muus was difficult to carry out by an assembly as large as the congregation. As had already been experienced, even with participants' goodwill, the investigation would take far too long. The congregation couldn't act as the fact-finding committee. Besides, it was in the Synod's best interest to avoid more publicity about the Muuses' personal affairs. Acting on a suggestion from the Synod's leadership, the meeting voted to establish an investigative committee. This committee's report should be the basis for the congregation's further consideration of the matter. Nothing more definite was said about the case at hand. Future church meetings would be closed to outsiders. The scandalous case in Holden needed to be brought under control—and to an end—as soon as possible.[1]

The Synod might have judged the matter to be a family disagreement. They may have thought that Mrs. Muus was to blame because she hadn't brought the matter to the congregation earlier. Her demand for money was unprecedented. She should never have filed a civil lawsuit against her husband. At the same time, Pastor Muus had been grossly thoughtless when he called his congregations to an open meeting. He initiated a public process that disgraced both the congregation and the Synod. The way the Muuses spoke about each other in public was deplorable; they were the exact opposite of an exemplary Christian couple. The Synod had a contentious issue on its agenda which required a swift solution. It concerned the Synod's honor—or rather, their leaders' impulse was to avoid further disgrace.

The marriage of Bernt and Oline Muus was an unhappy one. But which of the parties was to blame? Was anyone capable of mediating between them? After receiving the investigative committee's report, would the congregation be able to do anything to resolve the family dispute? A peaceable outcome must have been the Synod's secret hope, as it held marriage to be sacred and unbreakable and separation and divorce was sacrilege.

It was natural that Pastors Bøckman and Biørn, who had participated in the proceedings from the beginning, would serve on the investigative committee. Chairman Koren urged them to examine the case's testimony carefully. The committee consisted of fifteen men, all of whom belonged to the Synod: three chosen by Pastor Muus, three by Mrs. Muus, six by the congregation, and three pastors: Biørn, Bøckman, and August Hansen.[2]

The May 14, 1880, meeting minutes also document that neither Mrs. Muus nor Pastor Muus wished for the matter to be considered by a committee. Through spokesman Pastor Biørn, Mrs. Muus stated that she preferred to testify before the entire congregation. Pastor Muus insisted that the congregation should continue the church discipline case against Mrs. Muus, his consistent strategy after the first meeting.

Today's new information had strengthened his case considerably, so it must have been frustrating that the meeting still didn't go in his favor.

Pastor Muus was quite critical of his congregation and his colleagues. The way the matter had been handled had, unfortunately, yielded the most unpleasant consequences for the congregation and relationships among church members. In the future, Pastor Muus stated, the congregation must be led by God's word and rely upon clear testimonies. If nothing was proven, the congregation couldn't make a judgment.

In the end, Pastor Muus's congregation listened to the Synod. Pastor Muus clearly won the most votes in specific motions brought before the congregation, but this time it was a painful loss. The members with voting rights included about forty men, and they decided unanimously that an investigative committee should be established. Pastor Muus hadn't gotten his way.

About a week later, on May 25, 1880, *Budstikken* printed its commentary on the meeting's decision. For outsiders, the composition of the committee was of great interest. The committee members were duly considered: were they for or against Mrs. Muus?

Budstikken had only good things to say about Ludvig M. Biørn, who had been chosen as the committee's chair. Although Pastor Biørn had been Mrs. Muus's spokesman in the meetings, he had generally given the impression of impartiality. Thanks to him, the persecution of Mrs. Muus initiated by the congregation—under the guise of church discipline—was suspended. He had also made it clear that he didn't share Pastor Muus's understanding of a wife's obedience. *Budstikken* believed Mrs. Muus was in safe hands. Pastor Biørn was a straightforward, independent, and honest character; it seemed likely he would fulfill his obligations. According to *Budstikken*, as committee chair, he made certain that the implicit influence of Mrs. Muus's opponent couldn't be abused.

The second of the three pastors, August Hansen, was also given a favorable evaluation by *Budstikken*. He had hardly been mentioned in connection with the case, but he probably shared Biørn's personal interpretation of the scriptures. In the other corner, however, was Marcus Bøckman. Pastor Bøckman had not only supported Pastor Muus in everything, *Budstikken*'s editor believed, he had also been staunchly instrumental in creating the impression that Mrs. Muus was to blame. For the time being, there was nothing to indicate that Bøckman would change his mind. It was presumably safe to consider him one of Pastor Muus's men.[3]

This assessment was also true of Peder Langemo, one of the three parishioners chosen by Pastor Muus to participate in the committee. *Budstikken* concluded that Langemo had been faithful to his pastor at all the meetings where the newspaper had the opportunity to consider his participation. He said he was convinced of Pastor Muus's innocence, and he regarded Mrs. Muus's conduct with anything but an impartial view. *Budstikken* predicted Andrew Finseth would likely investigate the matter with integrity, with an intent to find the truth. During previous meetings Finseth's demeanor was calm and patient; he had followed the course of events without allying himself to either party. Still, it was assumed Finseth would still side with his pastor. *Budstikken* didn't comment on Pastor Muus's third appointed man, Erik E. Sævereide, nor is he found among the speakers in the meeting's minutes.

The newspaper's knowledge of the three parishioners chosen by Mrs. Muus was sparse. The first, Thom Rygh, belonged to one of the respected families in Goodhue County and was known for his thoughtfulness. The second, Osmund Wing, had from the beginning proved to be a freethinking and independent man, though his participation in the proceedings had been insignificant. *Budstikken* didn't comment on the third of Mrs. Muus's chosen men, Karl Andersen. But the paper lambasted the six members of the committee chosen by the congregation from its own. With the exception of Botulf Lie, and perhaps Nils F. Fenne, they all backed Pastor Muus. The remaining four, Ole H. Huset, Abraham Simpson, Ole Solberg, and Ole Erager, had so far followed their pastor through thick and thin, the newspaper claimed. *Budstikken* was in no doubt as to which of the parties they would support. The congregation could not have chosen more fanatical followers of Pastor Muus than these four. All in all, concluded *Budstikken*, Pastor Muus had a decided majority on the investigative committee. The report the committee eventually delivered would most certainly favor Pastor Muus.

When *Budstikken* prejudged the committee report, it was obviously a final push in the campaign to win public approval for Mrs. Muus. Editor Luth Jæger also created new, provocative news stories out of earlier reports. Pastor Koren's behavior at the May 13 meeting in Holden showcased his acting skills, for which he really deserved acknowledgment. Here *Budstikken* was referring to the scene when Koren had tried to demonstrate how one might, in a friendly manner, "anoint oneself with patience." In church, the performance had even been met with spontaneous applause. It was a lovely sight when one venerable leader stroked the other on the head, wrote Jæger, and it will be long remembered. But there had been a secret agenda behind the performance. Koren asserted that Pastor Muus had lovingly said "anoint oneself with patience," and the congregation had allowed Koren to persuade them. The Synod also made sure that Pastor Muus could refuse to present testimony that might result in allegations, such as the statement by Pastor Hansen's wife that had been thrown out. It's odd that Biørn tolerated this treatment, the report mused. "We dare say that Pastor Muus, if he had been in Biørn's position, wouldn't have been so restrained," wrote Jæger.

With this editorial commentary, Jæger wrote the last chapter of *Budstikken*'s editorial coverage of the matter between the spouses in the spring of 1880. But the story soon gained new life in a new format when the newspaper published a pamphlet entitled "Mrs. Oline Muus contra Pastor Muus," a collection of all its articles on the topic. This collection, thirty-five densely printed pages published while the case awaited verdict, testifies to the tremendous interest the scandalous case aroused. A short announcement noted that new subscribers who paid for *Budstikken* at least six months in advance would receive the pamphlet for free.[4]

43

Staging the Scandal

IN THE SPRING OF 1880 Marcus Thrane engaged in a dramatic writing frenzy. The result was a libretto for a Norwegian-language operetta entitled *Holden (eller: vær tålmodig! En Synode-opera i tre akter)* [*Holden (or: Be Patient! A Synod Opera in Three Acts)*]. It wasn't the first time Thrane had been involved with musical theater; in the late 1860s, he was a house playwright for his own Norwegian Theater of Marcus Thrane in Chicago. Terje Leiren notes that "the original plays of Marcus Thrane were probably among the most significant Norwegian-American literary works produced in America at this time. His plays not only represented the author's own vision, but also echoed the voices of Norwegian immigrants in their desire to accommodate themselves to their new home while remembering the land they left behind." The Muus case "not only stirred anew Thrane's ire at the church and fired his satirical sense of humor, but also appears to have been directly responsible for bringing him out of his self-imposed semi-retirement." In *Holden (or: Be Patient!)* Oline Muus became the tragic heroine, the wife who must undergo ever-new trials in her prison of a parsonage.[1]

Thrane's opera was an "opera comique," or what in England and America would soon become known as a musical. One example was Chicago's newest audience attraction, *H.M.S. Pinafore; or The Lass that Loved a Sailor*. The play, which premiered in London in the spring of 1878, created music history and was a thundering success. With great

sarcasm, lyricist W. S. Gilbert and composer Arthur Sullivan enter-
tained the public with scathing criticism of their own native land, the
queen of the British Empire. On board her majesty's warship, the heroine's love must be put to the test. Upper-class arranged marriages are
scrutinized, and until the very end the public is kept in suspense about
how the heroine fares. She gets the seaman she loves and the admiral,
the villain of the play, gets what he deserves.

Thrane, who may have seen *H.M.S. Pinafore* as early as 1879, was
undoubtedly also inspired by the play's social criticism. In Thrane's
Holden, just as in the real-life community, Mr. Bernt and Mrs. Bernt
were easily recognizable characters, as were others, such as the parishioners Ole Nauteby and Mr. Galgeberg and the pastors Ole Toskeberg,
Peter Ræveland, and Søren Fårelund. Thrane skillfully wove incidents
from "The Complaint" into his libretto. The second act, in which the
meeting's proceedings take place, is as if taken directly from articles in
Budstikken.

The opening scene is priceless. Mr. Press, an American newspaper
reporter, arrives in Holden, where he has been informed the Norwegian
congregation will be meeting. Outside the church, Mr. Press attempts
to talk to Ola Nauteby, who doesn't answer because he understands
only Norwegian, although he was born in Goodhue County, Minnesota, and has never been to Norway. Still, Thrane takes the liberty of
concocting a conversation between the American and the American-
born Norwegian. "Why in the hell should Ola learn English? The pastor," he explains, "forbids children to go to the public school, where the
devil's offspring attend."[2]

Then Mr. Press inquires whether Ola has heard of a pastor who has
been very cruel to his wife. "Cruel?" asks Ola. "What kind of talk is
that? A pastor must teach his wife to obey, for she has sinned against
the fourth commandment."

There's no way Ola can agree with Mr. Press, who believes Mr. Bernt
is the sinner because he broke the seventh commandment and took
$4,000 that belonged to Mrs. Bernt. The conversation ends with Ola
following Mr. Press to the saloon, where Ola is a regular.

In order to create further amusement in the plot, Thrane invented

Marcus Thrane, 1883.
Courtesy Norwegian Labour Movement Archives and Library

a German saloon owner, Schweinigel, and his daughter, Kätchen. The nationality was hardly coincidental, as the Norwegian Synod had received help and advice through the years from the German Lutherans in the Missouri Synod. Thus, Thrane was able to suggest that Norwegian and German Lutherans are cut from the same cloth. They allow themselves to be bullied by their clergy, retain their mother tongue and insist theirs is the best language in the world, and have no knowledge other than what their synod's religious school teaches. In addition, young people had to marry someone who belonged to their own church. It was a double standard, and Thrane intended to convey that religious dogma and fanaticism produce double standards.

While Mr. Press drinks beer in the saloon with Ole Nauteby and his thirsty comrades, he hears that Kätchen, a devilishly beautiful girl, has been visited by the pastor. According to this line of gossip, it seems the pastor wasn't solely concerned with converting her. Kätchen had confided to a friend that Mr. Bernt wanted to marry her when his wife died. The source was not entirely reliable, but as one of the beer-thirsty men says, "there's no smoke without fire."

Was there a hint of truth in what Thrane was insinuating: that the real-life Muus case also had a scandal behind the scandal, namely, adultery? Many rumors abounded in Pastor Muus's congregations, including one that Mrs. Muus had an affair with their family doctor and neighbor, Dr. Grønvold. But it's questionable whether the village gossip from Goodhue County reached as far as Chicago, where Thrane lived. It's an open question whether Thrane, in his eagerness to defend Mrs. Muus, had motive to turn the rumors of adultery against her husband.[3]

The premiere on Saturday, June 5, 1880, at Aurora Turner Hall in Chicago was packed to the rafters. The printed program tempted with the very latest news in the theater world; the American guest singer Miss Rawel was set to perform, and there would be a ball after the show. Miss Rawel in the role of Kätchen surpassed expectations. According to a review in the newspaper *Skandinaven*, she delighted the audience with her beautiful, clear, and full-bodied voice. During the performance, there was incessant laughter and applause, and later thunderous curtain calls for the play's author. The audience also appreciated the many comic scenes and dialogue, in addition to the powerful satire of the Synod in particular and Norwegian Americans in general.[4]

On Sunday, July 18, *Holden* was performed once again in Chicago, only to be quickly forgotten. As the final number of the choir praising freedom and progress faded, the audience and the play's many actors continued to enjoy themselves; the ball afterward lasted until four o'clock the next morning. It would be more than 125 years before *Holden* was published in English.[5]

Thrane had also returned to an earlier project that centered on Norwegian-Lutheran orthodoxy in America: *Den Gamle Wisconsin Bibelen [The Old Wisconsin Bible]*. Individual chapters had already been published in a serial in *Dagslyset [The Light of Day]*, the Norwegian American freethinkers' paper, in 1870 and 1872, without creating a fuss. But when Thrane published the entire work in 1881, *The Old Wisconsin Bible* triggered an uproar. In grandiloquent Old Testament style, Thrane portrayed a tyrannical synod clergy and foolish congregations. His satirical biblical pastiche reached far beyond the ranks of freethinkers and was constantly issued in new editions.

Thrane had most likely read *A Doll's House*, Henrik Ibsen's latest contemporary drama, when it was released in 1879. The play had received a very mixed reception, but liberal men and women read it as part of the women's cause. Ibsen had come down on the side of women's rights, with the main character, Nora, rebelling against marriage's sacred foundation and society's bigoted conventions. She pushes back against her husband, the man who treats her like a child, a doll in a dollhouse, Ibsen's metaphor for the humiliating and demoralizing conditions by which a married woman, legally a minor under Norwegian law, had to abide.

Thrane, who had already written plays in favor of women's rights in the 1860s, may simply have seen a Nora in Oline. In both *Holden* and *The Old Wisconsin Bible*, the Oline character shows an increasingly stronger opposition to her husband, Bernt; to the Synod; and to the dogmatic marriage doctrine before she finally emerges as a woman with the courage of her own convictions.

In Thrane's staging of the Muus case, the Oline character becomes, for a brief moment, a Nora. During a marital exchange, Mrs. Bernt bursts out that she will leave her husband to end twenty years of suffering. But since she doesn't dare leave, she has to endure even more cruelty from him. He refuses to buy ointment at the pharmacy to relieve the pain in her leg, telling her instead that she must anoint herself with patience. The Synod and the congregation offer Mr. Bernt unwavering support, while Mrs. Bernt is put under church discipline. As the pastor and parishioners in the musical interpreted it, she had been destroyed by American ways of thinking and the dangerous education of the time.

In one of the dialogues between the spouses, Bernt, who has found a washbowl broken because his wife left it overnight with water in it, exclaims: "Woman! Woman! What must I do with you? Haven't you read yet, that the wife should be submissive to her husband, and never insist on her rights?" To that Oline, who has become hardened, replies: "I have no more patience with which to anoint myself, and I refuse to believe that a husband has such a right over his wife. Give me my four thousand shekels of silver, and I'll go left, while you go to the right."[6]

In *The Old Wisconsin Bible*, the fictitious Oline, like the housewife Nora, realizes her marriage has been a delusion. But unlike Nora, who leaves her husband and child, Oline stays at home with her tyrannical spouse. Her choice must have disturbed Thrane, yet he didn't equip Oline with a suitcase or allow her the irrevocable words of farewell.

Case Dismissed

AS WEEKS PASSED and summer set in, from the investigative committee there was nothing but silence. This time no one leaked "news" about
the work of interrogating the spouses or the various witnesses. On
June 16–23, 1880, when the Minnesota District Synod held a meeting
in Le Sueur River Church in New Richland, Minnesota, the committee's report was the last item on a long agenda. Among the points the
meeting discussed were the Synod's doctrine on the spiritual authority
of the clergy and the Synod's stance on alcohol and the temperance
movement. On the afternoon of the second day, it was time to take
up the report from the Holden congregation. According to *Evangelisk
Luthersk Kirketidende*'s concise news story, the delegates discussed how
the Synod should approach Mrs. Muus's case against her husband and
Pastor Muus's accusations against her. But the case, or rather the consideration of the recommendation, was postponed.[1]

A fortnight later, on July 7–9, Pastor Muus convened a meeting in
Holden Church where the congregation was presented with the investigative committee's report. Six months had passed since Mrs. Muus's
case against her husband had been made public. What conclusions had
the fifteen members of the investigative committee drawn? None. Or,
as *Evangelisk Luthersk Kirketidende* noted, the committee hadn't been
able to come to any conclusion in the case. Incidentally, the report was
written by Pastors Preus, Koren, Frich, and, remarkably enough, Muus.

The committee's work resulted in not conclusions but rather resolutions, three in all.[2]

The lack of conclusions was certainly due to Mrs. Muus, who actively sabotaged the committee's work. She refused to respond when the committee attempted to meet with her. She refused to do anything until the lawsuit regarding her inheritance had been brought before the civil court and the verdict had been reached. Only then was she willing to appear before the church committee. Obviously, procrastination was now Mrs. Muus's plan. She sought to postpone the congregation's work so that the civil court could have the decisive word. After all, Mrs. Muus had already attended the congregational meetings several times, and she had appeared in front of the congregation and written a complaint to them. But after the meeting in mid-May, her strategy had changed.

In the end, however, Mrs. Muus met with the investigative committee. She had even provided written statements from witnesses, though she refused to disclose their names to the committee. Apparently, some of the witnesses had said they wanted to remain anonymous. When the committee held a meeting on a neighboring farm, three witnesses came forward. However, they said they hadn't forbidden Mrs. Muus to give their names. While one of the witnesses was waiting to be questioned, Mrs. Muus had come up to him and said, "You can go, you have no business here!"[3]

This tale was reported in *Evangelisk Luthersk Kirketidende*, which also printed a summary of the committee's resolutions. The committee stated that Mrs. Muus was guilty of three sins. First, she had made false and unjust accusations against her husband. Second, instead of confessing her sin and repenting, she had accused the congregation of being biased and untruthful. She even blamed the Synod, which hadn't done anything against her. Third, Mrs. Muus had refused to appear before the investigative committee and had also refused to present witnesses. This last resolution was demonstrably not true, but when she finally arrived, she was clearly reluctant.

At the congregational meeting on July 7–9, the three resolutions were read aloud to Mrs. Muus before the congregation admonished her to confess her sin and repent. The congregation also asked her to speak up, "lest God's word judge over those who wouldn't hear the congregation, should apply to her." This wording was crafty, a hint that the church had considered her excommunication. For the time being, the congregation would be satisfied with admonishing Mrs. Muus. According to the report in *Evangelisk Luthersk Kirketidende*, the congregation voted to give Mrs. Muus a transcript of the committee's resolutions. With that, they considered the matter closed.

Why hadn't the church discipline case ended in excommunication? Perhaps the congregation wished to avoid further public scandal. Since the beginning of January, *Budstikken*'s editor Luth Jæger had predicted that Mrs. Muus would be excommunicated: Should the congregation really admit that his assessment was right? That the pastor's wife was allowed to remain a member of the congregation testified instead to a community that took human considerations into account. In an attempt to preserve its public reputation, the Holden congregation paradoxically needed Mrs. Muus.

"The Complaint"—or rather the two complaints—that directed terrible accusations against the congregation and the Synod remained in force. The congregation got nowhere with Mrs. Muus. Pastor Muus wasn't easy to deal with either. At the meeting on July 7–9, "Pastor Muus's relationship with the person in question" was the second item on the agenda. First, the congregation requested the pastor explain his relationship with his wife, specifically "the extraordinary behavior" he had shown during the May 13–14 meeting, when he had said he hadn't spoken to his wife more than absolutely necessary for the past two or three years. Furthermore, he stated he wouldn't elaborate on the reasons for his conduct. He believed his rationale would become sufficiently apparent in due course.

As before, Pastor Muus replied in vague and abstract terms. It was his view that "such a relationship, which in ordinary circumstances would be a great sin, could in exceptional cases, be a duty." When no more could be said, he had sought to win his spouse by behaving piously. One thing he was certain of: he hadn't filed a case against his wife, nor would he.

But he reminded the congregation that Mrs. Muus had admitted to lying; she had proven herself to be a liar and malicious. And, he added, it was certainly not something she had become in one day or one year. Despite his own shortcomings and weaknesses, the pastor had nevertheless striven to live as a Christian spouse, following the same word of God that he asked his wife to.[4]

The congregation couldn't possibly have been satisfied with his answer. They had requested an explanation of Pastor Muus's testimony from the previous meeting; instead, he had again used his wife to excuse his own behavior. Before the meeting adjourned on the morning of the third day, the congregation deliberated whether the pastor should be suspended temporarily until the court had given its ruling. As recorded in *Evangelisk Luthersk Kirketidende*, a majority once again voted that he be allowed to remain in his position. The Holden congregation was attached to its pastor; there's no doubt about that.[5]

With that, the Synod's paper wrote about the Muus case for the very last time. The Holden congregation had now concluded a long and cumbersome judicial process—without coming to any conclusion. The question of guilt hadn't been settled. The congregation got nowhere with Mrs. Muus, and Pastor Muus remained in his position. The only thing that had emerged from the congregation's consideration of the Muus case was public scandal.

45

A New Judge Presides

....

THAT SAME SUMMER, Pastor Muus and the Synod received another intense round of press. On June 24, 1880, the *Red Wing Argus*, one of the local English-language newspapers in Goodhue County, caused an uproar when it asserted that the Norwegian Lutheran Church intended to institute ecclesiastical courts in America, where this type of court didn't exist. When a church only observed its own laws, it was an affront both to the country's legal system and to the constitutional right to religious freedom. The *Red Wing Argus* was merciless. It sarcastically posed the question: "What is the use in trying to prove anything before a jury whose verdict is made up beforehand?"[1]

Likewise, the *Goodhue County Republican* reported that it seemed Bernt Muus "was simply canonized and she [was] stamped . . . as a malicious liar of the deepest dye."[2]

On July 15, 1880, the *Red Wing Argus* went further, stating, "What was done during the three days session is yet unknown to the public. It was very likely some dirty business they had to deal with. Perhaps confessions of adultery or some bastardly cases of which those ecclesiastical courts claim jurisdiction." In the same edition, the paper published a translation of a letter sent to the Chicago *Skandinaven* and printed on June 29 which described Pastor Muus as "a fit subject for the bad place commonly called h—."[3]

However, the question of legal jurisdiction meant that the case of *Muus v. Muus* was also difficult for lawyers to predict. Would Minnesota

Georg Sverdrup, 1875.
MNHS collections

state law be the basis for the verdict? Before Pastor Muus could be judged, Mrs. Muus's lawsuit had to be approved by the Minnesota District Court in Goodhue County. But since neither the plaintiff nor the defendant were American citizens, it wasn't evident that the lawsuit would be heard there. The outcome could be that the judge dismissed the lawsuit because it concerned two Norwegian citizens. In that case, Oline Muus would no longer have a claim: current Norwegian law stipulated that Pastor Muus had the right to be his wife's guardian and manage her paternal inheritance as he had done until now.

Time passed. Summer turned into autumn, and then winter. Pending the court's decision, speculation and rumors had free rein among the public, and anyone could form new judgments. And then, in the last month of the year, a new someone entered the debate—and not just anyone. Since 1874, Georg Sverdrup had been president of the Conference Synod and a professor at Augsburg Seminary in Minneapolis. In December 1880, the Conference's journal, *Lutheraneren og Missionsbladet [The Lutheran and the Mission Paper]*, with Professor Sverdrup as editor, printed an explosive article in defense of Mrs. Muus. The text was sensational but perhaps not so surprising, as the Conference Synod had for years been very critical of the Norwegian Synod's dogma and zeal. Sverdrup could no longer remain silent; he had to speak on behalf of the Norwegian people and the Norwegian Lutheran Church in America.

The article stated that the way the case was handled was under so much criticism because it wasn't Mrs. Muus's case; it was Pastor Muus's case. Pastor Muus was the culprit, and he should have been defrocked a long time ago. A church that acted like the Synod had couldn't call itself the Church of Jesus Christ was Professor Sverdrup's verdict. Every Christian must have heartfelt sympathy for the wife of Pastor Muus, Sverdrup wrote. Her life seemed to be like a reed crushed under the weight of her domestic misfortune. No Christian could fail to feel the Church's sting of the ridicule in this matter, Sverdrup believed. The Synod had brought sorrow and shame upon the Norwegian people, sorrow in every Christian heart, and shame to every man.[4]

Not only the congregation but also the clergy should be blamed, since they sought to evade the responsibilities imposed upon them by the free church's laws. The Synod had a twisted understanding of what a free church is. Sverdrup referred to Paul's words that the overseer—that is, the pastor—should rule his household well and have obedient children with all honor. Apparently, neither the Synod nor Pastor Muus's congregations were familiar with this biblical passage, Sverdrup commented sarcastically. If a pastor can't preside over his own household, how can he provide for God's congregation? Neither the members of the congregation nor the Synod's leaders had seen the matter in its proper light: the disgraceful situation in Pastor Muus's home was his own fault.[5]

According to Sverdrup, Holden Church and the Synod had mishandled their duty. The congregation should have examined the main point of Mrs. Muus's lawsuit—the circumstances surrounding her claim to her paternal inheritance and to what extent her husband was at fault in that the suit had been filed at all. Why had Mrs. Muus taken the drastic step of suing her own husband? Did Pastor Muus live in keeping with God's word and "Love's eternal laws"? Did he, as befits a Christian, care for his family? Sverdrup believed the Holden congregation and the Synod's leaders should have focused on these questions. If the congregation had approached the matter properly and investigated it as Pastor Muus's case, perhaps a reconciliation between the couple could have been managed. Then, a court trial could have been avoided, and the congregation wouldn't have had a church discipline case against Mrs. Muus either.[6]

Professor Sverdrup doubted whether the congregation had any right at all to sentence Mrs. Muus to church discipline. He didn't have anything positive to say about the so-called investigative committee either. It was downright disgraceful that Pastor Muus had been involved in drafting the committee's report. It should be unheard of that the guilty party was involved in convicting the innocent. The whole case gave a terrible impression of a long, hateful victimization of the pastor's wife. Sverdrup was certain Mrs. Muus had the right of the miserable and oppressed. She had been wronged, violated, trampled upon, scorned, and treated with coldness and unkindness. Her own husband had called her vicious and deceitful.[7]

Given these heart-wrenching words, Professor Sverdrup hoped the Synod and the Holden congregation would reexamine closely the case of Pastor Muus and suspend him from his position. Only then would the two spouses be able to come to an agreement—or as Sverdrup put it in *Lutheraneren og Missionsbladet*, only then could their hearts be drawn to reconciliation and the peace of God shine in their unhappy, broken home.

46

Not Much Merriment

···

JUST AFTER THE NEW YEAR, the big day finally arrived. On January 5, 1881, more than twelve months after the lawsuit was first filed, the case of *Muus v. Muus* came before the Goodhue District Court in Red Wing. Residents were beside themselves. Since 1859, when the newly married couple arrived in Red Wing, the town had grown substantially. Several magnificent public buildings were constructed, including the courthouse on Oak Street, an impressive two-story brick building in heavy Romanesque style, with a towering, wide stone staircase leading up to the main entrance and a dome that rivaled the neighboring Presbyterian church. Red Wing had stores of all kinds, with lively shopping streets lining the boardwalk. There were hotels with restaurants and even more saloons. Milling was the city's most important commercial enterprise, although industrialization had long since begun. In 1860, the first of many shoe factories had been founded, and by 1881, the Red Wing Stoneware Company had been in business for three years. The city's pottery and leather boots had become popular American brands. The Haugean Synod had founded the Red Wing Seminary here in 1878–79.[1]

Many roads led to Red Wing. There was a waterway, the Mississippi River, and the railroad, which had a splendid new station with cast-iron columns and elaborate carpentry both inside and out, down by the riverbank. And people from Holden and neighboring areas traveled to Red Wing for the hearing. In all likelihood, Pastor Muus's parishioners

met in front of the courthouse in droves, lining up with all the spectators at the top of the stone staircase. Many were visitors, including
newspaper reporters, although on this particular January day city residents flocked to the courthouse as well.

The marriage scandal of *Muus v. Muus* was simply not to be missed.
Would Mrs. Muus appear in the courtroom? How would Pastor Muus
behave? The press suggested that a little bit of everything could be
expected. Perhaps there would be further juicy revelations about Pastor Muus's mistreatment of his wife and children, about Mrs. Muus's
alleged abnormal state of mind, about marital quarrels and uncomfortable family relationships. The large crowd that gathered inside the
courtroom awaited sensational entertainment.

The court was presided over by Judge Francis M. Crosby. He was
in his fifties and for nearly a decade had performed his duties with
great authority. His verdicts were based on thorough case research and
human discernment. Every decision of his had so far remained in effect,
none overturned by the Minnesota Supreme Court. F. M. Crosby, who
was a Republican, was reportedly the judge Mrs. Muus and lawyer
Andreas Ueland had wanted. Yet the judge's first decision was not what
the plaintiff or her lawyer had desired. Judge Crosby chose to dismiss
"The Complaint," the renowned appendix attached to the civil lawsuit.
The judge referred to the State of Minnesota's current law on spousal
property rights. "The Complaint" was neither relevant nor necessary,
as the lawsuit didn't require any justification, either morally or financially. Here in the courtroom, *Muus v. Muus* would only concern itself
with the question of money, inheritance, and financial amounts.[2]

The judge's decision probably confirmed what legally savvy observ-
ers had seen since the case's beginning: Mrs. Muus's much-publicized
addendum had no legal function. The lawsuit concerned a technical
matter. The accounts of suffering in the pastor's home had no bearing
on the outcome of the trial. Lawyer Ueland was well acquainted with
the state's laws and from the very beginning must have known that the
letter he attached was legally irrelevant. The purpose of "The Complaint" was different: it was meant to influence public opinion—and
it had succeeded beyond all expectations. Without "The Complaint"

as an attachment, Mrs. Muus's financial lawsuit would hardly have become sensationalized in the Norwegian and American press, nor a prestigious political case for the progressive lawyer.

On January 5, 1881, only Mrs. Muus's lawsuit for the right to manage her own paternal inheritance was the subject of legal proceedings. Judge Crosby stated that in this lawsuit the plaintiff didn't need to produce evidence of the kind that appeared in "The Complaint." The deliberations began with judicial peculiarities and continued in the same vein. It wasn't very entertaining for the audience; one newspaper reporter commented: "The case seems to have been an interesting one for the lawyers, but it did not afford much amusement for the spectators." The deliberations dragged on, and only facts that could shed light on the case, specifically the question of money, were put forward by Ueland or by Pastor Muus's lawyer, William C. Williston. Pastor Muus was present at the hearings, but Mrs. Muus was not.[3]

The lawsuit Ueland had filed with the court stated that the plaintiff, Oline Muus, simply couldn't accept that Norwegian inheritance laws should apply in Minnesota. The lawyer had enclosed a transcript of the state's act from July 31, 1854, concerning descendant heirs, which stipulates that the property of the deceased goes to the deceased's relatives and spouse in accordance with the provisions specified in the act. The law applied to relatives in direct descending and ascending lines regardless of age or title, and the law didn't differentiate between genders. It guaranteed for women, both married and unmarried, equal rights with men as heirs. The law, Ueland pleaded before the court, had been established five years before the Muuses' arrival in Goodhue County. Mrs. Muus's demand for her paternal inheritance was her full right according to Minnesota's inheritance law. But should Norwegian or American law apply in this case? Lawyer Ueland wisely avoided mentioning that the couple were not US citizens. Instead, he argued that American law should apply to the case because the spouses were determined from the outset to immigrate to Minnesota.[4]

Norwegian American attorney Nils Michelet was called to the court as an expert witness. In Norway a married woman's assets had long been a legal controversy. In 1871, Søren Jaabæk, a parliamentarian and farmer, had introduced a bill to facilitate a wife's access to her own assets. But years went by without anything happening. In 1881, the liberal intelligentsia in Christiania was nearly bursting with impatience: there had to be a limit to how many political authorities should deal with a proposed law before Parliament could vote on it. When Michelet claimed before the court that confusion reigned about this law in Norway, it was almost in accordance with the truth.[5]

Bernt Muus's American lawyer believed that in the case of *Muus v. Muus* Norwegian law must apply. And, on that point, it was quite clear that a married woman's inheritance becomes the couple's shared assets. Oline and Bernt Muus hadn't entered into a prenuptial agreement when they married in Norway in 1859; thus, the spouses shared assets and property in common. In Williston's defense of the accused, the size of the inheritance also became a recurring theme. The defendant, Bernt J. Muus, denied that in 1863 he had received and retained the large sum valued at just under five thousand American dollars at the time, as the plaintiff claimed. He also denied that he had deceived the plaintiff. On the other hand, he acknowledged that he had managed and invested the inheritance funds. He couldn't recall the exact amount, nor could he account for interest earned on it. He had never kept records, and there was no documentation of how he managed the funds.[6]

Williston's defense emphasized that in the position of pastor Bernt Muus's income varied from year to year. Muus had never kept a record of the sums he had received or lent out, so it wasn't possible for him to disclose information regarding his income. But he denied taking possession of controlled property or anything else belonging to the plaintiff. These facts were recorded in December 1879. Further, the defendant wasn't in possession of the funds he obtained from the plaintiff's inheritance from her father in Norway. According to Williston, one main argument for applying Norwegian law as the basis for the judgment was that the plaintiff and the defendant were both Norwegian citizens. The two were both immigrants—foreigners. They hadn't applied, nor were they planning to apply, for US citizenship.[7]

Williston defended Pastor Muus in the American court by applying Norwegian law. Ueland tried to cast doubt on what Norwegian law was. He pointed out that even under Norwegian law a husband is only entitled to receive an inheritance accruing to his wife if there are joint assets. If there isn't joint ownership, the husband has no right to his wife's assets. What was actually the case concerning the Muus couple?[8]

The day in the Red Wing courtroom was over. Judge Crosby announced that the verdict on the case would have to wait until the district court received a copy and English translation of the documents from the Pind estate. As a result, the trial stretched out for an additional eight months. Not until September 8, 1881, almost two years after Mrs. Muus first filed the lawsuit against her husband, was the verdict in the *Muus v. Muus* case finally reached.

Bernt Muus had plenty of time to provide documentation about the inheritance in Norway, so it may be that he deliberately slowed the legal process to delay the inevitable—that his wife would leave the Holden parsonage for good. The reason Oline Muus stayed in the parsonage as long as she did was most likely due to finances. She lacked money to start a new life somewhere else.

47

A Troll of a Wife

··

JUST A MONTH BEFORE THE TRIAL for Oline Muus's inheritance began, in December 1880, none other than "B. B." arrived in America. Bjørnstjerne Bjørnson was a Norwegian of great stature. A poet, politician, public educator, journalist, public speaker, and social debater, he spoke everywhere, loudly and resoundingly. He had now arrived in the land of opportunity. Like his old friend Kristofer Janson, he was bursting with excitement even before his departure from Norway. One of the first things Bjørnson did upon arrival in America was to buy a broadbrim hat, put it on slightly askew, and visit a photographer. His hair, once fiery red, had become speckled with gray. His short reddish beard likewise showed signs of gray, but his eyes glowed as in his youth. He was young, although he approached fifty with furious speed, and women adored him. It was an open secret that he was having affairs. His faithful wife, Karoline, had borne his infidelity early on. Right after she gave birth to their first child, her husband had a relationship with a Danish actress. Over the years Karoline had become a sedate married woman, while B. B. became a notorious philanderer. But he always came home to Aulestad, their grand estate in Gausdal.[1]

At the beginning of January 1881, Bjørnson was in Norwegian America, and from well-informed sources he knew all about the marriage scandal in Holden. In Minneapolis, he had been duly celebrated by the Norwegian American cultural elite, and Luth Jæger was planning to print Bjørnson's lectures in *Budstikken*. His visit was widely anticipated

Bjørnstjerne Bjørnson, 1880.
Courtesy National Library of Norway

in local English-language newspapers as well: the *Minneapolis Tribune* featured an article with the headline "A CELEBRITY" on January 11, 1881.[2]

The Muus case had become a scandal in the old country as well, and Bjørnson had surely read about the tyrannical Pastor Muus in the Norwegian *Verdens Gang*. Bjørnson was fascinated by the case and couldn't help but visit the parsonage at Holden. He was determined to speak to Mrs. Muus and Pastor Muus in person. Like a schoolmaster, Bjørnson would talk to each of them separately. Perhaps he had begun to doubt whether Oline Muus was completely without fault.

His self-imposed task during his lecture tour was to enlighten and convince his compatriots that they lived in the new age; that every man was free to believe and to think what they wanted. They had to live in truth, in accordance with their consciences, and they had to cast off the yoke of the clergy and fundamentalist Christianity. Like Kristofer Janson, Bjørnson was a missionary for progress, freethinking, and common sense. However, the two friends no longer had the same beliefs as in their days at Vonheim, the Grundtvigian folk school. The bright and cheerful Christianity they once preached was a thing of the past.

When Bjørnson wrote home to his wife, Karoline, on January 25, 1881, he was in Lanesboro, one of southern Minnesota's many small towns. He was to give a speech in a church and had been welcomed at the railway station by a band. The Norwegian musicians played very well, he wrote; she could rest assured that the Norwegians in America were skilled. But he wasn't quite well; he had a head cold. Still, his voice remained good, if not at its very best. The night before he had spoken in La Crosse, Wisconsin, with his customary thunderous authority. There was a large crowd—many people had poured in; they just had to see and hear Bjørnson himself—and afterward a choir sang. He held the day of judgment over the Norwegian immigrants in America. He explained to Karoline that the day of reckoning had come; it was only a question of how long ignorance would prevail. He shifted abruptly to the Muus case. Everyone was engrossed in it, and he believed public opinion had turned against Pastor Muus. "Pastor Muus is denounced by *all*!" Bjørnson wrote to Karoline. Everyone he talked to, those in the Synod and those on the outside, condemned the pastor.[3]

An enormous amount of snow had fallen, and Minnesotans were enduring storm after storm. Due to a blizzard, Bjørnson had to cancel some engagements and change his plans for his tour. For several days, he remained snowed in and unable to travel as scheduled; the *Goodhue County Republican* wrote about "the great author fast bound, a prisoner, imprisoned by feathery snow flakes." Unfortunately, some locals went to great lengths to attend events they thought would still happen.[4]

By mid-March, Bjørnson had arrived at Fort Dodge, Iowa, where he gave a two-hour lecture. But before he could take to the stage, a pastor gave an entire lecture speaking out against him. He recounted this event in a new letter to Karoline on March 19. Angered, Bjørnson used all his authority when addressing the crowd. There was an all-out battle, as he wrote in the letter, but there was also gratitude, because what he spoke about was what people in the old settlements had been longing to hear. Apparently, Bjørnson not only wanted to hold judgment in the case but also perceived himself as a kind of savior, and such people can be difficult to have as visitors.[5]

He finally arrived in Northfield, where he spoke at St. Olaf's School, to a packed house. In Red Wing, which he described as "Pastor Muus's neighborhood," it was "ditto ditto." In other words, a packed house there as well.

The exact circumstances of his visit to the Holden parsonage are not apparent from the letter to Karoline. Maybe he stopped by unannounced? Mrs. Muus was at home; he had expected that. Pastor Muus, whom Bjørnson knew from his early years in Christiania, wasn't. Their adult daughter was there, and Bjørnson was able to meet her during his visit. She was sweet and, as he remarked, as clean and meticulous as her father.

The meeting with Mrs. Muus made a strong impression. It was the first time they met. He previously knew her only from publicity in the papers. He wrote to Karoline that Mrs. Muus, the woman who had endured a man who had neglected and abused her for years, was neither small nor graceful. He was shocked by how she behaved and spoke. She wasn't timid, not at all. If Bjørnson had expected to meet a petite, pale, and thin woman, he was thoroughly mistaken. "She's large, burly, and stout," he wrote in the letter. "She was beautiful, still was." In addition, she was "very sharp"—that is, bright and intelligent. But he declared that she was a troll, a mountain troll, through and through.

In Bjørnson's day, angry old women were often referred to as trolls. For ages, women who made their husband's life a living hell were considered trolls. Malice and spite were specialties mastered to their very fingertips. And, as it appears from the subtext in Bjørnson's letter, in this case Mrs. Muus's husband hadn't been able to tame the troll.

Bjørnson could imagine how Pastor Muus had struggled with the old woman, "that crone." Bjørnson didn't spare his criticism. Mrs. Muus was only about worldliness, indifference, defiance, literally wanting to cause a hubbub. In her own way, Mrs. Muus was as strong as her husband, Bjørnson thought. The spouses lived under the same roof in the parsonage, competing to assert their own opinions, their rights. Bjørnson didn't get the impression that one side was weaker than the other. Mrs. Muus was anything but Christian, responsible, or selfless. She seemed self-centered and self-indulgent. And, when Mrs. Muus was in the mood for trouble, in his assessment, it was because she enjoyed causing a commotion over nothing.

What shocked Bjørnson most during his visit was how unkempt Mrs. Muus was. He must have arrived unannounced. Had she known Bjørnson himself was coming to visit, wouldn't she have made an effort to look her best? The once-beautiful young woman from Fet appeared to be a fat, sour-smelling wife. Bjørnson confided to Karoline that Mrs. Muus was so dirty, "so slovenly," that her petticoats stank, and to manage a conversation with her, he had to light a cigar.

He took action either so that the smoke would cover the stench or because he needed nicotine to calm his nerves and have an intelligent discussion. His letter described Mrs. Muus as starting off by speaking respectably, piously, and calmly. But he quickly understood the lay of the land. Soon, she raised a fuss about the Bible and her husband and holiness, and she laughed heartily. Mrs. Muus had suddenly become nothing but gaiety.

The letter writer had formed a clear opinion on the question of guilt. His letter implied that the troll of a wife was the cause of the couple's misery. But Bjørnson actually wrote that it was Pastor Muus who was mostly to blame, without a doubt. What mattered now, he wrote, was to separate the two, and that is exactly what he would try to talk to Pastor Muus about. Bjørnson never lacked self-confidence, not even as a marriage counselor. To Karoline, he reported that he would advise Pastor Muus to agree to separation, perhaps even divorce. In other words, it was Mrs. Muus, the troll, who wanted separation and divorce.

"Oh, Karoline, how I suffer on this journey," Bjørnson exclaimed. "I find life here crude, boring, and uninspired. Ugh!" Norwegian America was not a good place to visit, according to Bjørnson. His lecture tour was not motivated by pure idealism; there was a lot of money to make from ticket sales. He admitted to Karoline that he regretted leaving, and he ended his letter with "your B.B."[6]

48

Intentional Malice

IN THE POST–CIVIL WAR PERIOD of mass emigration, when thousands of Norwegians came to America, Norway extended to both sides of the Atlantic. For Bjørnstjerne Bjørnson and other writers on tour, Norway, whether west or east of the Atlantic Ocean, was the same project: a cultural-political project in the spirit of progress and liberalism. What was news in Norwegian America was also news in Norway, and that was very true of the Muus case. In February of 1881, Augsburg seminary's Georg Sverdrup's scathing article first printed in *Lutheraneren og Missionsbladet* in December 1880 was reprinted in Christiania, in the journal *Ny Luthersk Kirketidende [The New Lutheran Times]*, with theologian Jakob Sverdrup as editor in chief. In introducing the piece, he noted that most readers were aware that the Norwegian American Pastor Muus's domestic relations had been of a very troubled nature. Furthermore, the pastor's wife had sued her husband in court concerning her inheritance and during the lawsuit made strong accusations against him. He had, in turn, summoned her before the congregation to have her excommunicated. The deliberations held in church meetings and in a committee had been so significant for the Norwegian Synod's spirit that the editor believed readers would appreciate some clarification.[1]

The ties between America and Norway remained strong during the time of mass migration due to tight familial relationships. Jakob and

Sven Oftedal, date unknown.
MNHS collections

Georg Sverdrup were brothers, and their uncle Johan was the unofficial leader of a radical political movement. Three years later, Johan Sverdrup would become prime minister of Norway and Jakob Sverdrup minister of education and church affairs. Sven Oftedal, Georg Sverdrup's colleague at Augsburg Seminary (later Augsburg College and then Augsburg University) in Minneapolis, was also born into an influential liberal family. He was the brother of Lars Oftedal, the most famous pastor of Norway's revivalist movement. From Minneapolis, Professors Sverdrup and Oftedal led a large free-church movement on both sides of the Atlantic. America was in Norway, and Norway was in America.

"Bjørnson," "Muus," and the "grace election controversy" are among the keywords in the article "From North America," printed on June 4, 1881, in *Luthersk Ugeskrift [Lutheran Weekly]* a high church publication in Christiania edited by J. C. Heuch and M. J. Færden. The two editors were delighted that even *Skandinaven*, the liberal Norwegian American newspaper in Chicago, criticized Bjørnson. The quote reprinted stated that in his lectures the author rambled wildly on politics and religion, making a pitiful figure to the sorrow of his friends and the joy of his enemies. Further, his glory days as a poet were fading, and the previously highly esteemed and popularly beloved Bjørnson was, in the end, nothing more than a dreamer stumbling aimlessly and confused from one extreme to the other.[2]

For Heuch and the Færden, this review was money in their pockets. In America, people didn't think highly of Bjørnson. Initially, Bjørnson said he wanted to come to America to learn. Then, he declared that if there was strength in the movement among the people to cast off the yoke of the clergy, he would certainly come. When Bjørnson eventually learned that a lecture tour could secure him a total of a hundred dollars, he went.[3]

In *Luthersk Ugeskrift*, however, the greatest focus was placed on Pastor Muus. Heuch and Færden defended him wholeheartedly, while at the same time refuting the Sverdrups' support of Mrs. Muus. The editors declared that the church's enemies always use the same tactics, attacking by circulating suspicion and all kinds of unreliable rumors in

American and Norwegian publications. Consequently, it wasn't unexpected that the church's enemies threw themselves voraciously at the Muus case. *Luthersk Ugeskrift*, on the other hand, saw the matter as it was. It was simply a question of money. Editors Heuch and Færden grasped exactly the point that Pastor Muus's congregation didn't want to deal with and judge.

Heuch and Færden were well informed of the facts in the case. Among other things, they could reveal that Pastor Muus had inherited some money from his father, and the amount was about the same as that which Mrs. Muus inherited from her father. In accordance with Norwegian law when spouses have common property, Pastor Muus was her guardian and managed the assets they owned together. But his wife had quite a different opinion, including how much should be spent on food, clothing, furniture, and so forth. The spouses also had great differences in outlook and temperament, differences that over the years made married life more and more difficult.[4]

The two editors claimed to be too moral to go into details, let alone "convene a court." But wasn't that exactly what Heuch and Færden were doing? They continued a process in which the main objective was to clear Pastor Muus of all charges of ignoble conduct. The two editors stated as fact that Muus had "a very solid character," which frequently appeared as obstinacy. Moreover, Muus expressed his convictions in a rather thoughtless manner, so he certainly had a weaker side, too. But, Heuch and Færden noted, "no one who has had the opportunity to know Muus well is in doubt: within the hard shell there is a genuine heart." As a pastor, Muus was highly esteemed. He had worked with great skill and tireless diligence to build up the Lord's church in the far west. Members of his congregation still regarded him with respect, and many also with affection.

After their defense, Heuch and Færden went on to attack Mrs. Muus. "It seems that she hasn't been able to appreciate her husband's good essence," they wrote, and it didn't surprise them that discord had arisen between the couple. Heuch and Færden gave Mrs. Muus the benefit of the doubt, and they could sympathize with her: she may have experienced the pastor as he often behaved in meetings. Yet *Luthersk Ugeskrift* couldn't vouch for Mrs. Muus. It was regrettable that she had to declare several points in her Complaint to be false. Worse still, according to the editors, her later complaint to the congregation contained "several points" that also weren't true. Heuch and Færden concluded with a hope that it was sorrow and distress, and not deliberate maliciousness, behind why it "goes round for her" as it had.[5]

Aasta Hansteen, ca. 1888.
Oslo City Museum

Ghosts

WHAT OLINE MUUS WROTE in her letter to the pioneer feminist Aasta Hansteen in the spring of 1881 isn't known. Perhaps it was an act of friendship? Hansteen lived at the time in Boston, where she had arrived a year earlier with her adult foster daughter. Hansteen had had enough of Norway. In her hometown of Christiania, the daughter of a well-known professor, Christopher Hansteen, had for many years been ridiculed and bullied for her pamphlets, newspaper writings, and public appearances. It was back in the 1860s when she laid down her paintbrush and took up her pen to become the champion of Nynorsk and women's rights that people began to really notice her. In 1878, her seminal work, *Kvinden skabt i Guds Billede [The Woman Created in the Image of God]*, written in the spirit of biblical feminism, was suppressed by the press. Aasta Hansteen was seen as the epitome of a shrew, a man-hating old spinster. For an early feminist that label was inevitable. At the age of fifty-six, she immigrated to the land of women: America. Norway was a country for men. Norwegian writer and feminist Camilla Collett had long since faced the consequences of that reality. For three decades, Collett had lived as an intellectual nomad on the European continent. Hansteen traveled even farther.[1]

On American soil, Hansteen resumed her work as an artist, making her living in Boston as a portrait painter. But one of the first things she did after arriving in America was reach out to several of the activists in the American movement for women's rights. Her great role model was

Elizabeth Cady Stanton, who, during the landmark meeting in Seneca Falls in 1848, had defined the cause of women as a human cause, while at the same time putting criticism of the church on the agenda. Hansteen likewise anchored herself ideologically in biblical feminism. In her American exile, she continued her fight against conventional Christianity and for women's rights.

Before leaving Christiania, Hansteen had contracted with the Norwegian newspaper *Verdens Gang* to write five articles about her impressions of conditions in America. In this way, she could earn some income while at the same time improving her poor English skills. She also submitted two articles to *Budstikken* in Minneapolis. In both publications, she commented on the Muus case. With these articles, Hansteen became the first woman to write publicly about Oline and Bernt Muus. None of the male commentators had explicitly made the Muus case a feminist case. Hansteen, however, did. In a letter to *Budstikken* in August 1880, she used the key word "slavery" in a feminist sense: she called the Muus matter "this new slavery case," and she embroidered details of it with furious wit, while scoffing at the Synod's interpretation of the Apostle Paul. They had used Paul's words regarding the duty of women to submit to their husbands to justify their own actions.[2]

On September 14, 1880, six weeks after her commentary appeared in *Budstikken*, a reply was printed in the paper. An anonymous writer wondered how Hansteen, a newcomer to America, could be so familiar with the conditions here. Even though she was far away from the scene of events, she acted as if she knew intricate details that even within the immediate circle were unknown and unanswered. This salvo hit a sore spot; Hansteen knew she should familiarize herself with the conditions in the case and become acquainted with Oline Muus. So, in the summer of 1881, Hansteen was able to kill two birds with one stone. She went on a lecture tour of Norwegian America.[3]

It was rare to hear a woman speak in public in the Midwest, and for the audiences who attended her lectures it must have been an extraordinary experience. Hansteen spoke on women's rights in multiple locations. It's not known precisely when or where she and Oline became acquainted with each other. They could have met in town or at the parsonage, though their private conversations aren't known. Hansteen didn't reveal anything about her personal relationship with Oline Muus when she sat down and wrote a travel article during her lecture tour among her compatriots in America. The piece was written at the invitation of the editor of the influential magazine *Woman's Journal*, founded by Lucy Stone and her husband in 1870. It functioned as the mouthpiece of the radical faction of the women's movement. "Norwegians in the Northwest—letter from Mrs. Aasta Hansteen," printed on July 30, 1881, wasn't uplifting. The entire article centered on Pastor Muus and the Norwegian Synod. With or against her will, Oline Muus became the face for women's rights—the rights of American women.

First Hansteen declared that the Norwegian Synod consisted of "very zealous adherents of slavery; and now that black slavery is abolished, they try, with all their power, to keep up the white slavery." In congregational meetings, the clergy proclaimed that a wife shall be a slave to her husband. Hansteen also stated, and it was pure imagination, that the same pastors had previously declared that a father had the right to punish his children with death. Although the death penalty had been outlawed, the pastors were still fervent supporters of slavery: "the slavery of the wife is their favorite idea." Hansteen went further to state that the Synod considered themselves "to be the only true and pure Christians in the world."[4]

In this Norwegian American Synod, continued Hansteen, Pastor Muus is one of the most "prominent and powerful rulers and chiefs. . . . He has for twenty years shown himself, not only in theory but in practice, to be a slave-owner of his wife and children." He uses his clerical authority and rules over his family as a master over his slaves. It is, Hansteen commented, both

a domestic and clerical tragedy, but it has, nevertheless, just like the tragedies of Shakespeare, many comic details. For instance, one day, Mrs. Muus was put under church discipline, and forbidden to go to church to participate in the communion (the Lord's supper), by her husband, the powerful and imposing clergyman, because a waterpot had frozen and gone to pieces. The reason why the waterpot had frozen was that Mr. Muus had forbidden his wife to make a fire, so that not only the waterpot but the wife and the children too were frozen. But the reverend husband did not care a bit for them; he cared very much about the waterpot; and therefore he used his clerical authority to punish his wife.[5]

For twenty years, Oline Muus and her children were made to suffer, and it was only then that her husband gave her housekeeping money, fifteen dollars a month. Readers of the *Woman's Journal* knew that wasn't much money, and Hansteen pointed out the unreasonableness of Pastor Muus's pettiness by mentioning that Mrs. Muus had inherited over $4,000 from her late father in Norway. Mrs. Muus had repeatedly asked her husband for her inheritance; she needed the money for blankets, clothes, and food. But from her husband she received no answer except a "scornful smile and a declaration that he did not know anything about her inheritance. At the same time, other people told her that Mr. Muus had placed her money in some business or some bank."[6]

Hansteen continued to expound and comment on the case. It had been sixteen months since she had first heard of Mrs. Muus's civil lawsuit and complaint. Hansteen knew about the case from the Norwegian press, but the detail that Mrs. Muus hoped Mr. Crosby would be appointed judge in the case she presumably learned from Oline herself. Incidentally, Hansteen gave a disturbing update from the parsonage: "Her husband does systematically everything to annoy and humiliate her. She is kept like a penitent in her own home, being put under interdict or banishment of the church." All this punishment because she had declared that she didn't believe in the Synod's teaching that a wife is her husband's slave and must obey him in all things. When she neither would nor could accept this doctrine, her husband said she denied God's word.[7]

Hansteen thought readers of the *Woman's Journal* would find her piece interesting. She was surely right. East Coast feminists thought highly of the American settler-colonist women in the Wild West; they were tough, strong, and independent. Because Hansteen's travel letter concerned first and foremost the clergy in the Norwegian settlements, readers didn't learn anything more about the women than that they were completely suppressed. Hansteen refers to the Norwegian immigrant men as "antiquated people," explaining that they are like ghosts "from the dark middle ages, living in the last decades of the nineteenth century, in the prosperous and thriving States of Wisconsin and Minnesota, in the midst of free America. I do not feel very proud, in telling you about this Norwegian church party, and I wish you not to think all the Norwegians are in that way—without brains and without hearts."[8]

50

Verdict and Departure

....

IF AT THE BEGINNING OF AUGUST Oline was sent the latest issue of the *Woman's Journal*, it was probably left unread, wrapped in its gray paper and string. She had something far more serious on her mind. When Bjørnstjerne Bjørnson visited at the end of March, he had fortunately not noticed anything. He had met Birgitte and had a good impression of her. The Muuses' oldest and only daughter, who had turned twenty in November 1880, still lived at home and cared for her younger brothers and contributed to the work of the household. It was probably sometime after Bjørnson had visited that Oline discovered her daughter was expecting a child. Soon everyone would be able to see. Birgitte, the pastor's unmarried daughter, was about to have a baby. Yet another scandal would plague the Muus family. The village gossips would have even more dirt to dish about unseemly circumstances at the parsonage—first Mrs. Muus, then her daughter.

Birgitte might have been secretly engaged, although no public announcement had been made in Holden Church. Would the man who had impregnated her come to acknowledge his child? Was he prepared to marry her? The child's father was Johannes Olsen Kongsvik. On August 10, 1881, the two secured a wedding license in Red Wing, but they never married. The *Daily Minnesota Tribune* reported later that "Mrs. Muus threatened to kill three of the children if the eldest daughter married a certain man, which she did not do." Despite this shocking statement, similar reporting is not found in any other publication.[1]

Two weeks later, on August 27, 1881, Birgitte Muus gave birth to a son. Sverre Muus, as he was baptized, was born out of wedlock, and in church records such children were commonly labeled "illegitimate." At home in Norway, an unwed mother was a disgrace; this shaming was also upheld in the Norwegian American settlements. Her parents could refuse to have anything to do with their daughter and an employer could fire her.

In the old days, some girls took their own lives; others tried to hide their circumstances, giving birth in secret. "Child murderer" was a tragic reality, and frequently depicted in art. The punishment was a long prison sentence. But if the girl had a sweetheart who married her, preferably before or just after the child was born, she was accepted. It was customary among farmers to get married quickly when a woman was with child. Such marriages weren't unknown among the upper classes, although it was said that a bride must be a virgin. The parents typically arranged for the daughter to go away well in advance of the birth, and the child was placed with strangers. If the couple married, the child born out of wedlock usually remained a family secret.

Birgitte Muus raised her son, at least in his very early years. She continued to live at the parsonage, and her son remained there with her. Pastor Muus could have sent her on her way or placed her with a family far away from Holden parsonage. He could have forced his daughter to make an adoption plan for her son. But he didn't. As a father, Pastor Muus showed compassion by allowing his daughter and grandson to live at the parsonage. Oline Muus hardly had a say in the matter as the spouses were not on speaking terms with each other. In the dramatic conflict between her parents, Birgitte supported her father. Pastor Muus obviously believed his wife was an unfit mother. When their daughter became pregnant without being married, he would have had one more confirmation.

In August 1881, when Sverre was born, his grandparents were living unhappily together at the parsonage. On September 8, 1881, just four days before Sverre's baptism, F. M. Crosby announced the final verdict in the lawsuit at the county courthouse in Red Wing. Almost two years of waiting had finally come to an end. The conclusion was a great victory for Oline Muus. Judge Crosby's verdict was decisive: Oline Muus's inheritance had been paid out in the State of Minnesota. Therefore, local law was applicable, and according to Minnesota law a married woman has the right to manage the wealth and assets she has inherited. Norwegian marriage law should not determine the case on American soil. For immigrants, even if they were Norwegian citizens, American law, in this case Minnesota's marriage law, applied.[2]

The court upheld Mrs. Muus's claim against her husband. He was ordered to repay a portion of her inheritance, the total of which was 4,675 Norwegian spesidaler, which based on the exchange rate the judge used equaled 4,955 American dollars—over $150,000 at the time of publication. Bernt Muus wasn't ordered to repay this entire amount because the first payment from the inheritance settlement in Norway was affected by the statute of limitations. It was too late to claim it now. Oline Muus was entitled to the sum that had been paid to the defendant on September 20, 1874. In addition, the defendant was to pay the plaintiff for six years of lost interest, which was set at seven percent.[3]

The amount was more than two years' salary for Pastor Muus: a nice little fortune. Oline Muus had been awarded about a quarter of the inheritance left by her father, $1,115 ($34,000 today). With that amount plus interest ($117) she now had modest funds—enough that she could begin to think of a life on her own, even if she couldn't demand too much of that life. Her husband, on the other hand, allegedly had an estate valued at as much as $25,000 ($752,500 today). Oline wouldn't be responsible for anyone but herself, but still, she must have known that it remained for the court to rule on a further financial claim against her husband of more than twenty years. Their civil cases weren't yet over.[4]

Court records state that the two youngest children, three-year-old Harald and seven-year-old Petter, were "abducted from the plaintiff's custody" on November 3, 1881, and placed with a family in the congregation some four miles away from the Muus family residence. Records further state that Oline Muus believed this action was taken "with the sole intent of injuring plaintiff's feelings and [to] cause her great suffering of body and mind." The custody battle must have been the final straw for Oline, because on the twenty-eighth of that month, she took the next steps to leave her marriage and her home.

There must have been a considerable amount of luggage: boxes of clothes, books, letters, and music. The last words the spouses exchanged concerned precisely these belongings. Her husband insisted on examining what was in the boxes because he suspected his wife had packed things that weren't hers. And, when he searched through the luggage, he found two things that didn't belong to his wife: their daughter's confirmation Bible and her muff. He was angry, but Birgitte assured her father that she had given both as gifts to her mother, who was then allowed to take them with her. In Mrs. Muus's final exit from the parsonage, there were no heartbreaking scenes of weeping children clinging to their mother.[5]

Nearly two years had passed from when Andreas Ueland had filed a civil suit with the court to when Oline Muus left the parsonage at Holden. Just as Ibsen's Nora had done, she left her husband and children. But unlike Nora, Oline Muus didn't depart in the wake of a sudden realization. Her departure was well prepared and deliberate—and a long time coming.

PART III

Disgrace

51

Helpers in a Time of Need

....

AT THE BEGINNING OF 1882, the local press reported that Mrs. Muus was living in Minneapolis and that she would file for divorce. Oline had connections with resourceful Norwegian immigrants in the city. Among her most important friends were undoubtedly Georg Sverdrup and Sven Oftedal, both of whom lived just one block away from her in what is today known as the Cedar-Riverside neighborhood. It was Sverdrup who in a December 1880 periodical, *Lutheraneren og Missionsbladet,* had fiercely defended her and demanded her husband's resignation as a pastor. The two professors from Augsburg Seminary were her supporters during this difficult time. In the fall of 1881, when she left the parsonage to establish herself in Minneapolis, she was able to borrow money from them. In fact, her residence was just off the Augsburg campus. Thanks to their support, Oline Muus was not destitute, though she later gave that impression.[1]

In 1881, Kristofer Janson's travel book *Amerikanske Forholde [American Conditions]* was published at the prestigious Gyldendalske Publishing House in Copenhagen. Much of it was devoted to the Muus case, and while Mrs. Muus was vigorously defended, criticism poured down on Pastor Muus, the Synod, and members of the congregation. If Janson had been surprised by anything during his travels, it was that his fellow countrymen, liberated and influenced by democratic institutions in so many ways, were completely backward when it came to religion. Their motto seemed to be: the Church must and shall remain intolerant.[2]

Religious intolerance was Janson's explanation for the state of affairs in the Norwegian Lutheran Church in America, which now found itself divided into five synods. The Norwegian Synod, the [Norwegian-Danish] Conference Synod, the [Danish-Norwegian] Augustana Synod, the Haugean Synod, and the Eielsen Synod, as he wrote, were constantly in each other's business and fighting with one another, in the name of faith and brotherly love. The doctrinal disputes between them were meaningless; it was enough to note that all were faithful to the Augsburg Confession. But the greatest evil the Norwegians dragged over to America was the Norwegian Synod. Even though its model was the American free church, essentially a democratic congregational church, the Synod managed to create an aristocratic church, ruled by the clergy. Moreover, the clergy had entered into a covenant with the German Synod, where Professor Carl Ferdinand Wilhelm Walther, who believed in a literal interpretation of the Bible, was considered as infallible as the Pope. Janson criticized the Synod for promoting anti-Americanism, what he called æskepolitikk [box politics]. The Synod operated with a system to isolate Norwegian immigrants as much as possible from American and other people's influence, putting them in boxes filled with the clean air of "true doctrine" and closing the lid so that no other air could reach them. This strategy is why Synod pastors fought the American public school and stood in opposition to almost the entire American-Scandinavian press.[3]

But the most abhorrent thing about the Synod, according to Janson, was how it abused church discipline. A pastor ruled over the congregation with an iron fist. Once when a man was participating in a congregational meeting where slavery and the observance of the sabbath were on the agenda and the man didn't agree with the Synod's view, the pastor punished him with a scathing report. "For these false teachings, this denial of our Lutheran teachings, these blasphemous and false claims against his former pastor," the report began, resulting in a case of church discipline against the man. The situation in the Synod's congregations is scandalous, Janson wrote. People who leave the congregation are no longer allowed to have the graves of their deceased ancestors remain in the church cemetery. Janson told an outlandish story from a settlement in Winchester, Wisconsin, where the Synod and the Conference had separate churches, each with their own cemetery. Several longtime Synod members went to "the enemy," the Conference congregation, after a falling out with their pastor. Then, at night on the day of their resignation, members of the Synod's congregation came to the cemetery. They dug up the remains of the relatives of the members who had withdrawn and threw them over the fence to the Conference's cemetery. The next day, everyone in the settlement could see exhumed bodies from the Synod cemetery within the fence of the Conference cemetery.[4]

"Abuse of authority" and "power mad" were words Janson used to describe the pastors in the Synod's pastoral aristocracy. "While Our Lord is blamed for locusts, Indian unrest, plague, and famine," Janson pointed out polemically, "it is the devil who is blamed for people going and listening to a Methodist or Conference Pastor," for members of the Synod's congregations were forbidden to listen to pastors other than their own. "What a spirit of bondage and cowardice this must create within the congregations!" Janson exclaimed, continuing with a new story. One evening, a Baptist minister preached in a public schoolhouse with a large turnout of rural people. But when he was to meet at the school again the next night, "someone" tried to prevent him from entering. The Baptist minister managed to get into the schoolroom anyway, so the town pastor declared that anyone who went to hear the minister would be placed under church discipline. Only five or six people showed up to the meeting, and others didn't dare go in. Instead, they stood outside the schoolhouse, pressed up against the windows and doors, to hear the Baptist minister preach.

When Janson thought of Norwegian American common folk in a religious sense, he always imagined them in this way: "They hang around the doors and windows, in somewhat forbidden places, but they don't dare go in—don't dare, don't dare, so they have saved (and that's the main thing) their good reputations." Janson was certain that church discipline had become one of the clergy's most vital weapons.

The congregation trembled under the threat, for nothing ate at a Norwegian farmer more than public humiliation. And it wasn't a mere handful of wrongdoings the Synod's pastors considered enough to put a parishioner under church discipline. Janson reeled off a long list: secret engagements and marriages, participation in lotteries and establishment of life insurance, membership in secret societies and collection of interest on loans, marriage to one's late wife's sister, and so on.[5]

Janson was merciless in his criticism of the Synod. Nowhere was the tyrannical thinking so evident as in the view of relations between parents and children and husband and wife. During his 1879–80 lecture tour, he had heard a great deal about two marriage cases in Synod congregations. The first concerned a farmer who had abused his wife so horribly over a long period of time that she was about to lose her mind. In desperation, she fled to her two brothers, where she began to recover. Soon after, their pastor came to visit. He threatened her brothers with eternal damnation if they didn't send their sister back to her husband. For the wife who had run away from home, there was nothing she could do but to return and live with her husband. The pastor admonished her to obey God's word and completely disregarded her plea to be left in peace where she was. Upon her return home, the husband continued to abuse her, tormenting her even more than before— but now, as Janson remarked, with the church's blessing.

The second marriage case he'd heard about was the Muuses'. It was rehashed in all its embarrassing details and unfolded over ten printed pages. It had been shocking and disgusting to witness the Synod's prejudgment of the defenseless woman, and the Synod, as well as the congregation, should have acted more nobly and protected Mrs. Muus. Janson came to the same conclusion Professor Sverdrup had in his article the previous year: the congregation should have fired Pastor Muus. Janson predicted the congregational meetings in Goodhue County would stain the region's reputation.[6]

It was strange that a community in the name of Christianity could produce and defend a man like Pastor Muus and that this same community gave him the right to abuse his wife and children. Janson hoped the Norwegians in America would awaken to independent spiritual life, to a greater ethical moral conduct, and to break the Synod's bonds. If the Muus case had shown one thing, it was that the Norwegians in Goodhue County were still spiritually immature. They were blind servants under the clergy's inane literal domination. In conclusion, Janson asked if the Synod, with its organizational talent and sacrificial work, could persist in recruiting immigrants and continue to flourish. He thought it could, but that would not be the end of the story. Eventually, the Synod would suffer a terrible setback because children of the most severe and irrational pietists usually become drunkards and haters of religion. Kristofer Janson's prediction was that the great-grandchildren of the men who, in the Muus affair, so fanatically guarded a husband's right to be his wife's oppressor would perhaps throw all of Christianity overboard.[7]

52

New Legal Proceedings

....

WHEN THE VERDICT IN Mrs. Muus's lawsuit had finally been confirmed on November 28, 1881, Bernt Muus's lawyer, William C. Williston, appealed the decision to the Minnesota Supreme Court. Attorney Andreas Ueland did so as well on behalf of his client. Oline Muus demanded payment of her entire inheritance, plus seven percent annual interest.

In December 1881, Oline filed a third civil suit, from her new residence in Minneapolis, with the Hennepin County Court. She requested that her marriage to Bernt Muus be dissolved. If a divorce were not granted, she requested separation. She wanted "to be forever separated from the bed and board of the defendant." At the same time, she requested that the court order her husband to provide her with temporary alimony.[1]

Back at the Holden parsonage, Pastor Muus sat with shame and town gossip. He was disgraced as a husband and father, as a pastor, and as the Minnesota District president of the Norwegian Synod. Bernt Muus had admittedly always been a controversial figure, but the events of the past two years had seriously shaken his authority as a pastor and religious leader. Yet he continued his work in the congregation and the Synod. He could have left Holden and sought a call elsewhere, either in Norwegian America or in Norway. But the likelihood that Pastor Muus was wanted as a pastor in another congregation was perhaps slim. And if his wife's divorce lawsuit was granted, his career as a pastor and Synod leader would definitely be over. A divorced man couldn't serve as a pastor, that was for certain. The only thing Pastor Muus could do was fight to keep the religious positions with which he had been entrusted within the church. March 15, 1882, when he turned fifty, couldn't have been a day of celebration.

A month earlier, in mid-February 1882, the Holden congregation had convened a meeting in which Pastor Muus, and only Pastor Muus, was on the agenda. The meeting had set aside a full three days to discuss whether he could continue to serve as the congregation's pastor— the third time in two years a meeting was called to consider whether Pastor Muus was fit to lead. The church council, made up of laymen, was determined that the matter should be dealt with in the presence of experts. Accordingly, five theologians attended the meeting. Pastor Muus's old friend Professor Thorbjørn Mohn from St. Olaf's School was one of them, as was his former assistant pastor and supporter Pastor Bøckman. Moreover, Pastor Biørn, Mrs. Muus's spokesman during the congregational meeting in 1880, was present. The final two experts were younger theologians with the surnames of Thorsen and Hanson. So, it was Hanson (with an o); Pastor Hansen (with an e) had since resigned his post. Presumably, the Muus case was a strong contributor to August Hansen's decision to resign, since he and his wife, Kristine, had supported Mrs. Muus and thus had fallen out with both Pastor Muus and the Synod's leadership. In 1881, just a year after August and Kristine Hansen immigrated to America, they returned to Norway.

At the congregational meeting in Holden in mid-February 1882, the two younger theologians spoke against Pastor Muus and demanded that he voluntarily resign his position as pastor. It probably wasn't surprising that Haldor Hanson, a faculty member at Luther College, advocated for resignation. That Markus Thorsen, vice president of the Synod's district assembly and Pastor Muus's right-hand man, also followed suit was more striking. When Thorsen and Hanson, as theological experts, requested that Pastor Muus resign, the reason was said to be "his family relationships." The two experts felt it would be beneficial for the congregation and the Synod if Pastor Muus stepped down as pastor. They may have campaigned in league with the press. In any case, the local

Red Wing Argus made a big fuss about the case: "Holden Church Troubles," the headline announced on February 16, 1882. The newspaper reported that two pastors stood up and demanded the resignation of Pastor Muus at the church meeting, so that peace and harmony might again be secured within the congregation and church community. But Pastor Muus also had supporters among his parishioners who wished him to continue as pastor. They believed Pastor Muus "ought not to be responsible for the acts of his family," the newspaper noted.[2]

When the congregational meeting, after lengthy and thorough discussion, held a vote on the agenda's only matter, whether Pastor Muus could continue as pastor, a total of 110 voting men rendered their verdict. Again, the majority supported the old pastor, albeit by a smaller margin than before. While seventy-three parishioners voted that Pastor Muus should remain in his position, thirty-seven, a significant minority, voted against. After two decades, the time when the entire Holden congregation stood behind their pastor was over. Accordingly, the thirty-seven parishioners wouldn't accept the congregation's majority vote. In a letter of protest to the Minnesota District of the Synod, they demanded that Pastor Muus temporarily resign from his position as pastor. The minority tried to appeal the majority decision, but the democratic votes had to be respected, and the letter of protest was not taken up by the district assembly, where Pastor Muus was president. The Holden congregation's dissenting members had to put up with their old pastor.[3]

Synod president H. A. Preus and the two district presidents Ulrik Koren and J. B. Frich took action. First, they tried in vain to persuade Pastor Muus to resign as president of the Minnesota District. But Pastor Muus was on his way out of the Synod's leadership anyway. In 1883, when the Synod held presidential elections, Bernt Muus was not reelected as district president, the esteemed position he had held since 1876.

Pastor Muus had fallen into disgrace in his own Synod, mostly thanks to his highly censurable marital relationship, which the whole world had now heard about. It was also well known, though the press hadn't mentioned it out of respect for privacy, that his twenty-year-old daughter, Birgitte, had borne a child out of wedlock. Not only that but Bernt Muus allowed both his daughter and his grandson to live at home in the parsonage. All these things must have worked against Pastor Muus, both within the Synod and in his congregations. An unmarried mother and an illegitimate child—it was a scandal on top of the even larger ones that had unfolded in public with the pastor and his wife as the main characters. In the fall of 1881, Mrs. Muus had left her husband and children, and instead of returning home, she had filed for divorce.

The divorce case gave the town gossips yet another scandal to grab on to. In connection with the lawsuit, the judge needed testimony on the circumstances at the parsonage, on the relationship between the spouses, and on how Mrs. Muus had performed her duties as a mother. The testimony was given over several sessions, the evidence to be used as grounds for the verdict in Mrs. Muus's divorce suit before the Hennepin County Court. Both parties in the suit had to call witnesses, and people in the neighborhood as well as in the Muus household were to testify at a hearing with the justice of the peace in Goodhue County, John Naeseth. So, in 1882, Pastor Muus began to fall into disfavor, and he also had his wife's divorce lawsuit looming over him like a dark cloud. The civil suit was first heard by the court on December 3, 1882.

Everything said by the various witnesses in Justice Naeseth's hearings inevitably reached Pastor Muus's ear, and again he was confronted with testimony declaring him a bad husband. Even Knut Haugen, the farmer with whom the couple had lived when they first arrived in Holden in 1859 and one of the congregation's prominent members, testified that when the congregation had discussed whether Mrs. Muus should be placed under church discipline, Pastor Muus had said that they could be pleased to get rid of someone like her. And, at a later meeting, Haugen had noted Pastor Muus's harsh words about his wife, that she was "sinful, ungodly, and malicious."[4]

Haugen was not the only one in the congregation with little positive to say about Pastor Muus. Two members recalled the pastor had defended slavery, even explained that he himself had slaves, namely, his wife and children. Ole Solberg, on the other hand, vouched for Pastor Muus. In his testimony, Solberg confirmed that when Mrs. Muus broke her leg, Pastor Muus had arranged to send for Dr. Grønvold. Muus had asked one of his farmhands, who had already saddled a horse, to fetch the doctor. But Ole Simpson's testimony of how Pastor Muus had combed through Mrs. Muus's luggage at the time of their breakup wasn't merciful.

Birgitte Muus was called as a witness by her father. All in all, she painted a poor image of her mother. At one point, her mother had no longer wanted to be a housewife, and she left the housekeeping to the parsonage's maid, and later to Birgitte herself. When Justice Naeseth questioned how her mother reacted when Pastor Muus placed the two youngest sons with a family in the congregation, Birgitte answered forthrightly that her mother seemed glad that the two were being cared for by another family. The day her little brothers were sent away, they had asked for their mother. And, Birgitte added, it didn't seem like her mother took it so hard. She was sad for half a day, not longer.[5]

The parsonage's older domestic servant, Maren Ramstad, was more diplomatic. She explained that the relationship between the couple was cold and that Bernt Muus rarely spoke to his wife. Ramstad also stated that she couldn't remember the pastor ever uttering one kind word to Oline. But she hadn't ever heard him scold his wife either. To the justice's question as to whether Mrs. Muus behaved more kindly to Pastor Muus than he did to her, Ramstad replied that she didn't believe so. Another witness from the parsonage's household, Søren Monsen, the family's private tutor, gave Mrs. Muus a good reference. He believed Mrs. Muus was a capable organizer and housewife. His assessment, unlike that of Birgitte Muus, was that Mrs. Muus took it very hard when her sons were sent away.[6]

During Judge Naeseth's examination of the witness, the question of whether Mrs. Muus was a good mother was also raised. In her divorce suit, she didn't ask for custody of her two minor sons. In 1882, Petter was eight and Harald was three and a half. The law was clear; in the event of divorce, the children's father was granted custody unless he had committed criminal acts. Attorney Ueland had certainly explained this to Mrs. Muus, so she was aware that it was futile to ask that the little boys remain in her care. Nor was it ever questioned whether Pastor Muus was a bad father. The reason he had earned a poor reputation as head of the family was because he was a bad husband.

53

Divorce?

....

IN THE SPRING OF 1881, the *Goodhue County Republican* briefly noted that Oline Muus traveled to Boston. Joseph Shaw raises "the intriguing possibility that she could have met leaders in the American women's movement there." A year later, on March 14, 1882, *Budstikken* had a short mention of Oline Muus giving a lecture in Chicago, where Aasta Hansteen, the Norwegian pioneer feminist, now resided with her foster daughter. In that same edition, *Budstikken* also reported that Hansteen was expected to visit Minneapolis and the surrounding area.[1]

A few weeks later, on March 28, the newspaper advertised that Hansteen would give a lecture on the theme of women's rights and its development among Norwegian Americans. According to *Budstikken,* the talk would surely be interesting, given Hansteen's history of advocating for this cause in her native land. The person who invited Hansteen to Minneapolis was none other than Oline Muus. Hansteen did not need to be asked twice, from Chicago the journey was fairly easy. This time, perhaps, Oline Muus wanted to provide a favor for Hansteen, although the invitation was probably not an entirely selfless act. Oline didn't know what would happen in her divorce case, and she might need additional support from the pioneer feminist.[2]

Saturday evening, April 1, when Hansteen arrived by train in Minneapolis, she traveled straight to Oline Muus's home. The next day, the lecture took place at Norden Hall, home of the Scandinavian

Dramatic Society, with an audience of nearly a hundred people. Janet E. Rasmussen notes that Hansteen's diary reported problems that had arisen: she had to make do without either a manuscript or her silk dress. Nor did she get any share of the entrance tickets. Oline attempted to straighten up the mess. The following week, on April 10, she arranged a concert with the women's quartet Freja at Harrison's Hall, at the corner of Washington and Nicollet Avenue, where Hansteen would provide her commentary on the times and the present situation. But even though 180 people attended, the profits were far from satisfactory. Instead of continuing her planned lecture tour, Hansteen cut her trip short.[3]

Back home in Chicago, Hansteen wrote a travelogue to *Woman's Journal*, and for Oline Muus the piece must have come as manna from heaven. First, readers were reminded that Hansteen had previously written about how backward the Norwegian immigrants were in regard to religion, and that the Norwegian Synod defended slavery in everything. "The subjection of the wife is now discussed eagerly, while one of their most prominent leaders, Rev. Mr. Muus, is now before the courts with his wife," Hansteen stated. Pastor Muus, one of the foremost church leaders, was on trial, as she explained in some detail, and the situation had created a stir both in Norwegian America and in Norway. Hansteen added that Pastor Muus appealed the case to the Minnesota Supreme Court. She withheld that Mrs. Muus had also appealed the verdict in the Goodhue County District Court and, furthermore, had filed for divorce in Hennepin County District Court.[4]

Her article explained why Pastor Muus's wife had "rebelled"— mainly due to her husband's refusal to satisfy her needs for carpets, clothing, and other necessities. Finally, after the unhappy wife had for twenty years been obedient to her husband according to the words of Paul, she had revolted against his marital control. No one could say that Mrs. Muus hadn't shown implicit obedience, Hansteen pointed out. Even her husband's friends and supporters could testify to that. Hansteen referred to two of Pastor Muus's friends, namely, Pastors

Preus and Bøckman, who had both sworn that they knew nothing of the Muuses' marital unhappiness and misery until they read about it in the newspapers. Hansteen defended Mrs. Muus with a quote from the book of Paul that had been mentioned in one of the church meetings and which the Synod didn't seem to take into consideration: that a husband should love his wife even as Christ loved the church and sacrificed himself for it.

"Pastor Muus is a very orthodox man," Hansteen declared. He was also known to be cold as ice, as she had heard the most fanatical pastors in Muus's religious community say. While he was considered an exalted and irreplaceable pastor and a husband entirely in accordance with God's word, Mrs. Muus was criticized for being so brazen that she complained about her situation—after twenty years. Hansteen pointed out that the wife was required to "suffer silently all her lifetime beside her husband, with all possible (and impossible) love and respect for that piece of ice." This case, according to Hansteen, reveals Lutheran orthodoxy at its worst. It was shocking to see how the Synod misused Paul's words and made slavery the foundation of both Christianity and marriage. Aasta Hansteen had come to the end of the road. She pondered what a female acquaintance of hers had once said: "If these are Christians, then I will try the heathen for awhile."[5]

In the May 20, 1882, issue of *Woman's Journal*, Oline Muus's case was once again used to benefit the call for women's rights. Four days earlier, on May 16, she had been able to celebrate a small victory when the Minnesota Supreme Court dismissed Bernt Muus's appeal for acquittal. It also upheld the judgment of the Goodhue County District Court: the defendant, Bernt Muus, was required to pay his wife, Oline Muus, the portion of the inheritance that didn't fall under the six-year statute of limitations. Oline Muus hadn't won her appeal in its entirety. She didn't receive her full inheritance from her father. Whether her husband would be required to pay his wife temporary alimony was not yet clear. Until the verdict in the divorce suit was final, she was still to be regarded as Pastor Muus's wife.[6]

On January 3, 1883, the District Court of Hennepin County began proceedings on Mrs. Muus's divorce case, presided over by Judge A. H. Young. On January 4, the *Daily Minnesota Tribune* reported, "The main room at the court house was thronged yesterday afternoon with ladies and gentlemen of the Scandinavian persuasion who were attracted by the announcement that the Muus divorce case was to be heard."[7]

Seventeen days later, on January 20, 1883, Oline Muus won another victory. The final verdict read: "plaintiff is entitled to be forever separated from the bed and board of the defendant on the ground that defendant's conduct towards plaintiff has been such as to render it unsafe and improper for plaintiff to continue to live and cohabitate with him." The court had granted Oline Muus a legal separation known as a limited divorce, presumably because Bernt Muus refused to agree to a divorce or because the judge lacked the required evidence of spousal abuse, adultery, or immoral conduct. There was no evidence that the two parties had been guilty of "moral delinquency," as Andreas Ueland would later write in his memoir.[8]

The verdict granted Oline Muus alimony set at $150 per year for ten years. The alimony was in addition to the inheritance Bernt Muus was required to pay to her. He was also required to pay all the expenses his wife had incurred with her two lawsuits, a total of $161.93. Finally, the verdict made clear that the defendant, Bernt Muus, was awarded custody of the minor children, Petter and Harald.

Whether the press's many commentaries on the scandal influenced the outcome is difficult to ascertain, but it would be strange if they didn't. The settlement between the couple ended far better for Mrs. Muus than seemed likely in the summer of 1881. She was awarded a total of $2,575, which included a portion of her father's inheritance, interest, legal fees, and other compensation, equivalent to $77,500 today. She acquired a small nest egg that she could use as she wished or to invest in the future. The alimony was hardly enough to live on, but she earned income from teaching piano students as well.[9]

On January 20, 1883, the *Muus v. Muus* civil cases were brought to an end. It had been three full years since Oline Muus filed the civil lawsuit to gain control over the inheritance her father left her. Now that the religious and court proceedings were complete and the press was less attentive, she could finally move on. Three years after it all began, the couple was legally separated.

While Oline Muus settled in Minneapolis, Bernt Muus continued to work as a pastor and reside at the parsonage in Holden. For the remainder of their years, the two would live separately, even though the marriage wasn't formally dissolved.

54

The Three Pastor's Wives

....

WHEN DRUDE KROG WED Kristofer Janson in 1868 in Fana, Norway, they agreed that they would be equal partners, share everything, and keep nothing from one another. Drude Krog Janson was an adherent of the so-called modern marriage. Marriage should not be old-fashioned, based on lies and hypocrisy. She would have preferred for the two of them to remain in Norway, but in 1879 and again in 1881, her husband departed on a lecture tour to the Midwest. During their fourteen-year marriage, Drude bore seven children. Their first child, Sigmund, died just before Kristofer's second departure for America.[1]

Kristofer Janson considered it his calling to serve as a Unitarian clergyman and missionary in Norwegian America, and Drude allowed herself to be persuaded to join him in 1882. She had dreamed of becoming a writer all these years, and in Minneapolis that vision would become a reality. Her husband secured an apartment on Franklin and Thirteenth Avenue, in the middle of a large Scandinavian community in Cedar-Riverside. But she was unhappy from the very first moment, even though there were immigrants from Norway and the rest of Scandinavia everywhere—in the streets and on the streetcar, behind and in front of the counter at the grocery store, and in her husband's congregation. The problem was that Drude Krog Janson had nothing in common with these immigrants. If they weren't poor people, they were simple people, people without culture and education.[2]

Writing letters was her comfort in these unfamiliar surroundings. She longed for home and was often overwhelmed by feelings of loneliness. For long periods of time, her husband was out of town, doing extensive lecturing and serving both new and old congregations. Even Janson felt sorry for his wife; in a letter to his friend Bjørnstjerne Bjørnson in Aulestad, Norway, he admitted that his wife's life was by no means easy.

While he had many irons in the fire and could rejoice that his work bore fruit, Drude was at a standstill. But she was not relegated to the four walls of her home. She was doing important work for her congregation. She taught the children in Sunday School and instructed the girls in needlework and led the women's association. However, Kristofer noted in his letter to Bjørnson, Drude lacked the stimulation of the artistic and intellectual milieu she was accustomed to at home in Norway.[3]

Things went a little bit better over time. In 1883, the family could move into a Venetian-style villa on Nicollet Avenue in the Whittier neighborhood, where the upper middle class lived peacefully within their own front yards and each in their own personally designed house. On Nicollet Avenue, the couple held a salon every Sunday evening, and Oline Muus was often one of the participants. She knew Kristofer, who had been her fearless defender during the trials in Holden, and now she became acquainted with his wife. Oline and Drude, who was eight years younger, became friends.

In Minneapolis, Kristofer Janson was a cultural institution within a circle of both Scandinavian and American friends. Before Nazareth Church was completed in 1886, the congregation was housed in a rented room or even at the Jansons' residence. Although his Unitarian congregation had few members, he attracted large audiences for both church services and evening meetings. And among those who came were people who mattered, such as attorney Andreas Ueland and his American fiancée, Clara Hampson, and the Norwegian doctor Karl Bendke. Ueland was impressed with Janson's energy and enthusiasm. Ueland also read Janson's books, though he thought they were a bit overblown, almost political propaganda. In 1882, Ueland, with his former partner Luth Jæger, were in the forefront of founding the organization Fram

[Progress], and together they gave Johan Sverdrup's liberal movement, which was on the march in Norway, their unreserved support. Two years later, in 1884, when Sverdrup founded Venstre [the Liberal Party] in Norway, Ueland and Jæger founded a liberal organization in Minneapolis, Norskamerikanske Venstreforening [the Norwegian American Liberal Association], which was to work for cooperation between politically like-minded Norwegian Americans and Norwegians.[4]

At the Janson home, there was a read-aloud of fiction on Monday evenings and a house concert on Friday evenings. The women's association that Janson founded and his wife led held meetings there. The story goes that women in Janson's congregations were naturally full members equal to men. In the land of religious feminism, Janson was able to blossom as a pastor of the new school. His missionary activity was criticized in most publications in Norwegian America, with one exception: the newspaper where Luth Jæger was editor, *Budstikken*.[5]

At the Jansons' Sunday salons, guests were provided with tea, dramatic readings, and artistic entertainment. Drude often played piano pieces, or she accompanied Kristofer, who was a talented singer. And when Kristofer or one of the guests read aloud, it was from new Norwegian novels and plays. Both famous and unknown musicians and speakers on tour in Minneapolis were invited to the Jansons' home to contribute to the salon. One of the guests was a young Norwegian by the name of Knut Hamsun, who wanted to be a writer. (Hamsun would later become one of the most highly esteemed writers of his time, and was awarded the Nobel Prize in Literature in 1920.) Janson had met him after a lecture out of town in the summer of 1883 and immediately employed him as a secretary. For nearly a year, Hamsun lived with the Jansons on Nicollet Avenue, and Drude spent a lot of time in his company. She read what he was writing, encouraged him, and gave him advice. Hamsun also admired her, writing in a letter to a friend that she was a very gifted woman.[6]

Oline Muus may have met Hamsun at the Janson home or at least heard a great deal about him. When she visited, she also met Drude's close friend Valborg Stub. The culturally refined Valborg, born Hovind, retained her maiden name as her middle name, as did her friend Drude.

All three were pastor's wives. Since 1872, Valborg's husband, Hans Ger-hard Stub, had served various congregations in the Synod, but in recent years, he was a professor at Luther Seminary in Madison, Wisconsin. Valborg, on the other hand, lived in Minneapolis.[7]

Drude Krog Janson, Valborg Hovind Stub, and Oline Muus shared many attributes and interests. All held the position of and knew the cost of being a pastor's wife. They all felt alienated in the society of which they were a part. And none of them had the best reputations. There were rumors that Drude was infatuated with her husband's secretary, the considerably younger Knut Hamsun. She had become so involved with him and was allegedly so serious about the relationship that she asked her husband for a divorce. Valborg lived hundreds of miles away from her husband and did not share a table or bed with him. And, of course, Oline had recently become separated and during the church proceedings had been accused of adultery.[8]

Although the three friends weren't in the forefront of the great political cause of the day, woman's suffrage, they had firsthand acquain-tance with at least one of its activists. Clara Hampson, whom Andreas Ueland would marry in 1885, was one of the leaders of Minneapolis's Woman Suffrage Association. Oline Muus contributed music to the cause when, on a Sunday evening in 1884, she played piano pieces at the Norwegian Women's Society bazaar organized by Drude Janson. And after Kristofer Janson gave a speech, Oline Muus accompanied a male violinist. Drude would later write to her friend Bjørnstjerne Bjørnson that the convention the Woman Suffrage Association held in Minneap-olis in 1885 was the greatest experience of her life. Her enjoyment was seemingly fueled through her friendship with like-minded Norwegian American pastor's wives.[9]

55

A Dangerous Man

....

BERNT JULIUS MUUS CONTINUED to serve as pastor at Holden Church, even though in 1882 a significant minority in the congregation considered him unfit because of the conflict in his family and the eventual spousal separation. That summer a door opened in Norway for Bernt Muus when he received a death notice from Snåsa: his seventy-seven-year-old father had passed away. As Ingebrigt Muus's oldest son, Bernt had the right to inherit Krogsgården farm. It would cost him a journey to Norway, but it was worth it if he could resign from his call as pastor and leave Holden. The problem was that the farm belonged to his half brother, Martinius Muus, and Bernt had to buy him out. The assessment was high, 54,500 crowns (equivalent to $14,509 at the time), roughly equal to the entire amount Bernt would inherit from his father. Martinius, on the other hand, had taken over the farm at a much lower appraisal, namely, 12,000 crowns ($3,200 at the time). In the end, Bernt didn't exercise his right to own the family farm, reportedly because the asking price was too high, although he stated that, by mistake, he hadn't registered the petition for his father's farm in time. The door for him to return to Norway was again closed.[1]

Muus continued his ministry in Holden, and he continued to be faithful to his church. President H. A. Preus and others in the leadership learned that getting rid of Pastor Muus was easier said than done. He defied the Synod, which didn't want anything to do with him because of his stance regarding the doctrine of predestination, which became a pivotal division in the Synod.

Joseph Shaw explains, "election or predestination means that God from eternity chooses who will be saved." Within the Norwegian American settlements dispute on the doctrine raged. While one faction, the Missourians, maintained that God has chosen some individuals to be saved and have eternal life, the other faction, the Anti-Missourians, maintained that man can be saved by faith alone. In intensity and strength, the conflict divided the Synod far more than any previous theological rifts. Clergy were removed from their churches, and pastors left the Synod.[2]

The controversy over the doctrine of election was undoubtedly about more than just theology. An account by Jens Hansen, a parochial schoolteacher at Our Savior in Chicago, Illinois, offers testimony. When the dispute wreaked havoc in his own congregation in 1887, not a single parishioner actually understood what the controversy entailed. Hansen insinuated that the parishioners had no idea what they were talking about. When a rigid Anti-Missourian was asked which points in the Missouri Synod doctrine he disagreed with, he answered that the Missourians preached something called "tutte fide," in which he absolutely could not believe. Hansen explained, the parishioner had heard the expression "intuitu fidei" and had misunderstood the Latin expression meaning innate faith; he considered "tutte fide" to be a particularly stubborn form of heresy. The doctrine of innate faith was precisely what the Anti-Missourians fought for, and the parishioner was so uneducated that he didn't understand his own fellow Anti-Missourians were supporters of the doctrine of "intuitu fidei."[3]

In 1887, at a meeting held in Kindred, North Dakota, a majority of the participants determined that Pastor Muus should no longer be a member of the Synod. For one, he opposed the Synod in the debate over the doctrine of election. Another issue was that his congregations in Holden and in other communities had broken away from the Synod. In truth, the Synod regarded Pastor Muus as "a dangerous man" to have in their midst, as Pastor Biørn, Mrs. Muus's spokesman during the church discipline case in 1880, later wrote in a commemorative publication. He and Pastor Bøckman were also among the many clergy who submitted resignations to the Synod in 1887. They joined "the enemy" alongside Georg Sverdrup and Sven Oftedal at Augsburg Seminary in Minneapolis.[4]

In the fall of 1888, *Evangelisk Luthersk Kirketidende* ascertained that secession from the Synod's ranks was fairly large. In the early 1880s, the Synod had begun to receive a smattering of withdrawal notices from congregations. By 1887, these departures had become almost a daily occurrence. The Synod, established in 1853, had rapidly grown into the largest Lutheran religious body in Norwegian America, but it was now losing its position of power. It was no secret; *Evangelisk Luthersk Kirketidende* was constantly printing statements from congregations that no longer wished to belong to the Synod. An announcement from the Norway congregation in Iowa in 1887 read, "Because of the doctrinal dispute there is so much disagreement in the Norwegian Synod, the Norway Congregation no longer finds it beneficial to remain in the Synod."[5]

In just one Synod meeting in the summer of 1888, close to one hundred congregations and thirty-five clergy declared their resignations. There was a steady membership exodus. But the Norwegian Synod, where H. A. Preus was still president, didn't lose its composure. Even such upheaval didn't cause Preus or Pastor Koren to reconsider the Synod's doctrine. The two men, who were also editors of the Synod's paper, confirmed the mass exodus. They did not accept any accusation that the Synod was tyrannical, for the Synod was fully justified when it refused to allow congregations to substitute another doctrine for the established Lutheran one. After all, congregations couldn't adopt a new doctrine on their own.[6]

Despite the dissension Pastor Muus stirred, he refused to leave the Synod. "He was an avid member of the Synod the entire time," Biørn later recalled, "and he used a big sledgehammer against the Synod's religious opponents." When Bernt Muus was finally expelled from the Synod, it was a heavy blow for him. "He mourned this decision more than many people believed," Biørn contended. Many of Muus's Synod brothers saw him standing quietly smoking his pipe outside the church where they had cast judgment upon him. Strangely enough, in the Synod's history, Bernt J. Muus was listed as a member up until 1898;

only then was his "expulsion" a fact. So, for more than fifteen years he lived in disgrace in the Synod, and all these years he had also been able to remain the pastor for Holden Church. As a result of his continued outspoken opposition, a schism between the Synod and the Anti-Missourians formed. This split resulted in the Synod denouncing the founding of an alternative theological seminary at St. Olaf in 1887.[7]

The controversy over the doctrine of election that led the exodus was presumably the expression of a lay revival, a rebellion of the people against the pastor and authority of the clergy. Regardless, in 1888, Professors Sverdrup and Oftedal, who had helped Oline Muus, were able to delight in the many congregations that left the Synod and whose members debated how to understand a shared doctrine. There was much to argue about in determining what the new Lutheran doctrine actually was. Biørn collaborated with Sverdrup and Oftedal to create a new joint organization for Norwegian American Lutherans. Meanwhile, Synod leaders were anxious to regain lost souls by making alliances with other Norwegian American communities. In the end, in 1890, Pastor Biørn managed to implement the union. The United Norwegian Lutheran Church of America was the newly created church body. There was room for both theologians and laypeople who distanced themselves from the old Lutheran doctrine. The Synod was consequently excluded.

Oddly enough, despite theological and personal disagreements, Biørn and Muus remained friends. Or rather, Biørn seems to have taken it upon himself to care for Bernt Muus. Biørn was unable to persuade Muus to join the new free church. Family relationships, arthritis, divisions in society—all weighed heavily on Muus, wrote Biørn in a 1906 memorial article. He added that Bernt Muus, after the scandal and crises he endured, was never the same.[8]

After many years of doctrinal disputes with Bernt Muus, who was often characterized as "the perpetual gadfly who questioned virtually all of the Synod's theological positions," the majority of Norwegian Lutheran church bodies sought unity as one great, common organization. This vision resulted in a 1917 merger establishing the Norwegian Lutheran Church of America, now known as the Evangelical Lutheran Church in America (ELCA).[9]

56

Lonely and Abandoned

OLINE MUUS WAS LIKELY WELL INFORMED about how her children were doing. Over all the years since she left Holden, we know she was in frequent correspondence with her old friends and acquaintances. Her eldest son, Nils, who attended Luther College, didn't follow in his father's footsteps as a theologian and pastor. In 1886 he married Josephine Sortedal, the daughter of a Norwegian farmer, and became a farmer himself; the couple raised ten children. Nils, who was also a businessman and a man of deep faith, became a pillar of society in Minnesota. He visited Norway, but America was and remained his native land. Birgitte Muus, on the other hand, immigrated to Norway. In the fall of 1887 she married her second cousin, merchant Lorentz Diderik Klüver, in Steinkjer. The two were married in the church in Snåsa, where her great-grandfather had stood in the pulpit. She left her son, Sverre Muus, at the parsonage in Holden, where his grandfather, Pastor Muus, took care of him. After Sverre was confirmed, his grandfather, Bernt, paid his tuition at St. Olaf's School, where he was a student for a brief time. In her marriage to Klüver, Birgitte had three children, the third named Bernt Julius after his grandfather.

Paul died without descendants, only living to be eighteen years old. Oline was living in South Dakota when, in 1890, she received the sad news. He died of consumption, as tuberculosis was still called; like his younger brother he had weak lungs since boyhood. Petter turned out to be strong enough to live a fairly long adult life. After he had graduated from St. Olaf College in 1896, he attended medical school. From 1901 until his death in 1913, Petter Muus practiced medicine in Minnesota. The youngest in the Muus family, Harald, who was three years old when his mother vanished from his life, later became a student at St. Olaf's School for a short time.

For sons and daughters in Norwegian America, college or university education was highly valued. The second generation of Norwegian immigrants became teachers, librarians, lawyers, doctors, or businessmen, and if they weren't already Americanized, they became so eventually. During the three decades following the Civil War in America, often described as "the Gilded Age," a transformation was underway as America shifted from being an agricultural country to the world's largest industrial nation. Big business, industry, and banking barons ruled the country, the days of many small and medium-sized farms were numbered, and the countryside was becoming depopulated.

It was a sign of the times that none of the Veblen family's sons took over their father's farm and, in 1893, it was sold to strangers. Thomas Veblen, who had stood in opposition to Pastor Muus, lived in a house in Blooming Prairie near Nerstrand in his older years. Thomas and Kari Veblen had a rare legacy. In 1934 the couple was included in a book titled *Eminent Pioneers*. Of the nine Veblen children, only Thorstein, the one who did not receive an Americanized name, found a spouse outside his own milieu. When in 1888 he married Ellen Rolfe, the daughter of a wealthy businessman, he also married into the American upper class, a social rank he came to both love and hate. The other Veblen children followed the example of the two Muus sons: they married children of Norwegian immigrants. However, the children of Bernt and Oline Muus did not have a farm to inherit. The parsonage remained property of Holden Church.[1]

In 1889, Oline Muus decided to move. She was fifty-one years old. The decision may have been part of a major departure for her. In Minneapolis, she left behind private letters from Bernt Muus and other family members, entrusting them to one of her helpers in need: Professor Oftedal. To this day, Oline Muus's collection of letters can be found in the archives of Augsburg University in Minneapolis, Minnesota.

In 1889, Aasta Hansteen returned from her American exile, moving back to Norway. It was a different Norway than the one she left. The Norsk kvindesagsforening [Norwegian Association for Women's Rights], which had been founded five years earlier and had become an important political force, was even supported by women in her social class. The feminist pioneer was finally among like-minded people in her own country. On her eightieth birthday, in 1904, Hansteen was hailed as an honorary member of the organization.

Of the 800,000 Norwegians who emigrated from Norway between 1830 and 1920, there were many like Hansteen. As many as a quarter of the immigrants returned. Drude and Kristofer Janson separated. And, in the course of the 1890s, their chapter in Minneapolis came to an end, and they both returned to Norway. Marcus Thrane, on the other hand, remained in America. In 1883, he traveled to Norway on a lecture tour, hoping to regain his lost honor. After a few months, he returned disappointed and disillusioned to Chicago, and in the last years of his life, he lived with his son in Eau Claire, Wisconsin. When Thrane died at the age of seventy-three, Kristofer Janson wrote a eulogy that was read aloud at the memorial service. Thrane's children fulfilled their father's last wish, which was to be buried without a religious ceremony and without a gravestone.[2]

"The Norwegian Hymn Period," as Marcus Thrane had once coined the era, persisted after his death. Did it ever end? In America, the pastors in the Norwegian Lutheran churches continued to have their work. Christianity hadn't been thrown overboard, as Kristofer Janson predicted in 1881. Around 1900, the Norwegian Synod still had a stable membership. In addition to missionary work and schools, it operated hospitals, children's homes, and retirement homes. It took a long time, at least two generations, for the descendants of Norwegian immigrants to become Americanized and integrated. And they had enough descendants, both laypeople and clergy, that the Norwegian immigrant church remained active in areas with large Norwegian American communities. The conservative interpretation of the Lutheran doctrine still had a future, although it was no longer preached or read in Norwegian.[3]

Oline Muus moved on and settled in Columbia, South Dakota, a

small town in Brown County, where she opened a coffee shop. Subscribers to *Decorah-Posten* were informed of her situation when a letter she had written was published. Oline Muus wrote enthusiastically
about Pastor Sven Ulsaker, who belonged to the Anti-Missourians and
was the opposite of a modern ecclesiastical combatant. Not only did
he preach God's word with great composure, he also tried to live in
covenant with the word of God. As Oline Muus wrote, his approach
was far preferable to useless arguments over differing concepts and
various memorized orthodox phrases. However, the main point in her
letter was a business matter, specifically the future of her coffee shop in
Columbia. Brown County was newly open to settlement, and the news
was that Aberdeen would be the capital there. For a long time, Columbia had been a leading candidate, so Oline Muus, like everyone else in
the business community, was very disappointed with the outcome. She
felt the entire city suffered financially.[4]

The coffee shop only managed to break even, and for seven years,
she was one of the women who ran a small-scale business in Columbia. Then, in the fall of 1896, when Oline Muus was fifty-eight years
old, she moved again. With asthma and arthritis weakening her health,
she couldn't bear the long, cold midwestern winters anymore. On the
advice of her doctor, she moved south to Fruithurst, Alabama, where
a rather large Scandinavian colony of almost five hundred individuals
lived. "The Vineyard City," as it was referred to in the *Decorah-Posten*,
was a southern paradise. The cultivation of fruit was a main source of
income. Grapes to produce wine and other fruits that thrive in mild
climates brought prosperity to the city. Oline had managed her father's
inheritance well, and she purchased a hotel on the main street, which
she named Mrs. Muus' Hotel. Business flourished, and as a hotel man-
ager Oline experienced a period of great prosperity.[5]

The years took their toll on Oline; in a photograph from this time,
she is a mere shadow of herself. She is thin and broken down with arthritis, as her finger joints reveal. But she has a certain dignity as she sits in
front of the photographer in a gown of black patterned silk embellished
with a lace collar and brooch. Her hair, her pride, is styled according to
the rules of fashion with long corkscrew curls. Lacking a speck of gray,

Oline Muus in her later years.
MNHS collections

it probably had been dyed, or the photographer had retouched it. In contrast, her face's beauty has faded and is now marked with bitterness. Her cheeks are hollowed, possibly because she has lost her teeth. Her lips appear to sink into her mouth and form just a thin line.

Oline Muus was a survivor. She didn't lack determination or entrepreneurial spirit, and she adapted to situations along the way. Wherever she settled, she made friends in the city's Scandinavian religious community and was among the active members in her congregation. In small-town Alabama, hundreds of miles from Holden, Oline began yet another chapter in her life. Her twenty years at the parsonage certainly prepared her for work as a hotel proprietor. She was ostracized by her family; her husband made sure their children would have nothing to do with her. She wrote about this topic in a letter to Bjørnstjerne Bjørnson, who many years before had visited her at the parsonage in Holden. The letter, dated July 30, 1899, was eight pages long, written on the lovely lavender stationery of Mrs. Muus' Hotel. She told how in the eighteen years that had passed she had to struggle through adversity, sickness, poverty, and abandonment. At times she had felt she was about to perish in the maelstrom of life. The letter was a message of defense. When she left the parsonage, her so-called home, the two oldest children had taken their father's side, and they stood firmly by it. According to the letter, Pastor Muus had sent Birgitte and Nils to Norway so they could spread rumors about their mother. In addition, the two had managed to convince their younger siblings that their mother was to blame for all the terrible things that had happened, and their father was innocent. In Fruithurst, Oline was left lonely and abandoned. Could she have been mistaken in thinking that the sin and shame that had been brought upon her would rest twice as heavily on the pastors and leaders of the Synod?[6]

57

A Desire for Reconciliation

....

LIFE HAD GONE ON at Holden parsonage after Oline's departure. Bernt Muus even had the energy to write several small religious books. In 1891, he established an endowment, presumably with funds from his father's inheritance. Remarkably, the financial support given in "Inge-brigt Muus's Memory" was intended for residents of Snåsa: to alleviate poverty, fund youth who wanted to become teachers or clergy, and promote welfare by supporting the mining industry, cheese making, basket braiding, or the like. Even though Bernt Muus never became pastor at Snåsa, he became important there through the legacy he left in his father's name. In 1897, he also resumed an old project and wrote a supplemental preface to the book *Niels Muus's Æt [The Descendants of Niels Muus]*, which he had published nine years earlier. Ever since his youth in Snåsa, he had been interested in genealogy, and for that he owed a great deal to Paul Muus, his great-uncle, and other older relatives.[1]

In the original foreword, from Holden parsonage dated October 1888, Muus explained there were "circumstances" that led him to leave Snåsa and Norway. It wasn't that he didn't love his fatherland. He believed it was God's will that he should preach among his compatriots who had immigrated to America. When he parted ways with his beloved Norway, it was with deep sorrow. The preface from 1897 was written by a grieving man. Muus believed his days were soon coming to an end, and he used the foreword of his ancestral history book to say goodbye to his children and grandchildren. The majority of his descendants would probably remain in the United States, and he must have thought he would also be laid to rest there.[2]

"Blood is thicker than water," he declared in that same foreword. The old Viking concept of family had always seemed appealing to him. In those days, he explained, a family regarded itself as a political entity. The head of the family oversaw the well-being of all members. One prosecuted offenses inflicted on relatives, and in the worst case avenged murder with murder. In order to defend the family and its honor, one had to have the support of all who belonged to it. But through Christianity, family took on a different meaning. The scriptures teach that all are brothers and sisters in Christ, and that we are first and foremost to love those closest to us. Bernt Muus was clearly very proud of his ancestral lineage. The foreword may be his commentary on the legal proceedings his wife had brought against him.[3]

In the spring of 1899, the sixty-seven-year-old pastor was still living at Holden and had suffered two strokes, which left his body paralyzed on the left side. He believed he was dying. When he felt his mind was slipping, he called a meeting of the congregation and submitted his resignation. Pastor Biørn had informed Oline of Bernt's illness in a letter. He hoped the two could reconcile. Biørn urged Oline to return to Holden to help nurse and care for Bernt. In her letter to Bjørnstjerne Bjørnson dated July 30, 1899, she shared what Pastor Biørn had written. Biørn had been visiting his friend and former colleague in Holden, and Bernt Muus had confided that he hoped he and his wife could reconcile. What had happened was, in Pastor Muus's sincere opinion, both his and her fault. And now that his days seemed to be drawing to an end, he felt the need to make amends. May God forgive them, and may the two of them forgive each other, Oline wrote to Bjørnson.[4]

Oline Muus didn't reply to the letter from Pastor Biørn right away. He wrote again, urging her to travel to Holden. But for Oline Muus it was probably unthinkable to return; so much time had passed since she left her husband. Perhaps during the previous eighteen years Biørn had attempted to bring about a reconciliation between the spouses. If so, those attempts had failed, as did his effort in the summer of 1899.

In reply to Biørn, Oline explained that she lacked the funds to travel.

It would cost her fifty dollars to make the long journey from Fruithurst, Alabama, to Holden, Minnesota. But to Bjørnson she wrote that she had told Biørn that "nothing would be more dear to me than that there might be a reconciliation between us, and that I would do all that was in my power to help and serve him."[5]

Sometime later Oline received a new letter from Biørn informing her that Pastor Muus had recovered from his stroke, and in fact was doing so well that he no longer needed her help. Oline Muus wrote a letter to Pastor Muus, which she also shared with Bjørnson. She had told Muus, whom she still referred to as "my husband," that he committed a sin when he cast her aside. She had begged him to try to forgive her and to forget the large and small sins she had committed against him. But, she confided to Bjørnson, her husband hadn't answered her letter.

Bernt Muus wasn't able to complete the history of the Holden Church that he had begun in 1880; his patient and faithful friend Biørn would take up the task. Muus was preparing for his next big life's journey: returning to Norway. Four decades as a pastor in Minnesota had ended. Before his departure, Muus admitted to Biørn that it was difficult to come to terms with putting down the shepherd's staff and with the thought that his mortal life was drawing to a close. "All of my theology today is Jesus Christ and Him crucified," he declared during one of Biørn's last visits.[6]

Peter Floan recalls, "On a Sunday afternoon shortly before [Pastor Muus] left, the Congregation came over in a body to bid him a last farewell. Two of the old members went to the house to assist him out to the porch. He was not able to speak to them as his tongue was partly paralyzed, but he pointed toward heaven as if to say, meet me there, tears running down his cheeks." Then on a beautiful moonlit evening in July hundreds of locals bid Pastor Muus a final farewell at the train depot in Kenyon. His daughter, Birgitte, returned from Norway to accompany him on his journey back to his fatherland, where she would care for him in his final months.[7]

The congregation that called Bernt Julius Muus now embarked on a lengthy and agonizing process of choosing a new pastor. In 1899, John

Formal family portrait of B. J. Muus with daughter Birgitte and family, 1899.
B. J. Muus Papers, NAHA

*St. Olaf College president Sidney Rand and wife Dorothy
laying flowers at Bernt Julius Muus's grave in 1964.*
Municipal Archives of Trondheim. cc-by-2.0

Kildahl, who had been confirmed by Muus, was to return to Holden to serve as Muus's successor—only to find himself unexpectedly, and somewhat reluctantly, elected to serve as St. Olaf College's second president. The position of pastor was then given to N. J. Ellestad, whose daughter Bertha would later become the wife of Harald Muus.[8]

On May 24, 1900, after a fall outside Birgitte's home in Trondheim, Bernt Julius Muus died. The news was reported in Minnesota a week after his death; the Northfield newspaper headline read "HER FOUNDER DEAD."[9]

On September 16, 1906, when the Holden congregation commemorated its fifty-year jubilee, Pastor Biørn made a point to introduce the memorial publication with a tribute to Pastor Muus. "He had, for forty years, served the Holden Congregation," noted Biørn, praising Muus despite everything that had happened. With Pastor Muus at the helm, Holden Church had become the mother congregation for the majority of Norwegian American Lutheran congregations in Goodhue County and in Minnesota and Wisconsin. Biørn pointed out that, regardless of how one judged Pastor Muus, he had been a powerful personality. His name would be remembered by the Norwegian people in America, probably longer than many others who seemed important at the time. And Biørn was correct, as to this day Bernt Julius Muus is known to many as the founder of St. Olaf College.[10]

Bernt Julius Muus was laid to rest not in Snåsa but at the Nidaros Cathedral in Trondheim. Many individuals connected to St. Olaf College have since visited his grave site to pay their respects, and in 1974 the words "founder of St. Olaf College" were added to the marker to commemorate the college's centennial celebration. Fittingly, these words were chiseled into the side that faces the cathedral, where Olaf the Saint is also buried.

58

Mother and Daughter United

IN 1907, BIRGITTE KLÜVER, Oline Muus's forty-seven-year-old daughter, was one of many who crossed the Atlantic. She had left her husband and children in Trondheim and arrived in Fruithurst, Alabama, on December 24, Christmas Eve. How happy Oline must have been to reunite with her daughter. How much they had to talk about. Birgitte woke on Christmas Day to sunshine, birdsong, and the scent of violets as her mother served her breakfast in bed.[1]

Apparently, it took another marital conflict for mother and daughter to be reconciled. In 1907, Birgitte was about to be granted a divorce from the man she had been married to for twenty years. Her marriage lasted almost as long as her mother's. History had repeated itself, and after nearly thirty years, mother and daughter were reunited. The two got along so well that Birgitte settled down with her mother. There was plenty of room in Mrs. Muus' Hotel. As long as the hotel was profitable, the aging owner could certainly benefit from a helping hand.

When Birgitte arrived in Fruithurst, the city's prosperous times were beginning to wind down. Its main industry, wine production, struggled with sales, creating problems for all businesses in the region. Mrs. Muus' Hotel had to close its doors, presumably around 1910. But Oline didn't sell the building; she remained there with her daughter. The hotel still had frequent visitors, including sisters and brothers in the Scandinavian-Lutheran congregation where Oline Muus was an active member. In the absence of a church of its own, the congregation held services and meetings in the hotel dining room. The congregation appreciated Birgitte. She helped those who were sick and old, even if she could only read the Bible to them.[2]

Everything was in perfect order at Oline Muus's house. Mrs. Muus—or "Mrs. Muse," as people called her—was beloved and respected. She was known for her kindness and cheerfulness and was also gifted with indomitable optimism. She spent her days embroidering, reading, and writing letters. At some point, Birgitte traveled back to Norway. And then, in the spring of 1912, mother and daughter were again united when Birgitte accompanied her daughter, Else, from Norway to the United States to visit her grandmother and to study in New York and eventually in Minnesota.

Though Else and Sverre were the only grandchildren Oline is known to have met, large numbers of Norwegian Americans knew her as "Grandmother" through her almost-weekly contributions to the newspaper *Amerika*, where she regularly debated current happenings in her "Grandmother's Column." Among advertisements for the auction of twenty-five driving horses and timetables for the Cunard Line and other Atlantic ships, readers found Oline debating the salient issues of the time—women's rights, prohibition, and religion at the forefront. She wrote on general topics and also penned public rebuttals to editorial writers. In almost every edition from 1912 there is a response to "Grandmother" or directly to "Oline Muus." She often signed the column with her name, so it seems her pseudonym wasn't so secret. The title was an interesting choice, since she wasn't allowed to parent—or grandparent—after the separation some twenty-five years previous.

Oline's contributions stand out as a woman's voice in a sea of male and unsigned viewpoints. Some other women wrote in, but none contributed nearly as frequently. Maybe she found that writing was her forte. And maybe it was her way to hold on to her connection with the Norwegian American community in the Midwest that she had left behind so long ago. Perhaps the scrutiny she endured at Holden Church and in the civil court had given her the confidence she needed to express her opinions more widely.

Her writing was not limited to her beliefs. She reflected—in great detail—on what she had endured over the years, though some of her pieces offered versions of her past that differed substantially from what we know through so many earlier sources. Oline Muus apparently created a new narrative, one with which she could grapple. In 1906, she wrote what she called her life story, which began: "So it happened as my parents had hoped and wished, I was engaged to Bernt Muus. The day we were married in Fet Church, we had been given a bad omen. There was a terrible storm, so we barely made it across the Glomma river to the church. . . . At home I was the youngest, and as often happens with the youngest in the family, I was spoiled." Once again she felt the need to explain and defend herself publicly.[3]

She had now turned sixty-seven, and it was a quarter century since she left Holden parsonage. The newspaper's editor may have encouraged her to write about her life. Rasmus B. Anderson was a Norwegian American leader and historian and a professor of Nordic languages at the University of Wisconsin in Madison. He was opposed to Americanization, and he had long been the Norwegian Synod's ally. His great cause was to establish Norwegian-language literature and culture in America. Professor Anderson's work wasn't in vain; as late as the 1920s, Norwegian was the language used in many congregations in Norwegian America. The pastor officiated in Norwegian, the parochial schoolteachers taught in Norwegian, and youth could choose to be confirmed in either Norwegian or American English.[4]

Oline Muus may have still considered herself Norwegian. In all the years since her departure from Holden in 1881, she had continued her correspondence with friends and acquaintances in Norwegian. She had never applied for US citizenship; her native language was, as the many columns in *Amerika* suggest, intact after fifty years of living abroad.

In print, she retold her side of the scandal in Holden one last time, beginning with her childhood. If her parents were able to give her anything she wanted, they would do so, even if to her detriment. And as she matured, she realized her upbringing had made it more difficult for her to control her sinful desires. Therefore, after a great struggle and many deliberations she decided to marry a devout man of faith. If she were so fortunate as to partner with him, he could bear the burden for her. But, in retrospect, she didn't believe her love for him had been strong enough.[5]

Oline Muus wrote a life story akin to a Gothic novel. It seems inevitable that the marriage to Pastor Muus would be unhappy. And it's worth asking if the marriage had turned out as Oline Pind perhaps feared. There are some similarities between her own marriage and the one in the sinister serial article "My Lost Arlien" that Bernt had sent her so many years ago. When her husband acted in an abhorrent manner, Oline admitted she responded with righteous indignation. Later, she became more apathetic and indifferent and let things slide. In fact, she occasionally lost her senses and didn't know what was happening around her. In her description, it was as if she became a passive tool, a machine that is wound up and goes, until it comes to a stop.

She confided that the twenty years in Holden were nothing compared to what she had since suffered. All alone, she had struggled and fought her way forward in the world without a single human soul to support her. Nevertheless, the Lord had made everything for her own good; she had been blessed in her old age, more than she could ever have dreamed. She had her beautiful, comfortable home in the South. She was healthy and strong and had everything she needed for a living and, best of all, God's grace, peace, and blessing. But she had never regretted standing her ground twenty-five years earlier.

Oline ended this piece by correcting a widespread misconception, offering words for her friends and enemies. She had thought that time would probably be her best advocate, and it had been. She also thought that when she rested in her grave the full truth and right would come to light. Her consolation was that the truth always prevails in the end. "There are many who believe," she wrote, "that I sought a divorce from my husband." But it wasn't true; she had never filed for divorce and never wanted a divorce. When she left her husband, it was because she believed that without her, the home would be more peaceful for him and for their children. Besides, he was the one who wanted her to leave; he had made that clear both to her and to others.

But before she ended her letter in February 1906, she gave newspaper readers a puzzle by quoting a Bible story: "And as there is no rule without exception, of which our Savior has given us an example, in that he broke the law of the Sabbath and let his disciples eat of the shew-bread, so surely there must also be an exception to the law of marriage."[6]

Her letters also offer sage advice. In March 1912, she wrote, "with love, goodwill, and friendliness we can attract thousands into God's kingdom; with threats, coercion, and forcefulness we will only attract thousands into the Devil's kingdom. I have myself experienced—and not just minimally—what coercion and threats can lead a person to; but I have also experienced the impact of courtesy and goodwill on one's heart."[7]

Through her many columns she addressed her naysayers and aligned herself with those who shared her opinions. Several of her longer let-ters read as much like a confession as a defense. In her missive of April 5, 1912, Oline surprisingly declared that she had committed the greatest sin and was most at fault for the dramatic events that had once hap-pened to her. But her husband wasn't without fault; in all such cases, sin and error were committed on both sides. The main reason things went so wrong between her and her husband was because they didn't understand each other and they had completely different views on life. And when Satan finds a refuge between a married couple, peace and harmony disappear. The love between them chills to an icy crust, and their respect for each other dies out.[8]

She explained to *Amerika*'s readers that she was life's stepchild. She had been, and evidently still was, a subject of slander, malice, and gos-sip. She had been deprived of all that was dear and precious to her in this world—her children, her good name and reputation, and her honor. The parsonage had been a prison; she couldn't remain there when everything had been taken from her. She told the newspaper readers that she was a victim; as she had been crippled for life because of her husband's abuse. Nevertheless, she had managed to offer music lessons. She barely made it without going into debt. She wasn't seeking com-miseration and pity, for all the punishment and chastisement she had received and still received was well deserved and for her own good. In the course of her defense or confession, Oline Muus had transformed from a victim to a repentant and remorseful sinner.[9]

One wonders what Birgitte thought when she read her mother's letters in *Amerika*. Later that decade, in 1917, when war was raging in Europe and beyond, she lived with her mother in the abandoned hotel. But, in 1918, Birgitte Klüver returned to Norway. At that time her mother was no longer in good health. Nonetheless, the parting must have been peaceful, for Oline bequeathed both the house and possessions in Fruithurst to her daughter. The women in the congregation cared for Mrs. Muus in her final year. She was dependent on a wheelchair, and eventually she became bedridden. One of the women who sat with Mrs. Muus would later tell that she often sang hymns and that she knew long passages from the Bible by heart.

On Sunday, September 3, 1922, at a church service in the closed hotel's dining room, several congregation members were present when the pastor prayed for old Mrs. Muus. The next day she passed away. Oline Muus was eighty-three years old; she outlived her husband by twenty-two years. The memorial service was held in Norwegian and English, at her own request. Pastor Wilhelm Pedersen, whom she had come to know in Minneapolis, officiated at the funeral in a cemetery outside Fruithurst. She had decided that only "Oline Muus" should be written on her gravestone, nothing more. But the name inscribed on the gravestone was "Olene Muse." Such misspellings often happened when American stonemasons were commissioned for Norwegian American graves. The stonemason likely didn't understand Norwegian. Maybe it was a sloppy mistake, or perhaps he had only heard the name mentioned and carved it the way it sounded in English. In an irony of fate, Oline Muus first became Americanized posthumously. "Olene Muse" and "Oline Muus" sound alike, but the woman behind this name remains a mystery. In the fall of 1922, many details about her life seem to have been buried with her.[10]

APPENDIX

The Muus Descendants

AS TIME WOULD SHOW, it wasn't solely the lives of Bernt and Oline Muus that were fraught with hardship. All of their six children were born, baptized, and confirmed at Holden, but their lives took very different paths.[1]

Birgitte Magdalene Muus Klüver, the couple's first child, was born on November 24, 1860, and she was one of only two children to survive Oline. After her youth in Minnesota, she left her toddler, Sverre, at Holden parsonage and moved to Norway. In fall 1887 she married her second cousin, merchant Lorentz Diderik Klüver. The two were married in the church in Snåsa, where Birgitte's great-grandfather had stood in the pulpit. She lived in Trondheim and Steinskjær in Trøndelag, then Fruithurst, Alabama, with her mother and spent her final years in Oslo. Birgitte is also known for making a noteworthy book donation to the St. Olaf College library in 1931, including volumes that date back to 1634. Birgitte passed away in 1935 when she was seventy-one years old. She is buried in Vestre cemetery in Oslo.[2]

Birgitte and Lorentz had three children in Norway, all of whom came to America. The oldest, Johan Wilhelm Klüver, lived in New York beginning in 1916, but moved back to Norway shortly thereafter, becoming involved in his father's shipping business. During World War II Johan actively supported the Nazi Party, and he was imprisoned after the war. His son, Ole Wilhelm Kluwer, would later speak out on what it means to be a child of a Norwegian Nazi, eventually becoming the spokesman for the Organization of NS Children in Norway. The second son, Bernt Julius Klüver, named after his grandfather, became a renowned artist who traveled to Minneapolis and Northfield in 1932. Also a Nazi supporter, he died before World War II. Else Marie Berethe Klüver resided in the United States the longest of the three, living in New York, Alabama, and Minnesota from 1912 to 1917.[3]

Nils (Nels) Muus, the couple's second child and eldest son, was born on January 7, 1863. He was a student at Luther College from 1876 to 1879. In 1877 he wrote home to his mother saying he was so pleased to get her letter because he never received any from his father. In the same letter, he told her about the horrible stale bread the students were served and asked if his father would give permission for him to come home for Christmas. In 1886 Nils married Josephine Sortedal, the daughter of a Holden farmer, and became a farmer himself. Nils and Josephine would have ten children together. The couple is buried at the Holden cemetery along with some of their children. One of their daughters, Elizabeth Muus, was a student at St. Olaf College in the class of 1907. She is the only Muus grandchild to graduate from St. Olaf College.[4]

Jens Ingebrigt Rynning Muus, born on January 12, 1866, the couple's third child, was the first to pass away, in 1878, at only twelve years of age, after a battle with typhus. His death, although tragic, did not come without warning. He was a student at St. Olaf's School from 1877 to 1878. From 1878 to 1879 he was enrolled at Luther College, becoming very sick during that academic year. One month before his death, in October 1878, he penned a letter to his mother, remarking that he was too sick to attend class, with a horrible headache and stomach problems. His older brother, Nils, had asked if he might be allowed to go home. Although Jens enjoyed school at the outset, homesickness had set in, and he felt it had an impact on his deteriorating health. He must have been sent home soon after this letter, as he passed away from typhus on November 6, 1878, at the Holden parsonage. While his mother was at home caring for him, his father learned of the news from a messenger sent to Northfield, where he was celebrating the dedication of the first building on the St. Olaf campus, the Main, on that same day.[5]

Paul Johan Elster Muus, the couple's fourth child, also died before reaching adulthood. Born on March 22, 1872, Paul died of consumption in 1890, just before his eighteenth birthday. Ten years earlier, Oline had foreshadowed his death in the statement she wrote to the Holden congregation:

Our little son Paul in the fall and the beginning of winter 1878, according to orders from his father, had to walk to school every day two miles, that makes four miles to and from school, he was only 6½ years old and sickly. The boots that he has to wear should have been discarded long ago; but it wasn't possible to get anything better for the boy's feet, or wasn't his health worth much? The child became so ill and weak that at times he was unable to eat his noon lunch at school, and when he came home in the evening he would vomit because of illness and weakness. He became so seriously ill that he had to stay in all winter and take medicine, and most likely will never be really well again. I can call such a treatment of a child that age abuse and believe that this expression is justified.[6]

Petter (Peter) Herman Muus, the couple's fifth child, was born on December 12, 1874—an exciting time between the founding of St. Olaf's School and its opening day. Petter was a student at St. Olaf's School from 1887 to 1888 and St. Olaf College from 1892 to 1896. During this time, Bernt Muus exchanged a number of letters with Halvor T. Ytterboe, a faculty member at St. Olaf, inquiring about why Petter wasn't advancing in his studies as expected, commenting on his "rotten" Norwegian, and asking if he was too lazy. Petter was the only Muus child to graduate from St. Olaf College. He later studied briefly at the theological seminary of the United Norwegian Lutheran Church in Minneapolis, but then shifted to study medicine at Hamline University in St. Paul. Petter married Leonara Marie Rushfeldt and had two children, Virgil and Virginia. He received his MD in 1901 and practiced medicine in southern Minnesota. He died in 1913 at thirty-eight years old. Petter is buried in Albert Lea, Minnesota.[7]

Harald (Harold) Steen Muus (Moose) was the couple's youngest child, born in 1878. He was a student at St. Olaf's School from 1889 to

1890 and became a farmer, first in Minnesota and later in Petaluma, California. He married twice, first to Bertha Bendicta Ellestad in 1900. They had two children, Daphne Alberta and Harold Ellestad. In addition to his early years in Holden, records show him living in Illinois, Washington, and California. He also held many different occupations: he listed his profession as "brakeman for the railroad" in the 1910 census, as "(tire) vulcanizer" on his World War I draft card, and as "ranch laborer" in the 1940 census. He married a second time, to Annie Linebaugh, in 1919. Harald lived seventy-six years, dying in 1954. As he traveled farther west, away from the heart of Norwegian America, he seemed to become more Americanized. His grave marker spells his first name "Harold" and, perhaps most notably, his last name "Moose."[8]

Sverre Muus, Birgitte's first son, was raised in the Holden parsonage by his grandfather, Bernt Muus. Born in 1881, he was just three years younger than his uncle Harald, the youngest child of Oline and Bernt. One can only assume that Sverre experienced deep trauma from the early events in his life, most notably his unwed mother leaving him in the care of his grandfather, whose parenting ability had been brought into serious doubt. Based on Birgitte's marriage date in Norway, she departed before Sverre turned four years old.[9]

Sverre was a student at St. Olaf's School for a short time from 1891 to 1892, and then later at Luther College. Letters from Pastor Muus to the president of Luther, Laur. Larsen, indicate that Sverre had gotten into money troubles and was eventually expelled. Sverre resided in Oregon and Montana, marrying Hilda Sophie Eggen in 1905. On his marriage license he provided the name of his father as Johannes Muus, while his father's actual name was Johannes Olsen Kongsvik. Sverre and Hilda had a daughter, Leonora Muus, in 1904, a year before their marriage. On his World War I draft card in 1918, Sverre is listed as a cook in St. Paul, Minnesota. He named his nearest relative as Mrs. Oline Muus and wrote "mother" in parentheses next to her name, even though Oline was actually his grandmother. There is no record of Sverre and Oline ever connecting after Oline's departure from Holden when he was a toddler, so it is noteworthy that he didn't list another family member instead. It seems unlikely he was brought up to believe Oline was his mother. Instead, perhaps he wished to hide the fact that his mother was unmarried when he was born.[10]

Later accounts of Sverre's life also locate him in a Montana State Prison and a workhouse in Minneapolis. In 1923 he was declared "of unsound mind" in a report that states he had left his wife and daughter fifteen years earlier, had a sudden attack, and claimed Buffalo Bill hypnotized him in Birmingham, Alabama. He spoke incoherently and was sent to the Rochester state hospital in June 1923, but he immediately escaped.[11]

If there is any doubt surrounding Sverre's lack of acceptance into the Muus family, one need only examine any of the three family genealogies Bernt Muus authored and coauthored, which will prompt great sorrow on Sverre's behalf. Though devoted to documenting the family genealogy, Bernt excluded Sverre from the family tree. It is only noted that Birgitte had three children with her husband, and they are also left unnamed, unlike the other grandchildren. But there is no mention whatsoever of a fourth—Birgitte's first—child.

Bust of Bernt Julius Muus in Old Main, St. Olaf College.
Photo by Kari Lie Dorer

EDITOR'S AFTERWORD

MANY CONSIDER THE ESTABLISHMENT of St. Olaf's School, later to become St. Olaf College, to be Bernt Julius Muus's greatest achievement. There is no doubt the college has had a profound impact on the thousands of individuals who attended or were employed there over the next 150 years. But rarely during my tenure at the college have I heard any mention of Muus's other accomplishments—of which there were many. These achievements are all laid out in previous scholarship, but they aren't something with which the average person seems familiar.

When I began teaching at St. Olaf College in 2001, as I walked from my office to my classroom, I passed the bust of Bernt Julius Muus in Old Main at least ten times a day. At that time, students would come to Old Main just to rub his nose for good luck before an exam. But other than knowing where the founder was from, I too knew very little about the man with the shiny nose.

Bernt Julius Muus was Minnesota's *first* resident pastor for the Norwegian Lutheran church. In practice, because of the shortage of clergy, this role meant he managed twenty-eight congregations and was responsible for over 15,000 square miles, an area comparable to the entirety of Denmark. He was constantly on the move, especially in his early years before there were other pastors to share the burden. One source noted that from the first Sunday in Advent in 1860 until the same day in 1861, he traveled by oxen, horse, and buggy, and even sometimes on foot a total of 6,900 miles. All this movement was at a time when roads from point A to point B did not always exist. He also preached in German to a German congregation located between Zumbrota and Red Wing before it was able to acquire its own pastor.[1]

Bernt Julius Muus funneled his energies into his work. During his forty years in Minnesota, Muus performed 9,877 baptisms, confirmed 5,288 youth, married 1,268 couples, and buried 3,909 individuals. He was the president of the Minnesota District of the Norwegian Synod from 1876 to 1883, a total of seven years. In the midst of this, in 1878 he remained in charge of eighteen to twenty parochial schools with the help of two assistants. Such a work schedule left little time for his family.[2]

When the new church at Holden was dedicated in 1924, eight thousand people attended the celebration. Five years later, in 1929, and nine years after Pastor Muus had passed away, one immigrant scholar noted that everyone in Goodhue County still revered the name of Pastor Muus because his picture is found on a wall in every home. In 1937, a monument was erected at Holden Lutheran church commemorating his achievements. But somewhere his legacy was lost, including his contributions as a church founder.[3]

When a Sunday morning service begins at Holden today, it is truly apparent just how much the church has evolved in the 150 years since the events in this book. Today's pastor offers a children's sermon with a few lighthearted stories and, without hesitation, cuddles his toddler when they need comfort during the service—a striking, yet welcome, contrast from the hellfire and damnation services led by the authoritative Pastor Muus.

Inside Holden Church today, one finds a massive timeline depicting the congregation's history. Still, the majority of parishioners would not be familiar with Pastor Muus by name or know anything about him. Their knowledge of him was partially from oral histories, but very few are familiar with his work. Somehow his legacy, even as a church founder, has become lost. Holden Church still towers over the rolling hills, separated only by a windbreak from the vast area of farmland that encapsulates it. The church is surrounded by tombstones with names—mostly of Norwegian origin—of the deceased members of

Bernt Julius Muus monument at Holden Church.
Photo by Kari Lie Dorer

the congregation. Just west of the church is where Holden parsonage was built. Included in the National Register of Historic Places in 1978 because of its connection to Bernt Muus, the property has since been sold. A short distance farther west is where the Norway post office was located. Now a ghost town in Goodhue County, here is where the majority of Oline Muus's correspondence was sent and received.[4]

Oline Muus was never commemorated with monuments or given a prestigious title such as "first resident pastor for Minnesota" or "college founder," but her life was monumental. When Oline Muus took refuge in Minneapolis, in the area known today as the Cedar-Riverside neighborhood, she blossomed into a first-generation immigrant woman— an entrepreneur who used her talents for sewing and teaching piano to earn a living after having been an outcast tirelessly fighting against a patriarchal and unjust Norwegian American community. She didn't settle or give up; she believed in her pursuit of a better life. David Mauk notes that this area became the city's best-known and most densely populated Norwegian and Swedish immigrant quarter by the 1880s and that from the mid-1880s and to the mid-1900s, the heart of the area blossomed into a primarily Scandinavian neighborhood. This area also fostered growth of the suffrage movement. And the neighborhood has continued to house and employ wave after wave of new immigrants.[5]

Oline Muus lived for several years at Twenty-Second Avenue South and Sixth Street in Minneapolis, directly across from Augsburg University. Today on that same corner is a nonprofit store called Sisterhood Boutique. Its entrepreneurial program for East African immigrants is designed to empower young women to achieve their ambitious goals, develop valuable business skills, and make a positive impact in their communities. Its motto: "wrapped in confidence." These women represent a new generation forging their own path forward. While they make a life for themselves, they simultaneously pave the way for the next generation of immigrant women who are yet to arrive. Each wave benefits from the generations before them, sharing in sisterhood. Oline Muus's actions had a profound effect on the other women in her community and the following generation by demanding that her—a woman's—voice be heard.

Bodil Stenseth's book was published at a time when my curiosity regarding the founding of St. Olaf College had already been piqued. My initial research interest in the Muus family wasn't their marital drama; actually, I had not heard about it until well over a decade after joining the Norwegian Department at St. Olaf College. My research interests stemmed from a curiosity concerning Bernt Muus's ancestry—specifically if he possibly was of Sámi descent, which would not be unheard of given the history of Snåsa, where he was born and raised. I began my research where most people do, with the comprehensive historical inquiries by two esteemed retired colleagues: *Bernt Julius Muus: Founder of St. Olaf College* and *History of St. Olaf College, 1874–1974* by Joseph Shaw, professor emeritus of religion, and *The Promise of America: A History of the Norwegian-American People* and *Norwegian Newspapers in America: Connecting Norway and the New Land* by Odd S. Lovoll, professor emeritus of history and Norwegian. These four books continued to fuel my interest in the Norwegian American community that founded the college. In my search to answer that question, I found very little of what I sought and instead information I didn't know I was looking for.

Now, in my position as the chair of the Norwegian Department, I am constantly on the lookout for new and innovative ways to connect my students' understanding of Norwegian America with that of the experiences of recent immigrant groups in both Minnesota and Norway. The majority of our students come with the perception that Norwegian Americans, both past and present, hold Norwegian cultural and religious attitudes. My role is to affirm their past experiences with the heritage culture—but also to expand their knowledge and help them explore contemporary Norway, a culture often very different from that of their grandparents and great-grandparents. The story of *Muus vs. Muus* does an excellent job in pointing to a handful of similarities while also diving into and exploring the contrasts and the explanations for why, as well as how, cultures develop in divergent directions.

Stenseth's book captured my interest because it depicts these surprising contradictions within the Norwegian immigrant community. I began considering whether the book would be of interest to an

English-language audience, and how this work might fit in with that of my predecessors. The more I discussed it with colleagues, the more it became clear that only a select few, all of whom were older than me, had known this part of the Norwegian American community's past— and that the topic sparked interest.

One comment from professor emeritus of religion L. DeAne Lagerquist stuck. She said something along the lines of, "Have you ever thought about why we don't have a building named after our founder? Sometimes it's precisely what's missing that is the most revealing." No, I really hadn't, and framing the question in this way made me consider the value of bringing the story to an English-speaking audience—including many difficult topics in our community's past, of how and why Norwegians and Norwegian American leaders had acted for the good of themselves, for their religious or cultural milieu, and had actively worked to silence and shun those who stood in opposition.

While I was deciding whether to take up this assignment, I found a podcast interview with Bodil Stenseth in which she commented on the story's relevance for understanding newer immigrant communities in both Norway and the United States—specifically that the Norwegian American immigrant community did many of the things for which contemporary immigrant groups to both countries are criticized. And I think we could also include in that conversation how Indigenous peoples, specifically the Sámi and Dakota, have been impacted by Norwegian settlement. It was a good reminder regarding the significance of this story: that it doesn't end with the lives of a pastor and his wife. The value is found in having a historical understanding of how the Norwegian American community organized and developed, how it supported—and refused to support—individuals from outside communities and those within who didn't follow the group's norms. It's also the account of how a community acted counter to what the larger American society deemed acceptable and "American."

My hope is that as we prepare for two transformative commemorative events—200 years since the beginning of organized Norwegian American migration and 150 years since the founding of St. Olaf

College—that this story can serve as a springboard for a much-needed discussion of and reckoning with the past. Norwegian Americans need to engage with this history, to acknowledge both the accomplishments of our ancestors but also what they failed to do.

After working on this project for almost three years, I enlisted the help of my mother, Letty Homberger Lie, whose genealogy savvy I hoped might uncover something more on the lives of the Muus family and their descendants. She helped me find some interesting tidbits that I have included, but the far larger—and to me shocking—thing we discovered was an unanticipated ancestral link to the Muus family. Through my mom's maternal lineage, we are connected to the Muuses. While not recent or close by any means, our ancestral lines are intertwined through multiple marriages in the Klüver and the Muus families in the 1700s and 1800s. What began as an institutional connection for me at the outset of this project grew into researching my own ancestral past.

But for many this history isn't as personal: it involves reckoning with religious or institutional affiliations. And that reckoning has to include more than this story was able to fully capture; it should also include pushing ourselves to more thoroughly engage with the history of the Mdewakanton Dakota and the contributions of their leaders. Their land was stolen, their lives and culture uprooted and destroyed, for the progress and advancement of the Norwegian American immigrants. Engagement in this history would facilitate a deeper, more nuanced understanding of the lives and legacies of the Native Americans on whose land we live, work, and play.

Bringing this story to an English readership was a timely project as it coincided with an invitation to serve on the board of the Norwegian-American Historical Association (NAHA) and gave me an incredible opportunity to take a deep dive into the archives, to experience the value of the trove of resources. In addition to the time I spent in the Special Collections at St. Olaf College and the Norwegian-American Historical Association, I spent weeks digging in the archives at the Gale Family Library at the Minnesota History Center, at Luther College, at Augsburg University, and at Carleton College, in addition to many online archives. My research was complemented by inquisitive research students and incredibly helpful and knowledgeable archivists.

While this English edition is based on the original Norwegian *Fru Muus' klage*, there are a number of noticeable differences. As Stenseth points out, her research relied heavily on *Budstikken*'s reporting, which included both detailed accounts and summaries of English-language news reporting in Norwegian. For *Muus vs. Muus*, it was essential to utilize the original English-language newspaper articles in lieu of translated synopses. In the process of finding and understanding these journalistic pieces, I became engrossed in the sharp writing style of the reporters and the letters sent in as editorials, a handful of which are used within the text as they depict the case so vividly. I have also corrected a number of details centered on dates, names, and citations and added many details as well.

I am grateful that Bodil Stenseth saw the value in this story and took the time to write it. After discussing my interest in an English-language edition with her, I first sought to translate *Fru Muus' klage*. When focused on the translation, I found myself consulting with the primary English-language sources as much as Stenseth's text, which quickly resulted in so many details fueling my interest that my role shifted to that of an active researcher, intent on expanding her work in certain ways to make it come alive for an English-language audience. The more I researched, the less time I had to devote to the details of translation. I am forever indebted to Torild Homstad, who began as a proofreader and editor, and after some early helpful contributions, agreed to take on the much more time-consuming role of co-translator. Her keen attention to writing style in both Norwegian and English paired perfectly with her familiarity with St. Olaf College, Northfield and the surrounding community, and Norwegian American Lutheranism.

The English-language edition could not have been completed without the meaningful contributions of my students. I was awarded a Magnus the Good award from St. Olaf College to begin work in the summer of 2020 together with three students: Kristian Noll, Synneva Bratland, and Patricia (Tyga) Kinsumbya. We explored what makes a good translation (both human and computer-assisted) and developed a term base for the frequently used words in the text before testing it out on an article by the same author that has since been published in the journal *Norwegian-American Studies*. Student contributions continued with two editorial assistants, Erik Moe and Lance Halberg, who spent much time in a variety of archives and endless hours updating citations and finding primary sources. Then I taught a directed undergraduate research course in which students drafted a wide variety of resources to further explore topics in the book. The results of their work include a discussion guide available with and without their sample answers and insightful podcast interviews with scholars. These resources, in addition to many others, are available on the *Muus vs. Muus* website. Additionally, two students, Autumn Blackwell and Emma Gross, identified areas in the text that drew their curiosity, researched, and drafted short contributions to the book. Additional thanks to editorial work by Autumn Blackwell, Ryan Kiser, and Sam Hager, who diligently located original source materials in various archives, fact-checked, and rewrote the source notes and bibliography.

In addition to these students, I extend an enormous amount of gratitude to the archivists and librarians who helped locate many interesting articles and letters and gave so much advice along the way. A huge shout-out first to Kristina Warner, archivist at the Norwegian-American Historical Association, who helped me at many points in the project by digitizing, talking through questions, and offering advice, and who always had me on her radar when she found something she thought could be useful to me. Many thanks also to Kristell Benson, Jillian Sparks, and Karla Jurgemeyer at St. Olaf College, who worked with me and my students to identify sources and shared their breadth of expertise; Hayley Jackson at Luther College, who answered countless emails with enthusiasm; and Stewart Van Cleve at Augsburg University and Eric Hilleman at Carleton College, whose helpful contributions all made for interesting new tidbits in the English-language edition. Thanks as well to DeAne Lagerquist, who read an early draft and gave very helpful feedback.

To the individuals who met with me and my students or answered questions via email, I also extend my gratitude. This list includes DeAne Lagerquist, Odd Lovoll, Lori Ann Lahlum, Jeff Davidson, Pat Wickum Maisel, Joe Shaw, Nathan Muus, Eric Hilleman, and Jeff Sauve. And tusen takk to Amy Boxrud and Anna Peterson at NAHA.

I would also give a special shout-out to Shannon Pennefeather and the entire behind-the-scenes crew at Minnesota Historical Society Press. I'm so thankful I was paired with you for this project, and for all the thoughtful ways in which you engaged with it.

Thanks also to my family. First and foremost to my husband, Ben, who held down the fort while I worked long hours; to my son, Simon, for always changing the subject from work to ninjas or starting a dance party when I arrived home; and to Mocko, who would unapologetically jump on top of my laptop, reminding me that evenings are best spent playing with a puppy. Thanks also to my parents, Greg and Letty, for instilling a strong interest in my ancestral past. Ever since I can remember, they encouraged me to explore my roots. Together we spent many family "vacations" at cemeteries rubbing charcoal on paper to get dates from gravestones or at archives to look up records, about which my brother and I voiced our strong annoyance. I would never have anticipated that this project would explore my own personal ancestry—and further illustrate just how intertwined the Norwegian American community is.

TIMELINES

1832–1878 ⫶ *Part I: Hand in Hand*[1]

1832 Bernt Julius Muus born in Snåsa, Norway, on March 15.

1833 Bernt's mother dies. He moves in with his maternal grandparents.

1838 Kathrine Christiane (Oline) Pind born in Fet, Norway, on September 12.

1842 Bernt begins school in Trondheim.

1849–1854 Bernt attends Det Kongelige Frederiks University in Christiania.

1857 Bernt and Oline become engaged.

1858 Minnesota becomes a state.

1859 Bernt is ordained.

1859 Bernt and Oline marry on July 12 at Tien.

1859 Bernt and Oline immigrate to America in the fall.

1859 Bernt preaches his first sermon at Holden in the home of Ole Huset on November 6.

1860 The original Holden parsonage is built.

1860 The couple's first child, Birgitte, is born on November 24.

1862 The US–Dakota War begins on August 17.

1862 Oline's father dies in Norway.

1863 The estate of Oline's father is settled and Oline is bequeathed $4,955 (4,675 Norwegian spesidaler).

1863 The couple's second child, Nils, is born on January 7.

1866 The couple's third child, Jens, is born on January 12.

1869 Bernt opens Holden Academy in the parsonage's basement.

1871 The first Holden Church building is dedicated on November 7.

1872 The couple's fourth child, Paul, is born on March 24.

1874 St. Olaf's School is founded on November 6.

1874 The couple's fifth child, Petter, is born on December 12.

1875 St. Olaf's School opens for instruction on January 6.

1876 Bernt becomes the president of the Minnesota District of the Norwegian Lutheran Synod.

1877 Oline breaks her leg for the first time in the spring.

1878 The couple's sixth child, Harald, is born on July 2.

1878 Jens Muus dies on the same day as the dedication of St. Olaf's first building, the Main, on November 6.

1879–1883 ⋮ *Part II: Family Trials*

1879 Oline files a suit against her husband for the right to her inheritance on December 26 in Goodhue County. Case #1470 includes an appendix known as "The Complaint."

1880 Holden congregation has the first round of congregational meetings on February 18. There is disagreement about the agenda. Eventually, they vote to decide if Bernt should remain as pastor, with approximately a thousand in attendance.

1880 Holden congregation has their second round of congregational meetings March 10–11 to determine if Oline should be disciplined for not following the fourth commandment. Oline does not attend in protest because her conditions for her attendance are not fulfilled. She is brought to the church and her prepared statement is read.

1880 Holden congregation holds their third round of congregational meetings May 13–14, which the Synod leadership attends. It is determined that the assembly is too large, and an investigative committee is established.

1880 On June 5, *Holden (or: Be Patient! A Synod Opera in Three Acts)* is performed.

1880 The investigative committee meet at the Muus residence on June 7, 8, and 9.

1880 Holden congregation holds their fourth round of meetings on July 7, 8, and 9. Pastor Muus convenes the congregation to discuss the investigative committee's report, which determined that Oline committed three sins.

1881 Sverre Muus is born to Birgitte Muus and Johannes Olsen Kongsvik, out of wedlock, on August 27.

1881 Judge F. M. Crosby renders a verdict on Goodhue District Court Case #1470 on September 8, ruling that the statute of limitations had run out on the first of two estate payments. Bernt could keep the initial sum but would have to repay Oline the second portion, approximately $1,115.

1881 *The Old Wisconsin Bible* by Marcus Thrane is published.

1881 The two youngest children, Harald and Petter, are removed from the Muus family home and move in with a member of the church congregation four miles away on November 3.

1881 Minnesota State Supreme Court Case files #3189 and #3250 are filed by Oline and Bernt, respectively, for an appeal of Goodhue District Court's verdict on November 28.

LATE 1881 Oline withdraws membership from Holden Church after a meeting lasting several days.

END OF 1881/PRIOR TO JANUARY 3, 1882 Oline moves to Minneapolis with financial backing from Augsburg professors Sverdrup and Oftedal.

1882 Verdict is rendered in Minnesota State Supreme Court Case files #3189 and #3250 May 16 affirming the district court's decision on Oline's inheritance. In total Bernt is ordered to pay Oline $2,575 to account for the second inheritance payment, interest, legal fees, etc.

1882 Oline files for divorce in Hennepin District Court on October 17, 1882, Case #13571.

1883 Judge A. H. Young renders verdict on Hennepin District Court Case #13571 for a limited divorce (separation) on January 22.

1883 Bernt is not reelected president of the Minnesota District of the Norwegian Synod.

1887–1937 ⋮ *Part III: Disgrace*

1887 Birgitte marries Lorentz Diderik Klüver at Snåsa church on September 15.

1889 Oline moves to South Dakota.

1890 Oline and Bernt's fourth child, Paul, dies at seventeen years old.

1896 Oline moves from South Dakota to Fruithurst, Alabama, on October 22.

1898 Bernt is ousted from the Norwegian Synod.

1899 Bernt leaves Holden to live with his daughter, Birgitte, in Norway on July 21.

1900 Bernt Julius Muus dies in Trondheim, Norway, on May 5.

1922 Oline Pind Muus dies in Fruithurst, Alabama, on September 4.

1937 Monument of Bernt Julius Muus erected at Holden Church.

NOTES

Notes to Preface

1. Jan Eivind Myhre, "Utvandring fra Norge," Norgeshistorie, University of Oslo, last modified November 2, 2020, https://www.norgeshistorie.no/industrial isering-og-demokrati/1537-utvandring-fra-norge.html.

2. Hansen, "Migration and Puritanism," digital version, 1–9, 2; Erikson, *Wayward Puritans*, 73, 107; Alba, Raboteau, and DeWind, eds., *Immigration and Religion in America*, 4–8.

3. Ericson, "Triple Jeopardy."

Notes to Chapter 1: To America

1. Shaw, *Bernt Julius Muus*, 58.

2. Biørn, *Festskrift*, 10.

3. Letter from B. J. Muus to Laur. Larsen, July 5, 1859, Records of the Norwegian Synod, Luther College.

Notes to Chapter 2: A Call from God

1. Molland, *Norges kirkehistorie*, 1:192, 200.

2. Bernt J. Muus to Oline Pind [Muus], October 23, 1857, Sven Oftedal Papers, Augsburg University Archives.

3. Bernt Muus to Oline Pind [Muus], October 23, 1857, Sven Oftedal Papers.

4. Molland, *Norges kirkehistorie*, 1:191.

5. de Tocqueville, *Om demokratiet i Amerika*, 124.

6. de Tocqueville, *Om demokratiet i Amerika*, 120; *Norsk Kirketidende*, January 1857.

7. Bernt Muus to Oline Pind [Muus], October 23, 1857, Sven Oftedal Papers.

Notes to Chapter 3: Land Rush and Pioneer Life

1. Ulvestad, *Nordmændene i Amerika*; Shaw, *Bernt Julius Muus*, 63.

2. Lovoll, *The Promise of America*, 82.

3. "1851 Dakota Land Cession Treaties," treaties.matter.org, Minnesota

Humanities Center, accessed February 20, 2023, https://treatiesmatter.org /treaties/land/1851-Dakota.

4. Lovoll, *The Promise of America*, 17–18.

5. Bernt J. Muus, "Hon. Knut K. Finseth," *Kirkelig Maanedstidende*, January 15, 1870, https://babel.hathitrust.org/cgi/pt?id=wu.89077114791&seq=27.

6. Biørn, *Festskrift*, 47–48.

7. Biørn, *Festskrift*, 50; Mørkhagen, *Drømmen om Amerika*, 233; Peter O. Floan, "Reminiscences of the Early History of Singing in Holden Congregation, Goodhue County, Minnesota," 1938, Peter O. Floan Reminiscences, Norwegian-American Historical Association, Northfield, MN (hereafter NAHA).

8. Mørkhagen, *Drømmen om Amerika*, 236–38.

9. Hustvedt, "Vignettes from a Norwegian Settlement," 191.

10. Biørn, *Festskrift*, 48.

11. Günther, *The Little American*, 50.

Notes to Chapter 4: Oline's Disfavor

1. Louise Pind to Bernt Muus, March 28, 1858, Sven Oftedal Papers.

2. Grindal, *Unstoppable*, 44.

3. Grindal, *Unstoppable*, 44.

4. "Henrik Arnold Wergeland," Britannica, accessed June 11, 2023, https:// www.britannica.com/biography/Henrik-Arnold-Wergeland.

5. Ueland, *Recollections of an Immigrant*, 41.

6. Molland, *Norges kirkehistorie*, 198.

7. Molland, *Norges kirkehistorie*, 204.

Notes to Chapter 5: The Lay People's Church

1. Halvorsen, ed., *Festskrift*, 59.

2. Molland, *Norges kirkehistorie*, 2:52; Store norske leksikon, "menighetsråd," accessed June 11, 2023, https://snl.no/menighetsr%C3%A5d.

3. Biørn, *Festskrift*, 11.

4. Biørn, *Festskrift*, 11.

5. H. A. Preus, *Kirkelig Maanedstidende*, January 1, 1871, 6, https://babel.hathi trust.org/cgi/pt?id=wu.89077114825&seq=16.

6. Biørn, *Festskrift*, 48, 49.

Notes to Chapter 6: "My Lost Arlien"

1. Bernt Muus to Oline Pind [Muus], November 16, 1858, Sven Oftedal Papers.

2. Bernt Muus to Oline Pind [Muus], November 18, 1858, Sven Oftedal Papers.

3. Bernt Muus to Oline Pind [Muus], June 30, 1858, Sven Oftedal Papers.

4. Bernt Muus to Oline Pind [Muus], January 13, 1859, Sven Oftedal Papers.

Notes to Chapter 7: *Before Darkness Came*

1. Grindal, *Unstoppable*, 45.
2. Lovoll, *The Promise Fulfilled*, 14.
3. Bernt Muus to Oline Pind [Muus], September 29, 1857, Sven Oftedal Papers.
4. Norlie, *History of the Norwegian People in America.*

Notes to Chapter 8: *Hellfire and Damnation Sermons*

1. Østgård, *America-America Letters*, 113.
2. Bernt Muus to Oline Pind [Muus], March 13, 1859, Sven Oftedal Papers.
3. Halvorsen, *Festskrift*, 24.
4. Muus, "Hon. Knut K. Finseth."
5. Muus, "Hon. Knut K. Finseth."
6. Muus, "Hon. Knut K. Finseth."
7. Muus, "Hon. Knut K. Finseth."
8. Shaw, *Bernt Julius Muus*, 79, 104.
9. "Speech of P. M. Langemo at the 'Jubelfest' held at Holden, Sept. 12–16, 1906," translated by Julia Øredalen, S. O. Simundson Papers, NAHA; Norlie, *History of the Norwegian People in America,* 444, 454; Peter O. Floan, "Reminiscences from the Pioneer Days in Goodhue County, Minnesota," Peter O. Floan Reminiscences.

Notes to Chapter 9: *At War with the Dakota*

1. Peter O. Floan "Reminiscences of the Early History, circa 1938–1942," Peter O. Floan Reminiscences, P0096, box 1, folder 1, page 10.
2. Curtiss-Wedge, ed., *History of Goodhue County*, 186.
3. Curtiss-Wedge, ed., *History of Goodhue County*, 93; Tom Morain, "Spirit Lake Massacre," Teaching Iowa History, accessed June 6, 2023, https://teachingio wahistory.org/historical-essays/spirit-lake-massacre.
4. Floan, "Reminiscences of the Early History, circa 1938–1942."
5. "War and the Great White North," Some Dibble History, updated January 10, 2024, https://www.dibblehistory.org/history4.htm.
6. "War and the Great White North," Some Dibble History.
7. Rowberg, *The Aaker Saga*, 21; Curtiss-Wedge, *History of Goodhue County*, 335–36.
8. Holden Lutheran Church, Goodhue County, Minnesota, "Holden Lutheran Church," accessed June 18, 2023, https://sites.google.com/site/holdenlutheran.
9. Floan, "Reminiscences of the Early History, circa 1938–1942."
10. Douglas O. Linder, "The Dakota Conflict Trials: An Account," Famous Trials, University of Missouri–Kansas City, accessed July 2, 2023, https://famous-trials.com/dakotaconflict/1525-dak-account; "The Trials & Hanging," The U.S.–Dakota War of 1862, Minnesota Historical Society, accessed May 20, 2023, https://www.usdakotawar.org/history/aftermath/trials-hanging.

11. Wist, ed., *Norsk-Amerikanernes Festskrift*, 33; Østgård, *America-America Letters*, xxii.

12. White, "Indian Visits."

13. Bergland, "Norwegian Migration and Displaced Indigenous Peoples," 19, 30.

Notes to Chapter 10: The Churching of Women

1. Curtiss-Wedge, *History of Goodhue County*, 198; Floan, "Reminiscences of the Early History, circa 1938–1942"; Grose, *Fifty Memorable Years at St Olaf*, 19.

2. Shaw, *Bernt Julius Muus*, 261; Floan, "Reminiscences of the Early History, circa 1938–1942."

3. Hustvedt, "Vignettes from a Norwegian Settlement," 192.

4. Elisabeth Koren, December 2, 1862, record group 15, box 3, letter 107, Letters of Elisabeth Koren, Luther College, Decorah, IA.

Notes to Chapter 11: A Norwegian Rabble-Rouser

1. H. A. Preus, "Advarsel til alle Kristne mot Markus Thranes 'Norske Amerikaner,'" *Kirkelig Maanedstidende*, September 1866, https://babel.hathitrust.org/cgi/pt?id=wu.89077114676&seq=267&q1=thranes.

2. Bjørklund, *Marcus Thrane*, 307.

3. Bjørklund, *Marcus Thrane*, 305; Preus, "Advarsel til alle Kristne mot Markus Thranes 'Norske Amerikaner.'"

4. Gulliksen, *Twofold Identities*.

5. "Beecher, Henry Ward (1813–1887)," Encyclopedia.com, accessed February 10, 2023, https://www.encyclopedia.com/people/philosophy-and-religion/protestant-christianity-biographies/henry-ward-beecher; "Tilton v. Beecher (1875)," Encyclopedia.com, accessed February 10, 2023, https://www.encyclopedia.com/law/law-magazines/tilton-v-beecher-1875.

6. Hymowitz and Weissman, *A History of Women in America*, 94–95.

7. "Lucretia Mott," National Women's Hall of Fame, accessed August 15, 2023, https://www.womenofthehall.org/inductee/lucretia-mott/; Stanton, "Declaration of Sentiments."

8. Preus, "Advarsel til alle Kristne mot Markus Thranes 'Norske Amerikaner.'"

9. Preus, "Advarsel til alle Kristne mot Markus Thranes 'Norske Amerikaner.'"

Notes to Chapter 12: In Sickness and in Health

1. Karen Christophersen to Oline Muus, July 5, 1865, Sven Oftedal Papers.

2. Pauline Henschien to Oline Muus, October 10, 1864, Sven Oftedal Papers.

Notes to Chapter 13: The Mustard Seed of St. Olaf

1. This chapter revised and expanded by translator and editor Kari Lie Dorer.

2. Bernt J. Muus, "Akademi i Holden, Minn.," *Kirkelig Maanedstidende,* December 1, 1869, 383–84, https://babel.hathitrust.org/cgi/pt?id=hvd.ah6egk&seq=801&q1=holden.

3. Muus, "Akademi i Holden, Minn."

4. Benson, *High on Manitou,* 14–15.

5. Blegen, *Norwegian Migration to America,* 241, 243, 244, 248.

6. Jacob A. Ottesen, "Beretning om Skolelærermødet," *Kirkelig Maanedstidende,* September 1858, https://babel.hathitrust.org/cgi/pt?id=iau.31858045162033&seq=166.

7. Nydahl, "Social and Economic Aspects of Pioneering."

8. Blegen, *Norwegian Migration to America,* 248–49.

9. Ottesen, "Beretning om Skolelærermødet."

10. Ottesen, "Beretning om Skolelærermodet."

11. Babcock, "The Scandinavian Element in the United States," 11; Ravitch, "A Brief History of Public Education," 21.

12. H. B. Wilson, County Superintendent of Goodhue County, Minnesota Executive Documents, 1869.

13. Tavuchis, *Pastors and Immigrants,* 48.

14. Bernt J. Muus, "Skolesagen," *Nordisk Folkeblad,* May 11, 1870.

15. Tavuchis, *Pastors and Immigrants,* 48; Johnson, *Goodhue County, Minnesota,* 113; H. B. Wilson, "Our Public Schools," *Goodhue County Republican,* May 5, 1870.

16. Bernt J. Muus, "Schools and Good Schools," *Red Wing Argus,* May 12, 1870; "Education or Propagandism?," *Red Wing Argus,* May 12, 1870.

17. Tavuchis, *Pastors and Immigrants,* 50.

18. Fagereng, "Norwegian Social and Cultural Life in Minnesota," 99.

19. Rasmussen, *A History of Goodhue County,* 102.

20. Benson, *High on Manitou,* 19; Felland, "History of St. Olaf."

21. Benson, *High on Manitou,* 22.

22. Grose, *Fifty Memorable Years,* 28; *St. Olaf's School.*

23. Grose, "The Beginnings of St. Olaf College."

Notes to Chapter 14: In Her Husband's Long Absence

1. Oline Muus to Laur. Larsen, August 23, 1870, Laur. Larsen Papers, Luther College, Decorah, IA.

2. Muus and Muus, *Niels Muus's Æt,* 73.

3. Oline Muus to Laur. Larsen, September 17, 1870, Laur. Larsen Papers.

4. S. L. Floren to Oline Muus, September 28, 1870, Sven Oftedal Papers.

5. Shaw, *Bernt Julius Muus,* 260.

6. Bernt Muus to Oline Muus, August 15, 1870, Sven Oftedal Papers.

7. Pauline Henschien to Oline Muus, October 10, 1864, Sven Oftedal Papers.

8. Bernt Muus to Oline Muus, October 25, 1870, Sven Oftedal Papers.

Notes to Chapter 15: The Church and Women's Emancipation

1. "Kvindeemancipation," *Kirkelig Maanedstidende*, August 1, 1870, https://babel.hathitrust.org/cgi/pt?id=wu.89077114791&seq=248.
2. Hymowitz and Weissman, *A History of Women in America*, 92.
3. Hoff, *Law, Gender and Injustice*.
4. Hymowitz and Weissman, *A History of Women in America*, 184.
5. "Women's Suffrage in Minnesota," Gale Family Library, MNHS.
6. "Kvinder i Prædikeembedet," *Kirkelig Maanedstidende*, May 1, 1872, https://babel.hathitrust.org/cgi/pt?id=hvd.ah6egm&seq=154; "Kirkekronike," *Kirkelig Maanedstidende*, March 15, 1872, https://babel.hathitrust.org/cgi/pt?id=hvd.ah6egm&seq=91.
7. "Kirkekronike," *Kirkelig Maanedstidende*, March 15, 1872.

Notes to Chapter 16: A Precocious Confirmand

1. G. M. Bruce, "A Brief History," Valley Grove Preservation Society, accessed August 1, 2023, https://valleygrovemn.org/resources/newspaper-articles/brief-history; *Valley Grove Ministerial Bog 1867–1891*, 101.
2. Luther, *Dr. Martin Luther's Liden Catechismus*, 7.
3. *Valley Grove Ministerial Bog 1867–1891*, 101; Odner, *Thorstein Veblen*, 57.
4. Veblen, "Jul i Manitowoc-skogen," 145.
5. Veblen, "Jul i Manitowoc-skogen," 144.
6. Brodersen, "Thorstein Bunde Veblen," 7.
7. Romans 13:2 (ASV); Pontoppidan "Truth to Godliness," question 165; "Kirkekronike," *Kirkelig Maanedstidende*, October 15, 1870, https://babel.hathitrust.org/cgi/pt?id=wu.89077114791&seq=328.
8. Christianson, "Thorstein Veblen," 5; Odner, *Thorstein Veblen*, 59; Haas, "The History, Development, and Contributions of the Work of Thorstein Veblen." The house was located on Lot 5 in Block 2 (north of First Street, between Winona and Nevada, on the Winona side). The lot was then sold to Carleton College in 1877–78: Eric Hillemann, email correspondence, October 30, 2023.
9. Nils Muus to Oline Muus, October 2, 1877, Sven Oftedal Papers.
10. Veblen, *The Theory of the Leisure Class*; Minnesota SP Veblen Farmstead, National Register Database, object name 75001024, National Archives Catalog, accessed December 17, 2023, https://catalog.archives.gov/id/93202844.

Notes to Chapter 17: Clergy Shortages and Deceitful Preachers

1. Halvorsen, *Festskrift*, 259.
2. Olson, *The Norwegian Synod*, 29; Shaw, *Bernt Julius Muus*, 312.
3. "Möde of Theologer paa Universitetet i Kristiania Mandag Den 21de Septbr," *Evangelisk Luthersk Kirketidende*, November 6, 1874, https://babel.hathi

trust.org/cgi/pt?id=hvd.ah6ewg&seq=721&q1=21de+Septbr. In 1874 the Synod's publication changed titles from *Kirkelig Maanedstidende* to *Evangelisk Luthersk Kirketidende*.

4. "Möde of Theologer paa Universitetet i Kristiania," *Evangelisk Luthersk Kirketidende*.

5. O. Juul, "Fra New York," *Kirkelig Maanedstidende*, April 15, 1872, https://babel.hathitrust.org/cgi/pt?id=hvd.ah6egm&seq=124.

6. *Evangelisk Luthersk Kirketidende*, no. 13, March 29, 1878, 204, 205, https://babel.hathitrust.org/cgi/pt?id=wu.89077114684&seq=216.

7. "'Bogter eder for de falske Profeter, som komme til eder i Faarekläder, men ere indvortes glubende Ulve.' Matth. 7, 15," *Evangelisk Luthersk Kirketidende*, February 13, 1874, https://babel.hathitrust.org/cgi/pt?id=wu.89077114866&seq=107; *Evangelisk Luthersk Kirketidende*, no. 7, February 13, 1874, 97, 108.

8. F. A. Schmidt, "Satser om Splittelse i Kirken," *Evangelisk Luthersk Kirketidende*, May 25, 1877, https://babel.hathitrust.org/cgi/pt?id=wu.89077114718&seq=341.

9. Bernt J. Muus, "Fra Synodalkonferensen," *Evangelisk Luthersk Kirketidende*, November 1, 1878, https://babel.hathitrust.org/cgi/pt?id=wu.89077114684&seq=710.

10. Muus, "Fra Synodalkonferensen."

Notes to Chapter 18: The Family Gathered

1. Biørn, *Festskrift*, 10.

2. "Minnesota Distrikts Synodemode," *Evangelisk Luthersk Kirketidende*, July 11, 1879, https://babel.hathitrust.org/cgi/pt?id=hvd.ah6ewb&seq=457.

3. Shaw, *Bernt Julius Muus*, 261; Halvorsen, *Festskrift*, 366.

4. Janson, *Amerikanske Forholde*, 81–82.

5. Janson, *Amerikanske Forholde*, 81.

Notes to Chapter 19: Church Discipline on the Agenda

1. "Kirkekronike," *Evangelisk Luthersk Kirketidende*, December 19, 1879, https://babel.hathitrust.org/cgi/pt?id=hvd.ah6ewb&seq=816; "Et par advarende eksempler," *Luthersk Kirketidende*, 1879, 172–73.

2. "Kirkekronike," *Evangelisk Luthersk Kirketidende*, December 19, 1879.

3. Muus, "Kirkekronike," *Evangelisk Luthersk Kirketidende*, December 19, 1879.

4. Shaw, *Bernt Julius Muus*, 114.

5. "Om det kirkelige Embede," *Evangelisk Luthersk Kirketidende*, January 10, 1879, https://babel.hathitrust.org/cgi/pt?id=hvd.ah6ewb&seq=43.

6. "Om det kirkelige Embede."

7. J. M. Midboe, "Et Brev," *Evangelisk Luthersk Kirketidende*, December 12, 1879, https://babel.hathitrust.org/cgi/pt?id=hvd.ah6ewb&seq=789.

8. Midboe, "Et Brev."

Notes to Chapter 20: Hypochondria and Hysteria

1. "Diderikke Otteson Brand," Luther College Archives: People, updated September 5, 2022, https://www.luther.edu/library/archives/people; Jens Muus to Oline Muus, October 8, 1878, Sven Oftedal Papers.
2. Grønvold, "The Effects of the Immigration," 22.
3. Smith-Rosenberg, "The Hysterical Woman," 660.
4. Grønvold, "The Effects of the Immigration," 30.
5. "Packard, Elizabeth (1816–1897)," Encyclopedia.com, last modified February 4, 2023, https://www.encyclopedia.com/women/encyclopedias-almanacs -transcripts-and-maps/packard-elizabeth-1816-1897; "Packard v. Packard: 1864," Encyclopedia.com, last modified February 5, 2023, https://www.encyclopedia .com/law/law-magazines/packard-v-packard-1864.

Notes to Chapter 21: The Norwegian American Elite

1. Janson, En kvindeskjæbne.
2. Lovoll, Norwegian Newspapers, 102.
3. Draxten, Janson in America, 54; Ueland, Recollections of an Immigrant.
4. Ueland, Recollections of an Immigrant, 40.

Notes to Chapter 22: A Home in Deep Sorrow

1. Bernt J. Muus, "Taler ved Indvielsen af den nye Skolebygning for St Olafs School den 6te Novbr. 1878," Evangelisk Luthersk Kirketidende, November 22, 1878, 735, https://babel.hathitrust.org/cgi/pt?id=wu.89077114684&seq=751.
2. Pauline Henschien to Oline Muus, February 5, 1879, Sven Oftedal Papers; Shapell, "Mourning Stationery in 19th Century America," Shapell Manuscript Foundation, updated March 15, 2018, https://www.shapell.org/historical-per spectives/curated-manuscripts/mourning-stationery.
3. Anna [surname unknown] to Oline Muus, March 28, 1879, Sven Oftedal Papers.
4. Anna [surname unknown] to Oline Muus, March 28, 1879, Sven Oftedal Papers.
5. Shaw, Bernt Julius Muus, 300.
6. Pauline Henschien to Oline Muus, December 7, 1879, Sven Oftedal Papers.

Notes to Chapter 23: Battle on the Home Front

1. Hoff, Law, Gender and Injustice.
2. Oline Muus, "Til Holden Menighed," Budstikken, March 2, 1880.
3. Janson, En kvindeskjæbne, 46.
4. Muus, "Til Holden Menighed."
5. Muus, "Til Holden Menighed."

Notes to Chapter 24: The Complaint with a Capital "C"

1. Luth Jæger, "Oline Muus contra Bernt J. Muus," *Budstikken*, January 20, 1880; "Another Divorce Suit," *Pioneer Press* (St. Paul, MN), January 26, 1880.
2. "Another Divorce Suit."
3. Luth Jæger, "Oline Muus contra Bernt J. Muus."
4. "Another Divorce Suit."

Notes to Chapter 25: A Psychological Puzzle

1. Hymowitz and Weissman, *A History of Women in America*, 172; "Tilton v. Beecher (1875)."
2. Janson, *Amerikanske Forholde*, 51–53.
3. "Another Divorce Suit."
4. "Another Divorce Suit."
5. "Another Divorce Suit."
6. "Another Divorce Suit."
7. "Another Divorce Suit."
8. "Another Divorce Suit."

Notes to Chapter 26: Fifteen Days Before the First Congregational Meeting

1. Luth Jæger, *Budstikken*, February 17, 1880.
2. Erik L. Petersen, "Menighedsmödet i Østre Sogns Kirke, Goodhue Co den 18de Februar," *Budstikken*, February 24, 1880.
3. Luth Jæger, "Sagen Mrs. Oline Muus mod Pastor B. J. Muus," *Budstikken*, February 3, 1880.
4. Jæger, "Sagen Mrs. Oline Muus."
5. Jæger, "Sagen Mrs. Oline Muus."
6. Jæger, "Sagen Mrs. Oline Muus."
7. Luth Jæger, *Budstikken*, February 17, 1880.

Notes to Chapter 27: A Scandal Within the Scandal

1. "Another Divorce Suit"; "Goodhue County Scandal," *Goodhue County Republican*, January 29, 1880; "Mr. Muus's Muss," *Goodhue County Republican*, February 5, 1880; "GOODHUE County has a first-class scandal," *Owatonna Journal*, February 6, 1880.
2. As cited in "Af de forskjellige Blades Udtalelser," *Budstikken*, March 30, 1880.
3. Luth Jæger, *Budstikken*, February 17, 1880.
4. "Red Wing," *Pioneer Press* (St. Paul, MN), February 14, 1880.
5. "The Rev. B. J. Muus," *Red Wing Argus*, February 26, 1880.
6. "Muus Music," *Goodhue County Republican*, March 18, 1880.

Notes to Chapter 28: Out of Control

1. Petersen, "Menighedsmödet 18de Februar."
2. Romans 5:17–20 (ASV).
3. Halvorsen, *Festskrift*, 392.
4. Petersen, "Menighedsmödet 18de Februar."
5. Petersen, "Menighedsmödet 18de Februar."

Notes to Chapter 29: Who Was the Complainant?

1. Petersen, "Menighedsmödet 18de Februar."
2. Petersen, "Menighedsmödet 18de Februar."
3. Petersen, "Menighedsmödet 18de Februar."
4. M. O. Bøckman to H. A. Preus, February 27, 1880, Norwegian Synod Records, Luther College, Decorah, IA.

Notes to Chapter 30: Like a Bolt of Thunder

1. Gudmund Norsving, "Sagen mod Pastor Muus," *Budstikken*, March 9, 1880.
2. Norsving, "Sagen mod Pastor Muus."
3. Norsving, "Sagen mod Pastor Muus."
4. Norsving, "Sagen mod Pastor Muus."
5. Norsving, "Sagen mod Pastor Muus."
6. Norsving, "Sagen mod Pastor Muus."

Notes to Chapter 31: Personal Punishment

1. Luth Jæger, *Budstikken*, March 2, 1880.
2. Jæger, *Budstikken*, March 2, 1880.
3. Muus, "Til Holden Menighet."
4. Muus, "Til Holden Menighet."
5. Muus, "Til Holden Menighet."
6. Jæger, *Budstikken*, March 2, 1880.

Notes to Chapter 32: Under Church Discipline?

1. Erik L. Petersen, "Menighedsmödet i Holden Kirke, Goodhue Co den 10de og 11de Marts," *Budstikken*, March 16, 1880; Jæger, "Sagen Mrs. Oline Muus."
2. 1 Corinthians 13:4–7 (ASV); 1 Corinthians 13:11–13 (ASV).
3. Petersen, "Menighedsmödet den 10de og 11de Marts."
4. Petersen, "Menighedsmödet den 10de og 11de Marts."

Notes to Chapter 33: The Big Defense Speech

1. Petersen, "Menighedsmödet den 10de og 11de Marts."
2. Petersen, "Menighedsmödet den 10de og 11de Marts."

3. Petersen, "Menighedsmödet den 10de og 11de Marts."
4. Petersen, "Menighedsmödet den 10de og 11de Marts."
5. Petersen, "Menighedsmödet den 10de og 11de Marts."
6. Petersen, "Menighedsmödet den 10de og 11de Marts."
7. Lovoll, *The Promise of America*, 80.
8. Petersen, "Menighedsmödet den 10de og 11de Marts."
9. Petersen, "Menighedsmödet den 10de og 11de Marts."

Notes to Chapter 34: The Money Question

1. Petersen, "Menighedsmödet den 10de og 11de Marts."
2. Rasmussen, "Aasta Hansteen og Amerika," 131.
3. Petersen, "Menighedsmödet den 10de og 11de Marts."

Notes to Chapter 35: A Christian Husband?

1. Erik L. Petersen, "Mödet den 11te Marts," *Budstikken*, March 23, 1880.
2. Petersen, "Mödet den 11te."
3. Petersen, "Mödet den 11te."

Notes to Chapter 36: In the Backwoods

1. Petersen, "Mödet den 11te."
2. Gudmund Norsving, "Hr. Redaktør!," *Budstikken*, March 30, 1880.
3. Norsving, "Hr. Redaktør!"
4. Bernt J. Muus, "Kirkekronike," *Evangelisk Luthersk Kirketidende*, May 7, 1880, https://babel.hathitrust.org/cgi/pt?id=wu.89077114841&seq=304; M. O. Bøckman, *Evangelisk Luthersk Kirketidende*, May 28, 1880, https://babel.hathi trust.org/cgi/pt?id=wu.89077114841&seq=357.
5. "The Letter Killeth," *Goodhue County Republican*, April 29, 1880.
6. "Muus Correspondence," *Red Wing Advance*, March 24, 1880.
7. "Muus Correspondence."

Notes to Chapter 37: The Leadership Takes the Case

1. Oline Muus to H. A. Preus, April 15, 1800, Norwegian Synod Records, record group 13, series 1, subseries 3, box 1, folder 9, Luther College.
2. Oline Muus to H. A. Preus, April 29, 1880, Herman Amberg Preus Papers, record group 15, series 1, box 6, folder 5.
3. Oline Muus to H. A. Preus, April 19, 1800, Norwegian Synod Records, record group 13, series 1, subseries 3, box 3, folder 7.
4. Oline Muus to H. A. Preus, April 20, 1880, Herman Amberg Preus Papers, record group 15, series 1, box 6, folder 5, Luther College, Decorah, IA.
5. Oline Muus to H. A. Preus, May 4, 1880, Herman Amberg Preus Papers, record group 15, series 1, box 6, folder 5.

6. Information from Øyvind T. Gulliksen (July 7, 2018), who was told this in a meeting with Thomas Hanson, Østen Hanson's grandchild. The version of the manuscript dated April 2018 is in Stenseth's possession.

Notes to Chapter 38: A "Spectacle" at the Parsonage

1. Erik L. Petersen, "Menighedsmödet i Østre Sogns Kirke, Goodhue County, Minn. den 13de og 14de Mai," *Budstikken*, May 18, 1880.
2. Petersen, "Menighedsmödet 13de og 14de Mai."

Notes to Chapter 39: A Doctor, a Horse, and a Crutch

1. Petersen, "Menighedsmödet 13de og 14de Mai."
2. Petersen, "Menighedsmödet 13de og 14de Mai."
3. Petersen, "Menighedsmödet 13de og 14de Mai."
4. Petersen, "Menighedsmödet 13de og 14de Mai."

Notes to Chapter 40: In Loving Jest

1. Petersen, "Menighedsmödet 13de og 14de Mai."
2. Petersen, "Menighedsmödet 13de og 14de Mai."
3. Petersen, "Menighedsmödet 13de og 14de Mai."
4. Erik L. Petersen, "Menighedsmödet den 14de Mai," *Budstikken*, May 25, 1880.
5. Petersen, "Menighedsmödet den 14de Mai."

Notes to Chapter 41: False Accusation

1. Petersen, "Menighedsmödet den 14de Mai."
2. Petersen, "Menighedsmödet den 14de Mai."
3. Petersen, "Menighedsmödet den 14de Mai."

Notes to Chapter 42: The Question of Blame

1. Petersen, "Menighedsmödet den 14de Mai."
2. Petersen, "Menighedsmödet den 14de Mai."
3. Luth Jæger, *Budstikken*, May 25, 1880.
4. "Mrs. Oline Muus contra Pastor Muus," *Budstikken*, March 30, 1880.

Notes to Chapter 43: Staging the Scandal

1. Leiren, *Selected Plays of Marcus Thrane*, 1, 121.
2. Marcus Thrane, documents pertaining to Holden, manuscript 4 1758, National Library of Norway, Oslo. Stenseth uses Thrane's original text; Dorer uses Leiren's translated text.

3. Shaw, *Bernt Julius Muus*, 291.
4. *Skandinaven*, June 1880.
5. Leiren, *Selected Plays of Marcus Thrane*, 121.
6. Thrane, *Den Gamle Wisconsin Biblen*, 19.

Notes to Chapter 44: Case Dismissed

1. *Evangelisk Luthersk Kirketidende*, July 9, 1880, 437, https://babel.hathitrust
.org/cgi/pt?id=wu.89077114841&seq=450.
2. "Redegjørelse fra Holden Menighed, Minn," *Evangelisk Luthersk Kirketidende*, December 3, 1880, 774, https://babel.hathitrust.org/cgi/pt?id=wu.89077
114841&seq=785.
3. "Redegjørelse fra Holden."
4. "Redegjørelse fra Holden."
5. "Redegjørelse fra Holden."

Notes to Chapter 45: A New Judge Presides

1. "The Holden Church Troubles," *Red Wing Argus*, June 24, 1880.
2. "Wanamingo," *Goodhue County Republican*, July 29, 1880.
3. "Holden Church Troubles Not Yet Over," *Red Wing Argus*, July 15, 1880;
"Muus versus Muus," *Red Wing Argus*, July 15, 1880.
4. Georg Sverdrup, "Pastor B. J. Muus's Sag," *Lutheraneren og Missionsbladet*,
December 14, 1880.
5. Sverdrup, "Pastor B. J. Muus's Sag."
6. Sverdrup, "Pastor B. J. Muus's Sag."
7. Sverdrup, "Pastor B. J. Muus's Sag."

Notes to Chapter 46: Not Much Merriment

1. Felland, "History of St. Olaf."
2. *Muus v. Muus*, Goodhue District Court No. 1470 (September 8, 1881).
3. "Muus vs. Muus," *Red Wing Argus*, January 13, 1881.
4. *Muus v. Muus*, Goodhue District Court.
5. *Morgenbladet*, February 13, 1881.
6. Rodney Edvinsson, Portal for Historical Statistics, historicalstatistics.org.
7. *Muus v. Muus*, Goodhue District Court.
8. *Muus v. Muus*, Goodhue District Court.

Notes to Chapter 47: A Troll of a Wife

1. Hoem, *Villskapens år*, 264.
2. "A CELEBRITY," *Minneapolis Tribune*, January 11, 1881.
3. Bjørnson, *Breve til Karoline*, 249–50.

4. "A Number of Scandinavians . . . ," *Goodhue County Republican*, February 12, 1881.
5. Bjørnson, *Breve til Karoline*, 259–60.
6. Bjørnson, *Breve til Karoline*, 260.

Notes to Chapter 48: Intentional Malice

1. Georg Sverdrup, *Ny Luthersk Kirketidende*, February 23, 1881, 313–20.
2. J. C. Heuch and M. J. Færden, "Nordamerika," *Luthersk Ugeskrift*, June 4, 1881, 373.
3. Heuch and Færden, "Nordamerika," 373–74.
4. Heuch and Færden, "Nordamerika," 373–74.
5. Heuch and Færden, "Nordamerika," 375.

Notes to Chapter 49: Ghosts

1. Rasmussen, "Aasta Hansteen og Amerika," 131.
2. Rasmussen, "Aasta Hansteen og Amerika," 126; Aasta Hansteen "Sporgsmaal til rettes herved til den norske Synodes Formand,"*Budstikken*, August 3, 1880.
3. "Til Aasta Hansteen," *Budstikken*, September 14, 1880.
4. Hansteen, "Norwegians in the Northwest," 244.
5. Hansteen, "Norwegians in the Northwest," 244.
6. Hansteen, "Norwegians in the Northwest," 244.
7. Hansteen, "Norwegians in the Northwest," 245.
8. Hymowitz and Weissman, *A History of Women in America*, 176; Hansteen, "Norwegians in the Northwest," 245.

Notes to Chapter 50: Verdict and Departure

1. Shaw, *Bernt Julius Muus*, 272–73; "Muus v. Muus," *Daily Minnesota Tribune*, January 12, 1883.
2. *Muus v. Muus*, Goodhue District Court.
3. *Muus v. Muus*, Goodhue District Court.
4. Luth Jæger, *Budstikken*, March 2, 1880.
5. Shaw, *Bernt Julius Muus*, 275.

Notes to Chapter 51: Helpers in a Time of Need

1. "Holden Church Troubles," *Red Wing Argus*, January 5, 1882; "Picked Up," *Goodhue County Republican*, January 7, 1882. *Lutheraneren og Missionsbladet* 14, no. 26 (December 1880): 407–8; Oline Muus, "Brev fra fru Oline Muus," *Amerika*, April 5, 1912. Oline Muus is listed as residing at 616 Twenty-Second Avenue South, in 1886, Sverdrup at Twenty-First and Seventh, Oftedal at 712 Twenty-First

Avenue South: Ancestry.com, "U.S., City Directories, 1822–1995," accessed May 7, 2023, https://www.ancestry.com/search/collections/2469/.

2. Janson, *Amerikanske Forholde*, 212.

3. Janson, *Amerikanske Forholde*, 122, 139.

4. Janson, *Amerikanske Forholde*, 134.

5. Janson, *Amerikanske Forholde*, 136, 148.

6. Janson, *Amerikanske Forholde*, 153.

7. Janson, *Amerikanske Forholde*, 158.

Notes to Chapter 52: New Legal Proceedings

1. *Muus v. Muus*, Hennepin District Court No. 13571 (October 17, 1882).

2. Shaw, *Bernt Julius Muus*, 273; "Holden Church Troubles," *Red Wing Argus*, February 16, 1882.

3. Shaw, *Bernt Julius Muus*, 273.

4. Shaw, *Bernt Julius Muus*, 276.

5. Shaw, *Bernt Julius Muus*, 275.

6. Shaw, *Bernt Julius Muus*, 276.

Notes to Chapter 53: Divorce?

1. "Local News," *Goodhue County Republican*, May 7, 1881; Shaw, *Bernt Julius Muus*, 278; Luth Jæger, *Budstikken*, March 14, 1882; Rasmussen, "The Best Place on Earth for Women," 245.

2. Luth Jæger, *Budstikken*, March 28, 1882; *Muus v. Muus*, Hennepin District Court.

3. Rasmussen, "Aasta Hansteen og Amerika," 134; Rasmussen, "The Best Place on Earth for Women," 249.

4. Hansteen, "Scandinavians and Woman's Rights," 158.

5. Hansteen, "Scandinavians and Woman's Rights."

6. *Muus v. Muus*, Minnesota Supreme Court No. 3189 and 3250 (May 16, 1882).

7. "Muus vs. Muus," *Daily Minnesota Tribune*, January 5, 1883.

8. *Muus v. Muus*, Hennepin District Court; Ueland, *Recollections of an Immigrant*, 42.

9. *Muus v. Muus*, Hennepin District Court.

Notes to Chapter 54: The Three Pastor's Wives

1. Janson, *A Saloonkeeper's Daughter*, xii.

2. Draxten, *Janson in America*, 80; Janson, *A Saloonkeeper's Daughter*, xviii.

3. Janson, *A Saloonkeeper's Daughter*, xvii.

4. Mørkhagen, *Drømmen om Amerika*, 396; Mauk, *The Heart of the Heartland*, 212.

5. Draxten, *Janson in America*, 57.
6. Janson, *A Saloonkeeper's Daughter*, xxi.
7. Shaw, *Bernt Julius Muus*, 296.
8. Draxten, *Janson in America*, 160; Janson, *A Saloonkeeper's Daughter*, xxii.
9. Shaw, *Bernt Julius Muus*, 296; Grindal, *Unstoppable*, 253.

Notes to Chapter 55: A Dangerous Man

1. Biørn, *Festskrift*, 11; Muus and Muus, *Niels Muus's Æet*, 73.
2. Shaw, *Bernt Julius Muus*, 312.
3. Hovde, ed., *What Became of Jens?*, 87.
4. Biørn, *Festskrift*, 11.
5. "Udtrædelie af Synoden," *Evangelisk Luthersk Kirketidende*, July 15, 1887, https://babel.hathitrust.org/cgi/pt?id=wu.89077114882&seq=452.
6. "Bare Bygge-Arbeider," *Evangelisk Luthersk Kirketidende*, August 10, 1888, https://babel.hathitrust.org/cgi/pt?id=wu.89077114916&seq=506.
7. Halvorsen, *Festskrift*, 104; Olson, *The Norwegian Synod*, 71–72.
8. Biørn, *Festskrift*, 12.
9. Olson, *The Norwegian Synod*, 29.

Notes to Chapter 56: Lonely and Abandoned

1. Ylvisaker, *Eminent Pioneers*, 2.
2. Jan Eivind Myhre, "Utvandring fra Norge," Norgeshistorie, University of Oslo, last modified November 2, 2020, https://www.norgeshistorie.no/industrial isering-og-demokrati/1537-utvandring-fra-norge.html.
3. Bjørklund, *Marcus Thrane*, 323.
4. Oline Muus, "Hr. Redaktør" *Decorah-Posten*, March 13, 1889.
5. Shaw, *Bernt Julius Muus*, 297.
6. Oline Muus to Bjørnstjerne Bjørnson, July 30, 1899, Brevs. BB 2, National Library, Oslo.

Notes to Chapter 57: A Desire for Reconciliation

1. Muus and Muus, *Niels Muus's Æt*, 73.
2. Muus and Muus, *Niels Muus's Æt*, 4.
3. Muus and Muus, *Niels Muus's Æt*, 4, 8.
4. Floan, "Reminiscences of the Early History, circa 1938–1942"; Oline Muus to Bjørnstjerne Bjørnson, July 30, 1899.
5. Oline Muus to Bjørnstjerne Bjørnson, July 30, 1899.
6. Biørn, *Festskrift*, 12–13.
7. S. O. Simonson, "Rev. B. J. Muus as I Learned to Know Him," 1932, 9, Bernt J. Muus Papers, NAHA; Floan, "Reminiscences of the Early History, circa 1938–1942."

8. "Past Presidents," About St. Olaf, St. Olaf College, accessed August 5, 2023, https://wp.stolaf.edu/about/history/past-presidents/.

9. "Her Founder Dead," *Northfield News*, June 2, 1900.

10. Biørn, *Festskrift*, 7.

Notes to Chapter 58: Mother and Daughter United

1. Shaw, *Bernt Julius Muus*, 299.

2. Shaw, *Bernt Julius Muus*, 299.

3. Oline Muus, "Fra Mrs. Oline Muus," *Amerika*, February 23, 1906.

4. Lovoll, *Norske Aviser i Amerika*, 311; Hustvedt, "Vignettes from a Norwegian Settlement," 192; Hustvedt, *Rasmus Bjørn Anderson*.

5. Oline Muus, "Fra Mrs. Oline Muus."

6. Oline Muus, "Fra Mrs. Oline Muus."

7. Oline Muus, "Bestemors spalte," *Amerika*, March 29, 1912.

8. Muus, "Brev fra fru."

9. Muus, "Brev fra fru."

10. Shaw, *Bernt Julius Muus*, 306. Information from Øyvind T. Gulliksen, June 7, 2018. A version of the manuscript dated April 2018 in Stenseth's possession.

Notes to Appendix: The Muus Descendants

1. This appendix researched and written by Kari Lie Dorer.

2. "Fru Birgitte Muus Klüver," *Nordmanns-Forbundet* 28 (1935): 314.

3. *Minneapolis Tidende*, November 10, 1932; Lorentz Klüver, Hjemmeside for Lorentz D. Klüver, accessed August 20, 2023, https://www.kluwer.no/ldk/REF SAAS.61G1.html.

4. Nils Muus to Oline Muus, October 2, 1877, Sven Oftedal Papers.

5. Jens Muus to Oline Muus, October 8, 1878, Sven Oftedal Papers.

6. Shaw, *Bernt Julius Muus*, 302; Oline Muus statement, Bernt J. Muus Papers, P0559, box 2, folder 4.

7. "First 30 Years of Enrollment: 1600–1699," St. Olaf College, accessed December 6, 2023, https://wp.stolaf.edu/archives/first-30-years-of-enrollment-1600 -1699/; B. J. Muus to H. T. Ytterboe, February 2, March 31 1891, H. T. Ytterboe Papers, box 1, folder 1, St. Olaf College Archives, Northfield, MN.

8. US Census Bureau, *Population Schedule 1910*, Hillyard, Spokane, WA, roll T624–1669, page 26b, enumeration district 0207, FHL microfilm 1375682, image online at Ancestry.com, accessed January 29, 2023; Harold Steen Muus draft registration card, World War I Draft Registration Cards, 1918, digital image, *National Archives*, available at Ancestry.com, accessed January 29, 2023; US Census Bureau, *Population Schedule 1940*, Petaluma, Sonoma, CA, roll: m-t0627-00349, page 15A, enumeration district 49–29, image online at Ancestry.com, accessed January 29, 2023.

9. Shaw, *Bernt Julius Muus*, 303.

10. Shaw, *Bernt Julius Muus*, 303; State of Montana, Marriage License Record 17:8338, Sverre Muus and Hilda Sophia Eggan, January 16, 1905, image 569 of 924, online at Ancestry.com, accessed January 29, 2023; Sverre Muus draft registration card, World War I Draft Registration Cards, 1918, digital image, *National Archives*, Ancestry.com, accessed January 29, 2023.

11. State of Minnesota, Report of Probate Judge, case #6662, box 3, folder 2, NAHA.

Notes to Editor's Afterword

1. Blegen, *Norwegian Migration to America*, 279; Grose, *Fifty Memorable Years*, 18; Hans Olav Løkken, "1874: To store personligheter i Goodhue County," historiefortelleren, accessed August 23, 2023, http://historiefortelleren.no; Floan, "Reminiscences of the Early History, circa 1938–1942," 7.

2. Muus and Muus, *Niels Muus's Æt*, 73; [Research notes, no name given,] Bernt J. Muus Papers, P0559, box 2, folder 4.

3. Grose, *Fifty Memorable Years*, 19; Telemark to America II: Settlements, Bernt J. Muus Papers, box 3, folder 2.

4. Jeff Davidson and Pat Wickum Maisel, interview, October 4, 2023.

5. Mauk, *The Heart of the Heartland*, 164–65.

Note to Timelines

1. Timelines researched and created by Kari Lie Dorer.

Notes to Bibliography: A Note on Newspaper Sources

1. "A Note on Newspaper Sources" researched by Kari Lie Dorer. Lovoll, *Norwegian Newspapers*, 3, 9–10; Blegen, *Norwegian Migration to America*, 300.

2. Munch, "Authority and Freedom," 8; Fagereng, "Norwegian Social and Cultural Life in Minnesota"; Lovoll, *Norwegian Newspapers*, 65.

3. *Morgenbladet*, June 17, 1880; Oline Muus, "Pastor Muus og hans hustru," *Verdens Gang*, December 9, 1880.

4. Lovoll, *Norwegian Newspapers*, 101.

BIBLIOGRAPHY

A Note on Newspaper Sources

THE VALUE OF NORWEGIAN AMERICAN journalism can easily be seen when researching the case of *Muus v. Muus*. In *Norwegian Newspapers in America: Connecting Norway and the New Land*, Odd Lovoll explores the significance of the foreign-language press and its importance in immigrant communities, explaining that the newspapers "eased adjustment to the new society while retaining ties to the one left behind." The Norwegian American press was part of a much larger phenomenon among immigrant groups in the United States: Norwegian American immigrants eventually founded over four hundred newspapers in America. The first newspapers in the United States written in Dano-Norwegian began appearing in the 1840s with the rise of immigration. Some of the most prominent papers leading up to the twentieth century included *Skandinaven, Budstikken, Nordlyset, Decorah-Posten,* and *Nordisk Folke-blad*. Early goals for the Norwegian-language press included better informing and educating the Norwegian-speaking public about the happenings covered in English-language newspapers, along with providing readers news stories from Norway.[1]

The dichotomy between the authority given to pastors by the Norwegian Synod and the prevalence of the idea of freedom in America made for a complicated relationship between Norwegian American papers and church leaders. During the eighteenth century, there was significant tension between the Norwegian common folk and the elite (which included clergymen), and it was only from the mid-nineteenth century onward that peasants became a political and cultural force. However, many of the Norwegian American publications fell into comparative silence on the issue of women's rights and remained so into the mid-nineteenth century, with a few exceptions. Despite what seemed like an actively avoided topic, the majority of newspapers sided with Oline Muus while simultaneously condemning Bernt Muus's actions. It wasn't only the editors and regular columnists taking sides; many readers wrote editorials expressing their concern for Oline's well-being, with one writer to *Budstikken* in April 1880 pointing to "the absurdity of the master and slave relationship between husband and wife." Another such letter printed in *Decorah-Posten* in September 1880 from Chicago titled "To the Scandinavian women in America!" pled for financial donations to support Oline. This advocacy was in line with the empathetic attitude held by many immigrants at the time. Many Norwegians arrived in the United States in poor conditions and in dire need of help, and newspapers often fostered community by advocating for supporting others and making appeals for donations with the idea that "there was pride in giving aid." It makes sense that a portion of readers would give their aid and support in a written form that went out to the general public.[2]

Norwegian Americans were not only active readers of the press in the United States; they also read newspapers published in Norway. Oslo-based *Morgenbladet* printed a detailed account of the case in June 1880. Six months later, in December 1880, one can find a long rebuttal written by Oline Muus in the Oslo-based *Verdens Gang*, in which she explains that she had written a response to *Morgenbladet*, but months had gone by and still they had not printed her letter. So, she wrote to the editor of *Verdens Gang* requesting they publish it instead. Her letter includes details that hadn't yet come out in the press in the United States, namely, that she had confided in her lawyer and, without her permission, he had made public details she had wished to keep private. But now that many details had been made public, she knew the press would take the opportunity to scrutinize every detail.[3]

Lovoll further explains that the "ambitious young men who under unfamiliar circumstances shaped the Norwegian American press did so in a competitive spirit with rival Norwegian newspaper ventures; consequently, confident in their own judgment, their rivalry from time to time descended into heated personal accusations against competitors, even when the rivals shared political and religious faith. Nineteenth-century political discourse—in general, not limited to the immigrant press—was nothing less than strident." And it was this impassioned discourse that captured the attention of readers.[4]

Periodicals

Amerika (Madison, WI)
Arbeider-Foreningernes Blad (Drammen, Norway)
Budstikken (Minneapolis)
Dagslyset (Chicago, IL)
Daily Minnesota Tribune (later *Minneapolis Daily Tribune, Minneapolis Tribune*)
Decorah-Posten (IA)
Emigranten (Inmansville, WI)
Evangelisk Luthersk Kirketidende (Decorah, IA)
Goodhue County Republican (Red Wing, MN)
Kirkelig Maanedstidende (Madison, WI)
Lutheraneren og Missionsbladet (Minneapolis)
Luthersk Kirketidende (Oslo, Norway)
Luthersk Ugeskrift (Oslo, Norway)
The Manitou Messenger (Northfield, MN)
Marcus Thrane's Norske Amerikaner (Chicago, IL)
Minneapolis Tidende
Minneapolis Tribune
Morgenbladet (Oslo, Norway)
Nordisk Folkeblad (Rochester, MN)
Nordmanns-Forbundet (Oslo, Norway)
Norsk Kirketidende (Oslo, Norway)
Northfield (MN) News
Ny Luthersk Kirketidende (Oslo, Norway)
Owatonna (MN) Journal
Pioneer Press (St. Paul, MN)
Red Wing (MN) Advance

Red Wing (MN) Argus
Skandinaven (Chicago, IL)
Verdens Gang (Chicago, IL)
Verdens Gang (Oslo, Norway)
Woman's Journal (Boston, MA)

Archives

Augsburg University Archives, Minneapolis, MN.
Sven Oftedal Papers.

Evangelical Lutheran Synod Archives, Mankato, MN.

Hennepin County Library, Minneapolis, MN.
Minneapolis Star and Tribune Photographs.

Luther College, Decorah, IA.
The Letters of Elisabeth Koren. Record group 15, box 3, letter 107.
Records of the Norwegian Synod. Record group 13, series 1, subseries 3, box 1, folder 57.
Herman Amberg Preus Papers. Record group 15, series 1, box 6.

Municipal Archives of Trondheim.

National Library Norway, Oslo.
Letter, Oline Muus to Bjørnstjerne Bjørnson, July 30, 1899. Letters, BB 2.
Marcus Thrane, documents regarding the play *Holden*. MS 4 1758.

Norwegian-American Historical Association, Northfield, MN.
Peter O. Floan Reminiscences, P0096.
Bernt J. Muus Papers, P0559.
S. O. Simundson Papers, P0347.

Norwegian Labour Movement Archives and Library, Oslo.

Oslo City Museum.

St. Olaf College Archives, Northfield, MN.
St. Olaf College Academic Catalogs Collection.
H. T. Ytterboe Papers.

Interviews and Correspondence

Davidson, Jeff, and Pat Wickum Maisel. Interview, October 4, 2023.
Hillemann, Eric. Email correspondence, October 30, 2023.

Court Cases

Muus v. Muus, Goodhue District Court No. 1470 (September 8, 1881).
Muus v. Muus, Hennepin District Court No. 13571 (October 17, 1882).
Muus v. Muus, Minnesota Supreme Court No. 3189 and 3250 (May 16, 1882).

Books and Articles

Alba, Richard, Albert J. Raboteau, and Josh DeWind, eds. *Immigration and Religion in America: Comparative and Historical Perspectives.* New York: New York University Press, 2009.

Babcock, Kendric C. "The Scandinavian Element in the United States." *University of Illinois-Urbana Studies in the Social Sciences* 111, no. 3 (September 1914): 11.

Benson, William Clarence. *High on Manitou: A History of St. Olaf College, 1874–1949.* Northfield, MN: St. Olaf College Press, 1949.

Bergland, Betty. "Norwegian Migration and Displaced Indigenous Peoples: Toward an Understanding of Nordic Whiteness in the Land-Taking." In *Nordic Whiteness and Migration to the USA: A Historical Exploration of Identity*, ed. Jana Sverdljuk, Terje Mikael Hasle Joranger, Erika K. Jackson, and Peter Kivisto. London: Routledge/Taylor and Francis, 2021.

Bergland, Betty A., and Lori Ann Lahlum, eds. *Norwegian American Women: Migration, Communities, and Identities.* St. Paul: Minnesota Historical Society Press, 2011.

Biørn, Ludvig Marinius. *Festskrift: jubelfest holdt i Holden Menighed, Goodhue Co., Minn., fra 12te til 16de September 1906, i anledning af femtiaarsdagen for menighedens stiftelse.* Minneapolis, MN: Augsburg Publishing House, 1906.

Bjørklund, Oddvar. *Marcus Thrane: Sosialistleder i et u-land.* Oslo: Tiden, 1970.

Bjørnson, Bjørnstjerne. *Breve til Karoline, 1858–1907*. Oslo: Gyldendal, 1957.

Blegen, Theodore. *Norwegian Migration to America: The American Transition*. Northfield, MN: Norwegian-American Historical Association, 1940.

Brodersen, Arvid. "Thorstein Bunde Veblen 1857–1929." In *Den arbeidsfrie klasse: en økonomisk studie av institusjoners utvikling*, edited by Thorstein B. Veblen, translated by Per A. Hartun, 7–33. Oslo: Gyldendal, 1976.

Budstikken. "Mrs. Oline Muus contra Pastor B.J. Muus" [pamphlet]. Minneapolis: Budstikken, 1880.

Cadwell, Christopher. *Reflections on the Revolution in Europe: Immigration, Islam, and the West*. London: Allen Lane/Penguin, 2009.

Christianson, J. R. "Thorstein Veblen: Ethnic Roots and Social Criticism of a 'Folk Savant.'" *Norwegian-American Studies* 34, no. 1 (1995): 5. https://doi.org/10.1353/nor.1995.a799284.

Curtiss-Wedge, Franklyn, ed. *History of Goodhue County, Minnesota*. Chicago: H. C. Cooper Jr. and Company, 1909. https://archive.org/details/historyofgoodhue00curt/page/n8/mode/1up?view=theater.

Daae, Peter. *Om Chicago: Amerikas mest amerikanske by og den tredie største norske by i verden*. Kristiania [Oslo]: Alb. Cammermeyers Forlag, 1903.

de Tocqueville, Alexis. *Om demokratiet i Amerika*. Translated by Birgit Tønnesson. Oslo: De norske Bokklubbene, 2010.

Draxten, Nina. *Kristofer Janson in America*. Boston: Twayne Publishers; Northfield, MN: Norwegian-American Historical Association, 1976.

Erickson, William D. "'Something Must Be Done for Them': Establishing Minnesota's First Hospital for the Insane." *Minnesota History* 53, no. 2 (Summer 1992): 42–55.

Ericson, Kathryn. "Triple Jeopardy: The Muus vs. Muus Case in Three Forums." *Minnesota History* 50, no. 8 (Winter 1987): 298–308.

Erikson, Kai T. *Wayward Puritans: A Study in the Sociology of Deviance*. New York: John Wiley and Sons, 1966.

Fagereng, John A. "Norwegian Social and Cultural Life in Minnesota, 1868–1891: An Analysis of Typical Norwegian Newspapers." Master's thesis, University of Minnesota, 1932.

Felland, O. G. "History of St. Olaf: 1874–1899." Accessed June 11, 2023. https://wp.stolaf.edu/archives/quarter-centennial-souvenir-1874 -1899/history-of-st-olaf-college/.

Gatty, Margaret. *Parabler fra Naturen.* Translated by Bernt Julius Muus. Christiania [Oslo]: P. F. Steensballe, 1857.

Grindal, Gracia. "The Americanization of the Norwegian Pastors' Wives." *Norwegian-American Studies* 32 (1989): 199–207.

———. *Unstoppable: Norwegian Pioneers Educate Their Daughters.* Minneapolis, MN: Lutheran University Press, 2016.

Grose, I. F. "The Beginnings of St. Olaf College." *Studies and Records* 5 (1930): 110–21. muse.jhu.edu/article/799369.

———. *Fifty Memorable Years at St. Olaf, Marking the History of the "College on the Hill" from Its Founding in 1874 to Its Golden Jubilee Celebration in 1925.* Northfield, MN: Northfield News, Inc., 1925.

Grønvold, Christian J. "The Effects of the Immigration on the Norwegian Immigrants." In *Annual Report of the State Board of Health of Minnesota,* 6th ed. Minneapolis: State Board of Health of Minnesota, 1878.

Gulliksen, Øyvind T. *Twofold Identities: Norwegian-American Contribution to Midwestern Literature.* New York: Peter Lang, 2004.

Gulliksen, Øyvind T., and Harry T. Cleven, eds. *Norwegian-American Essays 2008: Migration and Memory.* Oslo: Norwegian-American Historical Association–Norway, 2008.

Günther, F. W. *The Little American: Den lille Amerikaner.* 2nd ed. Christiania [Oslo]: Feilberg and Landmarks Forlag, 1851.

Haas, Sean. "The History, Development, and Contributions of the Work of Thorstein Veblen." *Oxford Research Encyclopedia of Business and Management,* April 20, 2022. https://doi.org/10.1093/acrefore /9780190224851.013.245.

Halvorsen, H., ed. *Festskrift til Den norske synodes jubilæum, 1853–1903.* Decorah, IA: Den Norske Synodes Forlag, 1903.

Hansen, Marcus Lee. "Migration and Puritanism." *Norwegian-American Studies and Records* 9 (1936): 1–28.

Hansteen, Aasta. "Norwegians in the Northwest. Letter from Mrs. Aasta Hansteen." *Woman's Journal* 12, no. 31 (July 30, 1881).

———. "Scandinavians and Woman's Rights." *Woman's Journal* 13, no.

20 (May 20, 1882). https://iiif.lib.harvard.edu/manifests/view/drs :48880298$162i.

Haugen, Einar. "Language and Immigration." *Norwegian-American Studies and Records* 10 (1938): 1–43.

Hoem, Edvard. *Villskapens år: Bjørnstjerne Bjørnson, 1832–1875.* Oslo: Oktober, 2009.

Hoff, Joan. *Law, Gender, and Injustice: A Legal History of U.S. Women.* New York: New York University Press, 1991.

Hovde, Oivind M., ed. *What Became of Jens? A Study in Americanization Based on Reminiscences of J. C. M. Hanson, 1864–1943.* Decorah, IA: Luther College Press, 1974.

Hustvedt, Lloyd. "Images of the Minister in Norwegian-American Literature." In *Essays on Norwegian-American Literature and History*, vol. 2, edited by Øyvind Tveitereid Gulliksen, Ingeborg R. Kongslien, and Dina Tolfsby, 201–11. Oslo: Norwegian-American Historical Association–Norway, 1990.

———. *Rasmus Bjørn Anderson: Pioneer Scholar.* Northfield, MN: Norwegian-American Historical Association, 1966.

———. "Vignettes from a Norwegian Settlement." In *Nordics in America: The Future of Their Past*, edited by Odd S. Lovoll, 189–98. Northfield, MN: Norwegian-American Historical Association, 1993.

Hymowitz, Carol, and Michaele Weissman. *A History of Women in America.* New York: Bantam Books, 1978.

Ibsen, Henrik. *Nutidsdramaer 1877–99.* Oslo: Gyldendal, 1973.

Janson, Drude Krog. *A Saloonkeeper's Daughter.* Edited by Orm Øverland. Translated by Gerald Thorson. Baltimore, MD: Johns Hopkins University Press, 2002. First published in 1887 by C. Rasmussen, Minneapolis.

Janson, Kristofer. *Amerikanske Forholde: Fem foredrag.* Copenhagen: Gyldendalske Boghandel Nordisk Forlag, 1881.

———. *En kvindeskjæbne: Skuespil i tre akter med forspil.* Bergen, Norway: Ed. B. Giertsen Forlag, 1879.

———. *Hvad er Unitarisme?* Oslo: Oslo Prenteverk, 1900.

———. *Nordmænd i Amerika: Fortællinger.* Copenhagen: Gyldendalske, 1887.

―――. *Præriens saga: Fortællinger fra Amerika*. Copenhagen: Gylden-dalske, 1904.

Johnson, Frederick L. *Goodhue County, Minnesota: A Narrative History*. Red Wing, MN: Goodhue County Historical Society Press, 2000.

Joranger, Terje Mikael Hasle. "Lokale eller nasjonale kollektive iden-titeter? Etnifisering og identitetsbygging blant norske immigranter i Amerika." *Historisk tidsskrift* 89, no. 2 (2010): 233–47.

Leiren, Terje I. *Selected Plays of Marcus Thrane*. Northfield, MN: Norwegian-American Historical Association and Seattle: University of Washington Press, 2007.

Lovoll, Odd S. *A Century of Urban Life: The Norwegians in Chicago before 1930*. Northfield, MN: Norwegian-American Historical Association, 1988.

―――. *Norske aviser i Amerika*. Oslo: Scandinavian Academic Press and Spartacus Forlag, 2012.

―――. *Norwegian Newspapers in America: Connecting Norway and the New Land*. St. Paul: Minnesota Historical Society Press, 2010.

―――. *The Promise Fulfilled: A Portrait of Norwegian Americans Today*. Minneapolis: University of Minnesota Press, 1998.

―――. *The Promise of America: A History of the Norwegian-American People*. Minneapolis: University of Minnesota Press and the Norwegian-American Historical Association, 1984.

Luther, Martin. *Dr. Martin Luther's Liden Catechismus*. 1529.

Maranda, Jacob. "Saint Olaf: Man, Martyr or Murderer?" *The Olaf Messenger*, November 29, 2018. https://www.theolafmessenger.com /2018/saint-olaf-man-martyr-or-murderer/.

Mauk, David. *The Heart of the Heartland: Norwegian American Community in the Twin Cities*. St. Paul: Minnesota Historical Society Press and Norwegian-American Historical Association, 2022.

Molland, Einar. *Norges kirkehistorie i det 19. århundre*. 2 vols. Oslo: Gyl-dendal, 1979.

Munch, Peter A. "Authority and Freedom: Controversy in Norwegian-American Congregations." *Norwegian-American Studies* 28 (1979): 3–34.

————. "Norwegians." In *Harvard Encyclopedia of American Ethnic Groups*, edited by Stephan Thernstrom, Ann Orlov, and Oscar Handlin, 752–59. Cambridge, MA: Harvard University Press, 1981.

Muus, Alfred, and Bernt J. Muus. *Niels Muus's Æt: Muus-slegten i Snaasa, 1642–1942*. Trondheim: Aktietrykkeriet, 1942.

Myhre, Jan Eivind. "Utvandring fra Norge." Norgeshistorie, November 2, 2020. https://www.norgeshistorie.no/industrialisering-og -demokrati/1537-utvandring-fra-norge.html.

Mørkhagen, Sverre. *Drømmen om Amerika: Innvandringen fra Norge 1825–1900*. Oslo: Gyldendal, 2012.

————. *Farvel Norge: Utvandringen til Amerika 1825–1975*. Oslo: Gyldendal, 2009.

Norlie, Olaf Morgan. *History of the Norwegian People in America*. Minneapolis, MN: Augsburg Publishing House, 1925.

Norsk Biografisk Leksikon. https://nbl.snl.no/.

Nydahl, Theodore L. "Social and Economic Aspects of Pioneering as Illustrated in Goodhue County, Minnesota." *Studies and Records* 5 (1930): 50–60.

Odner, Knut. *Thorstein Veblen: Forstyrreren av den intellektuelle fred*. Oslo: Abstrakt forlag, 2005.

Olson, O. Rolf. *The Norwegian Synod 1853–1917: A Short History of a Premier Predecessor Church Body*. Minneapolis: Lutheran University Press, 2016.

Omdal, Sven Egil. "Paven av Stavanger har falt." *Aftenbladet*, April 6, 2010.

Pontoppidan, Erik. *Truth to Godliness*. Copenhagen: 1737.

Putnam, Robert D., and David E. Campbell. *American Grace: How Religion Divides and Unites Us*. New York: Simon and Schuster, 2010.

Rasmussen, C. A. *A History of Goodhue County Minnesota*. Red Wing, MN: Red Wing Print Company, 1935.

————. "When a Czar of the Church Ruled in Southern Minnesota." *The Pioneer Magazine*, May 28, 1939, 3.

Rasmussen, Janet E. "Aasta Hansteen og Amerika." In *Furier er også kvinner: Aasta Hansteen 1824–1908*, edited by Bente Nilsen Lein, 123–54. Oslo: Scandinavian University Press, 1984.

———. "'The Best Place on Earth for Women': The American Experience of Aasta Hansteen." *Norwegian-American Studies* 31, no. 1 (1986): 245–67.

Ravitch, Diane. "A Brief History of Public Education." In *Public Education: Defending a Cornerstone of American Democracy*, edited by David C. Berliner and Carl Hermanns, 21. New York: Teachers College Press, 2021.

Rowberg, Andrew Ansel. *The Aaker Saga: A Family History*. Northfield, MN: Mohn Printing Company, 1951.

St. Olaf's School: en evangelisk luthersk höiskole i Northfield, Minn., indviet den 8de januar 1875. Northfield, MN: St. Olaf College, 1875. https:// stolaf.eastview.com/browse/book/87754.

Shaw, Joseph M. *Bernt Julius Muus: Founder of St. Olaf College*. Northfield, MN: Norwegian-American Historical Association, 1999.

———. *History of St. Olaf College, 1874–1974*. Northfield, MN: St. Olaf College Press, 1974.

Smith-Rosenberg, Carroll. "The Hysterical Woman: Sex Roles and Role Conflict in 19th-Century America." *Social Research* 39, no. 4 (Winter 1972): 652–78.

Stanton, Elizabeth Cady. "Declaration of Sentiments." July 1848.

Sticklus, Adam. "Kai T. Erikson's *Wayward Puritans*." Book review, July 12, 2010.

Store Norske Leksikon. https://snl.no/.

Tavuchis, Nicholas. *Pastors and Immigrants: The Role of a Religious Elite in the Absorption of Norwegian Immigrants*. The Hague: Martinus Nijhoff, 1963.

Thrane, Marcus. *Den Gamle Wisconsin Bibelen*. Chicago: Scandia Publishing Company, 1938.

———. *Marcus Thrane's Manuscripts*, Vol. 2. Edited by Jorun Marie Jonassen. Trondheim: Privately printed, 1984.

Ueland, Andreas. *Recollections of an Immigrant*. New York: Minton, Balch and Company, 1929.

Ulvestad, Martin. *Nordmændene i Amerika: deres historie og rekord*. Minneapolis, MN: History Book Company, 1907.

Valley Grove Ministerial Bog 1867–1891. Northfield, MN: Norwegian-American Historical Association.

Veblen, Andrew A. "Det første skolehus i vart distrikt i Manitowoc County." *Samband* 92 (1915): 102–12.

———. "Jul i Manitowoc-skogen." *Samband* 93 (1916): 134–48.

———. *Veblen Genealogy.* San Diego: Privately printed, 1925.

Veblen, Thorstein. *The Theory of the Leisure Class.* New York: Macmillan, 1899.

White, Bruce M. "Indian Visits: Stereotypes of Minnesota's Native People." *Minnesota History* 53, no. 3 (Fall 1992): 99–111.

Wilson, H. B. "Annual Report of the Superintendent of Public Instruction, Sept, 30, 1869." In *Executive Documents of the State of Minnesota for the Year 1869,* 72–282. St. Paul, MN: Press Printing Co., 1870.

Wist, Johannes B., ed. *Norsk-Amerikanernes Festskrift 1914.* Decorah, IA: The Symra Company, 1914.

"Women's Suffrage in Minnesota: Overview." Gale Family Library, Minnesota Historical Society. Last updated December 20, 2023. https://libguides.mnhs.org/suffrage.

Ylvisaker, Erling. *Eminent Pioneers: Norwegian-American Pioneer Sketches.* Minneapolis, MN: Augsburg Publishing House, 1934.

Østgård, Bjørn Gunnar. *America-America Letters: A Norwegian-American Family Correspondence.* Translated by Donald L. Berg. Northfield, MN: Norwegian-American Historical Association, 2001.

Øverland, Orm. Introduction to *A Saloonkeeper's Daughter,* by Drude Krog Janson, xii–xxxiv. Baltimore, MD: Johns Hopkins University Press, 2002.

Øverland, Orm, Harry T. Cleven, Todd W. Nichol, and Susanne Nevin, eds. *Norwegian-American Essays 2004.* Oslo: Norwegian-American Historical Association–Norway, 2005.

INDEX

Page numbers in *italics* refer to images.

Lang, Dane H. P., 89
Langemo, Peder: February 1880 con-
    gregational meeting, 149–50, 153–
    55; Holden Church bylaws, 24; on
    Holden settlement, 15–17; inves-
    tigative committee, 219; March
    1880 congregational meeting, 167,
    169, 183–84; press's portrayal, 191;
    religious education, 28
Larsen, Peter Laurentius, 8, 71–73, 103,
    149, 310
laypeople, 24–25, 39, 84, 86–87,
    100–102
lecture tour, Bjørnson, 241–46, 247–49
lecture tour, Hansteen, 254–55, 275–76
lecture tour, Janson, 268
legal jurisdiction, 231–33
legal separation, 278–79
legislative reforms, 57, 78
Leiren, Terje, 221
Le Sueur River Church, 227
letter from Pauline Henschien to
    Oline Muus written on mourning
    stationery, *118*
"The Letter Killeth" article, 190
liberalism, 112–13
liberal movement of the 1860s, 282
Lie, Botulf, 211, 219
Lie, Letty Homberger, 319
Lilleskov, John, 185
limited divorce, 278–79
Lincoln, Abraham, 44–45
Linebaugh, Annie. *See* Muus, Annie
    (née Linebaugh)
London, England, 56
Lovoll, Odd, 174
Luther, Martin, 27, 64, 81, 84, 89, 172
Lutheran doctrine, 79, 127–28, 286–87,
    290
*Lutheraneren og Missionsbladet (The
    Lutheran and the Mission Paper)*
    (journal), 233, 247, 265
Lutheran orthodoxy, 172, 277

Lutheran tradition of literature and
    song, 21–22
Luther College, 85, 96, 99, 102, 103–4
Luthersk Ugeskrift (Lutheran Weekly)
    (newspaper), 249–51

Main, St. Olaf College, dedication of,
    116
Manitou Heights, Northfield, MN, 116
Mankato, 45
*Marcus Thrane's Norske Amerikaner
    (Marcus Thrane's Norwegian Amer-
    ican)* (newspaper), 53–58
marriage cases in Synod congrega-
    tions, 268
Married Women's Property Acts, 126
mass emigration, 8, 14, 112, 247
mass executions, 45
Mauk, David, 316
medicine chest, 73–75
meeting minutes, 101, 163, 183, 204,
    209, 211–12, 217–19
Methodists, 77–80, 88, 90, 102
Michelet, Nils, 238–39
Midbøe, J. M., 101–2
Mill, John Stuart, 110, 172, 175
Minneapolis, MN, 109–15, 249, 265,
    270–74, 275, 279, 280–83
Minneapolis Tribune (newspaper), 243
Minnesota District, 90, 92, 227, 272
Minnesota law, 78, 126–27, 134, 260
Minnesota's hospital for the insane, 107
Minnesota State Board of Health, 105
Minnesota Supreme Court, 237, 270,
    276–77
missionary societies, 93
Missouri Synod, 63–64, 285
Miss Rawel, 224
Mohn, Thorbjørn, 70, 148, 150, 271
Monsen, Søren, 274
monument at Holden Church, 315
Morris, Esther, 78
Mott, Lucretia, 56–57

Mrs. Muus' Hotel, 291–93, 300–305
"Mrs. Oline Muus contra Pastor
Muus" pamphlet, 220
musical. See *Holden (or: Be Patient!)*
(Thrane)
Muus, Annie (née Linebaugh), 310
Muus, Bernt Julius: American citizenship, 147; announcement of
lawsuit, 130–33; arrival in America, 32–35; and Birgitte, 259; and
Bjørnson, 243–46; Black (Negro)
communities, 90–91; *Budstikken's*
editorial commentary, 141–43, 145–
47, 161–62; *Budstikken's* reporting, 161–64; building Holden
Church, 47–49; bust in Old Main,
St. Olaf College, *312*; case heard
before Goodhue County District
Court, 236–40; church discipline,
98–101; Civil War, 45–46; confession associated with church
discipline, 38–39; criticism against
the Holden congregation, 37–39;
custody of children, 260–61; death
of, 299; defense speech, 171–77;
divorce case proceedings, January
1883, 277–79; doctrinal disputes
with Norwegian Synod, 87–89,
284–87; early life, 5–8; excluding
Sverre from the family tree, 311;
family portrait, *95, 96–97, 297*;
February 1880 congregational
meeting, ix–x, 148–56; fifteen days
before the first meeting, 140–43;
and Finseth, 14–15; first phase of
the conflict, 125–29; Georg Sverdrup's criticism, 233–35; Hansteen
on, 254–56, 276–77; Heuch and
Færden, 249–51; hierarchical
organization of the Norwegian
Synod, 86; *Holden (or: Be Patient!)*
(Thrane), 221–26; Holden congregation, 92–96; income, 98, 159,

239; inheritance settlement, 260,
277–78; investigative committee's report, 227–30; and Janson,
265–69; later years of, 294–99;
long journey, 71–76; Louise
Pind's letter to, 18–19; March 1880
congregational meeting, 165–86;
May 1880 congregational meeting,
199–220; money issues, 98–99;
monument at Holden Church, *315*;
new legal proceedings, 270–74;
Norsving's letter to the editor,
157–60, 187–88; Norwegian-
language press in America, 144;
Oline's final exit from the parsonage, 261; *Parables from Nature*, 20;
photograph, *6, 298*; predestination
controversy, 87; press's portrayal,
187–91, 231, 247–51; and Preus,
194–97; religious education,
62–70; reorganization of 1876, 90;
revival movement of the 1850s,
9–12; role of, 313–14; sending
children to Norway, 293; trials
faced at Holden parsonage, 116–21;
university examinations in prepa-
ration for America, 29–31; and the
Veblens, 81–85; women's role in the
congregation, 92–93. See also "The
Complaint"
Muus, Birgitte. See Klüver, Birgitte
(née Muus)
Muus, Elizabeth, 308
Muus, Harald (Harold) Steen
(Moose): birth of, 61; custody,
260–61, 274, 278; descendant overview, 309–10; early life of, 94–96;
illnesses at Holden parsonage,
117–20; wife of, 299, 310
Muus, Hilda Sophie (née Eggen), 310
Muus, Ingebrigt, 5–7, 284
Muus, Jens Ingebrigt Rynning, 60, 96,
103–4, 116–20, 308–9

Norwegian historian and writer **BODIL STENSETH** has a prolific authorship focusing on Norwegian and Western cultural history. For many years she was a regular columnist for the newspaper *Klassekampen*. Her most recent book, *Antikvitetshandler Watchman: familien som ble borte* (*The Antique Dealer Watchman: The Family That Disappeared*), is about the Jewish antiques dealer P. S. Watchman from Oslo and his family, who were killed in the Holocaust. She lives in Oslo.

KARI LIE DORER holds the King Olav V Endowed Chair of Scandinavian-American Studies at St. Olaf College and is president of Norwegian Researchers and Teachers Association of North America (NORTANA). She is the coauthor of *Sett i gang: An Introductory Norwegian Curriculum,* the foundational Norwegian language text used by the majority of North American students of Norwegian. She is also the project leader for *Godt i gang,* a collaborative online intermediate and advanced curriculum. She holds a master's degree from the University of Minnesota and a doctorate from The University of Texas at Austin. At St. Olaf College she teaches a wide variety of courses in Norwegian language, history, culture, and film. She lives in Minneapolis.